LIVE JESUS IN OUR HEARTS

THE PASCHAL MYSTERY

AND THE GOSPELS

High School Framework Course 3

CHRIS WARDWELL

saint mary's press

Thanks and Dedication

Thanks to May Lane and Brian Singer-Towns for laughing at my jokes and patiently guiding my writing in the right direction.

A very special thank you to our student contributors: Rosa and Duc from Totino-Grace High School in Fridley, MN; Colin from Father Judge High School in Philadelphia, PA ; Richard from Mater Dei High School in in Santa Ana, CA, and Olivia from New Smyrna Beach High School in New Smyrna Beach, FL.

Love to my wife, Christine, who has generously supported my recent adventures, both in writing and otherwise. Love also to my son, Jacob.

This book is dedicated to Joe Zarantonello, who continues to guide me through my little mysteries and into the Great Mystery.

The Subcommittee on the Catechism, United States Conference of Catholic Bishops, has found that this catechetical high school text, copyright 2019, is in conformity with the *Catechism of the Catholic Church* and that it fulfills the requirements of Course 3 of the *Doctrinal Elements of a Curriculum Framework for the Development of Catechetical Materials for Young People of High School Age.*

Nihil Obstat: Dr. John Martens, PhD
                Censor Librorum
                October 7, 2019

Imprimatur: † Most Rev. Bernard A. Hebda
              Archbishop of Saint Paul and Minneapolis
              October 11, 2019

The nihil obstat and imprimatur are official declarations that a book or pamphlet is free of doctrinal or moral error. No implication is contained therein that those who have granted the nihil obstat or imprimatur agree with the contents, opinions, or statements expressed, nor do they assume any legal responsibility associated with publication.

The content in this resource was acquired, developed, and reviewed by the content engagement team at Saint Mary's Press. Content design and manufacturing were coordinated by the passionate team of creatives at Saint Mary's Press.

Cover image © Markus Pfaff / Shutterstock.com

Printed in the United States of America

1167 (PO6464)

ISBN 978-1-64121-025-6

CONTENTS

UNIT 1: Old Testament:
United with God, Separated by Sin 8

CHAPTER 1: God's Original Plan 10

Article 1: The Fullness of Creation 11

Article 2: Creation Accounts: The Literary Form 17

Article 3: You Can't Un-Ring That Bell 22

Article 4: The Wages of Sin 28

Article 5: The Cycle of Sin Begins 33

CHAPTER 2: Bound to God: The Covenants 40

Article 6: Ending the Cycle 41

Article 7: The Promise 46

Article 8: Covenant: A Relationship and a Remedy 50

Article 9: The Covenants with Noah and Abraham 54

Article 10: The Covenants with Moses and David 60

CHAPTER 3: Pointing toward Christ's Sacrifice 70

Article 11: The Past: A Glimpse into the Future 71

Article 12: The Lamb of God 76

Article 13: Carrying the Sins of Others 81

Article 14: Love Requires Sacrifice 87

Article 15: The Prophets: Hints of the Coming Messiah 91

UNIT 2: New Testament: God's Plan Fulfilled. 108

CHAPTER 4: The Life and Teachings of Jesus 110

   Article 16: The Birth of Christ 111

   Article 17: In the Flesh 119

   Article 18: Bearing the Burden 125

   Article 19: Grabbed from the Grave 132

CHAPTER 5: Jesus' Death: Four Perspectives. 140

   Article 20: One Threat in Five Events 141

   Article 21: Why They Killed Jesus 148

   Article 22: Carrying the Cross 155

   Article 23: Crucifixion and Death 159

CHAPTER 6: Resurrection and Ascension 172

   Article 24: Nothing in the Dark? 173

   Article 25: What Is Resurrection? 178

   Article 26: Resurrection Appearances 184

   Article 27: The Ascension 191

UNIT 3: The Paschal Mystery: Christ's Saving Work 210

CHAPTER 7: Redeemed by God 212

Article 28: The Power of Love 213

Article 29: Paul's Theology of the Cross 218

Article 30: Resurrection of the Dead 225

Article 31: Becoming One 230

CHAPTER 8: Our Salvation 238

Article 32: Saved *from* What? 239

Article 33: Saved *for* What? 242

Article 34: Judgment Day 246

Article 35: Where Do We Go after Death? 250

UNIT 4: The Paschal Mystery and Real Life 264

CHAPTER 9: Personal Suffering and the Paschal Mystery 266

Article 36: Making Sense of Suffering 267

Article 37: Is Accepting Suffering a Sign of Weakness? 273

Article 38: Finding Strength in Times of Weakness 277

Article 39: How Do I Cope with Suffering? 281

CHAPTER 10: Communal Suffering 288

Article 40: Sinful Violence 289

Article 41: Human Failings 295

Article 42: God's Creation Suffers 302

UNIT 5: Prayer and Holiness 314

CHAPTER 11: Holiness and Union with God 316

Article 43: Being Holy 317

Article 44: Discipleship: The Path to Holiness 323

Article 45: Mysticism: Seeking Union with God 327

Article 46: The Church's Sacramental Life Unites Us 333

CHAPTER 12: Communing with God 338

Article 47: What Is Prayer? 339

Article 48: Forms of Prayer 343

Article 49: Expressions of Prayer 350

Article 50: Scripture: A Source and Guide 355

CHAPTER 13: Praying with the Triduum 360

Article 51: The Paschal Mystery and the Triduum 361

Article 52: Holy Thursday 365

Article 53: Good Friday 371

Article 54: Easter Vigil 375

APPENDIX: Challenge Questions 388

GLOSSARY 392

INDEX 401

ACKNOWLEDGMENTS 411

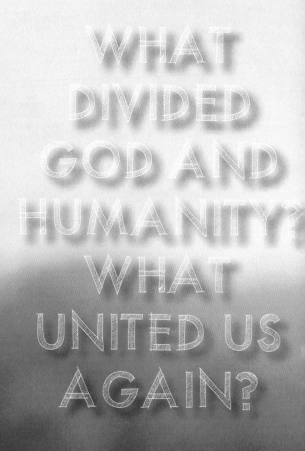

UNIT 1
Old Testament: United with God, Separated by Sin

WHAT DIVIDED GOD AND HUMANITY? WHAT UNITED US AGAIN?

LOOKING AHEAD

CHAPTER 1   Page 10
God's Original Plan

CHAPTER 2   Page 40
Bound to God: The Covenants

CHAPTER 3   Page 70
Pointing toward Christ's Sacrifice

In my opinion, disobedience and lack of faith in God are what divided God and humanity. I think Adam and Eve's giving in to temptation is an example of humans' defying God's rules because we don't think of God as present to us. But Jesus walked among us and lived with us. Jesus' close relationship with God shows us how we can become one with God. We can be united with God by following Jesus—living humbly, valuing people over profits, and acting as peacemakers.

COLIN
Father Judge High School

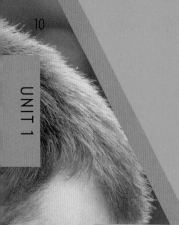

CHAPTER 1
God's Original Plan

IF GOD MADE EVERYTHING GOOD, HOW DID THINGS GET SO BAD?

SNAPSHOT

Article 1   Page 11
The Fullness of Creation
- Pre-read: Genesis, chapter 2

Article 2   Page 17
Creation Accounts: The Literary Form

Article 3   Page 22
You Can't Un-Ring That Bell
- Pre-read: Genesis, chapter 3

Article 4   Page 28
The Wages of Sin

Article 5   Page 33
The Cycle of Sin Begins
- Pre-read: Genesis 4:1–16
- Pre-read: Genesis 6:5–9:28
- Pre-read: Genesis 11:1–9

Article 1
The Fullness of Creation

Since the beginning of creation, God has planned for us to share eternal happiness with him through an intimate relationship of love. The disobedience of our first parents, however, disrupted this plan, and humanity's relationship with God has been wounded ever since. But God is ever faithful, and nothing can stand in the way of his love. The Bible's accounts reveal how throughout history, God has worked to bridge the gap that separates us. His saving plan is ultimately fulfilled through the Passion, death, Resurrection, and Ascension of Jesus Christ—the **Paschal Mystery**. To better understand the Paschal Mystery, let's start at the beginning: the Book of Genesis and the Creation accounts.

TAKE IT TO GOD

God who created me,
Help me to overcome the pressure of society
    and its "perfect" image of a person.
Help me to accept myself as I am, despite my failings.
May I become aware of just how wonderfully you made me;
    may I learn to live as the person you intend me to be.
May I remember my goodness and the goodness of others,
    to accept others the way you accept me.
Help me walk in your footsteps, which lead me to eternal life with you.
Amen.

Paschal Mystery ➤ The work of salvation accomplished by Jesus Christ mainly through his Passion, death, Resurrection, and Ascension.

Half Full or Half Empty?

Some would say that in general, there are two types of people. The first type sees life as a glass half full: life is full of beauty, goodness, joy, and love. When something bad happens, they look for something positive to take from it. The second type of person sees life as a glass half empty: life is full of disappointments, ugliness, prejudice, and division. When something good happens, they assume that something bad will soon follow.

Most of us probably see life somewhere between these two types, but we do tend to lean one way or the other. Which way do you lean? Which is the best way to see life and creation, glass half full or glass half empty?

The Creation accounts at the beginning of Genesis tell us that both views contain part of the truth. When we read them carefully, we understand that God created the world as a place of beauty, goodness, and love. However, human sin has marred God's intent and has brought ugliness, division, and hatred into the world. In this chapter we will explore this fundamental conflict and the deeper spiritual truths these accounts teach us.

It's All Good

"Looks good to me." "Good to know." "Sounds good." "It's all good!" You've probably heard or used these or similar words at some point in your life. But have you ever considered how well these common phrases could be used to describe the first Creation account in the Bible? Think about it. Genesis 1:1–2:4 details the six days of God's work of Creation and its goodness.

This is one of the most fundamental truths taught in the Bible: the goodness of all creation reflects the goodness and glory of God the Father, Son, and Holy Spirit. The goodness and perfection of the garden reflected the goodness and perfection of Heaven. This state of perfection was short-lived because sin entered the world, beginning with Adam and Eve's disobedience. But all is far from lost, and we live in the hope of God's providence. For, "The universe was created 'in a state of journeying' toward an ultimate perfection yet to be attained, to which God has destined it" (*Catechism of the Catholic Church [CCC]*, number 302). It's all good!

UNIT 1

The belief that creation is one way in which God connects Heaven and Earth is acknowledged in the Nicene Creed.

Heavenly Life on Earth

Creation is certainly one way that God connects Heaven and Earth. But creation is not limited to what we can see, hear, taste, smell, and touch; it also includes everything in the universe that we *can't* see. This belief is acknowledged in the Nicene Creed: God created "all things visible and invisible," in and on "heaven and earth."

So, what are some of the things that fit into the "invisible" category? Heaven, Hell, Purgatory, and angels are "invisible" things. You may recall learning about Heaven, Hell, and Purgatory in a previous course, but what about angels?

Angels are spiritual creatures with intelligence and free will. The word *angel* means "messenger" and describes their role: angels are the servants and messengers of God. From preventing Abraham from sacrificing his son, Isaac, to announcing the coming of Christ to the Virgin Mary, Sacred Scripture records the active presence of angels in the lives of God's people. We too can find the assistance of angels in our own lives! We can be comforted by the knowledge that "human life is surrounded by their watchful care and intercession"[1] (*CCC*, number 336).

---

angel ➤ Based on a Greek word meaning "messenger," a personal and immortal creature with intelligence and free will who constantly glorifies God and serves as a messenger of God to humans to carry out God's saving plan.

But Scripture also notes that not all angels were so . . . angelic. Saint Peter refers to a time when some angels disobeyed God (see 2 Peter 2:4). Like humans, angels have free will and were created good. By rejecting God, some of them became "fallen angels"; the most notable of these we call the **Devil** or **Satan**. Though fallen angels can and have negatively influenced humanity, they are still created beings, and have never had the infinite power that God has.

Another way God connects Heaven and Earth is through each of us! Every human being is a union of both the physical and the spiritual worlds. We are human, but we are made in the image and likeness of God. We are the summit of creation; that is, we are the only creatures on Earth that God has willed for our own sake.

It is important to note that it is not our physical appearance that "looks" like our Creator, but rather it is our soul that reflects God. For example, when we offer our lives in service to one another, we reflect God's faithfulness and loving kindness. In these moments, we are given glimpses of heavenly life here on Earth. (This subject will be studied further in a later chapter.)

The angel Gabriel brings a message to Mary from God, announcing that she will bear God's son through the Holy Spirit.

© Yakov Oskanov / Shutterstock.com

Devil ➤ From the Greek *diabolus*, meaning "slanderer" or "accuser"; refers in general to the fallen angels, those spiritual beings who sinned against God.

Satan ➤ The fallen angel or spirit of evil who is the enemy of God and a continuing instigator of temptation and sin in the world.

One Body

God created Eve from the rib of Adam in the second Creation account, and the two of them became "one body" (Genesis 2:24). This symbolic account of Eve's creation tells us that Adam and Eve were perfectly united before sin entered the world.

This passage reveals another fundamental spiritual truth: human beings are made for communion, that is, for intimate relationship. We see this most fully reflected in marriages. Consider the many ways in which a husband and wife become "one" after they get married. They are now one family and live in the same home. They are spiritually and legally bound to each other. They may share the same friends, bank accounts, and last name. Emotionally, they support each other. When one experiences joy or sadness, the other also feels its effects. Physically, their bodies become one in the sexual act of love, and their children are the physical manifestation of their love. Scientifically speaking, the characteristics of children are a result of the union of the DNA codes received from their parents.

Husband and wife become one through their deep mutual love, a love that mirrors the love God has for all his children. They know each other intimately and sometimes even finish each other's sentences. Their selfless nature allows them to put the other's wants and needs ahead of their own. A wholeness is created that could not have been made by either one of them alone. Their love steers them toward each other, guides their lives, strengthens their bond, and gives them the energy to share that love with others.

© nevodka / Shutterstock.com

As humans, we are social beings who are meant to be in relationship with one another.

No Shame

There is another spiritual truth to observe about Adam's and Eve's original holiness before sin entered the world: Adam and Eve felt no shame even though they were both naked (see Genesis 2:25). Can you imagine walking around naked in public without frantically trying to find something to cover yourself? Besides protection from the physical elements and societal norms for decency, why do we feel the need to cover our private areas? At the beginning of his papacy, Pope Saint John Paul II (1920–2005) gave regular weekly talks about the human body and sexuality. Now called the **Theology of the Body**, these presentations offered some fascinating insights into the second Creation account and why Adam and Eve "felt no shame."

Pope Saint John Paul II echoed the first Creation account when he emphasized that humans were made good—this includes every aspect of us, including our bodies. There was no shame before sin entered the world. And it was only after sin entered the world that lust became part of the human experience. Lust is selfish activity because it objectifies people. It sees others merely as a sexual object to be used for one's own pleasure. Now that lust was present, people needed to protect themselves from it. Pope Saint John Paul II identified shame as a type of fear ("General Audience," December 19, 1979). Shame reflects the fear we have of people seeing us merely as an "object." And when someone sees another person as an object to use, they take away that person's dignity.

Before sin, Adam and Eve felt no shame. They were not judging themselves or each other. They did not see each other as an object for their own pleasure. What a contrast to the pressures we often feel today!

We can get a glimpse of this acceptance of each other in the loving relationship of marriage. When a husband and wife know each other's value as a person, they feel safe. They do not feel shame around each other because they have fully given themselves to each other. In marriage they become "one body" united by love. ✳

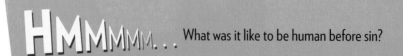

HMMMMM... What was it like to be human before sin?

Theology of the Body ➤ The name given to Pope Saint John Paul II's teachings on the human body and sexuality.

UNIT 1

Article 2
Creation Accounts: The Literary Form

"Little pig, little pig, let me come in," says the big bad wolf. The three little pigs respond, "Not by the hair of my chinny-chin-chin!" The wolf then warns, "Then I'll huff, and I'll puff, and I'll blow your house in!"

Imagine someone responding to this fairy tale by saying: "That story never happened! You don't really believe that, do you?! Pigs and wolves can't even talk!" They would be completely missing the point, of course. A fairy tale is not intended to be a historically and scientifically accurate portrayal of reality. It is intended to express some sort of teaching or moral. For example, in *The Three Little Pigs*, the third little pig works all day building his home out of brick, while the other two quickly finish their houses so they can have fun. Although this isn't a historically true story, it does teach the importance of investing time, resources, and hard work—a valuable truth in any day and age.

Similar criticism has been used to attack the two Creation accounts in the Book of Genesis. There are some who say: "Those stories aren't true! The Earth took billions of years to form, not six days!" Unfortunately, like the critic of the fairy tale, they are also missing the point. Through the Bible, God communicates his revealed truth. The Bible conveys the truth, which "God wants to reveal through the sacred authors for our salvation" (*CCC*, number 137). In some of the Bible's writings, like the first eleven chapters of Genesis, this takes the form of figurative or symbolic stories. These first chapters of Genesis are primeval history, meaning they cover a time before humans kept a written record of the events in their lives. Like a fairy tale, these chapters are symbolic; unlike a fairy tale, they are rooted in historical reality. They reveal spiritual truths that complement the truth revealed through science and history. We know

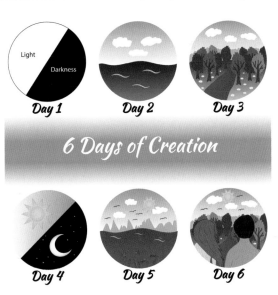

The first Creation account in the Book of Genesis uses figurative language—six days of Creation—to teach the religious truth that God created everything.

that because these chapters are written in figurative language. Before we look at more Bible passages related to the Paschal Mystery, let's revisit some important understandings for interpreting the Bible.

Figurative Language, Religious Truth

Figurative language is a literary form that uses symbolic images, stories, and names to point to a deeper truth. Figurative language can teach us religious truths, but it is not meant to be scientifically or historically accurate. For example, with the seven days of Creation, chapter 1 of Genesis uses figurative language to teach us an important religious truth: God created the world with order and purpose. We should not interpret this story to mean that God literally created the universe in six twenty-four-hour days. Nor should we interpret figurative language as pure fantasy; the first chapters of Genesis affirm real events that took place at the beginning of human history.

Another example of figurative language is in the second Creation account in Genesis, chapter 2: God places the tree of the knowledge of good and evil in the middle of the garden. This is not an actual tree that exists in nature. "The 'tree of the knowledge of good and evil' symbolically evokes the insurmountable limits that man, being a creature, must freely recognize and respect with trust"[2] (*CCC*, number 396). Eating the fruit of the tree of the knowledge of good and evil is how the human authors expressed humanity's entrance into sin. (Read more about the tree of the knowledge of good and evil in article 3.)

Adam's and Eve's names are also symbolic elements in the second Creation account. Adam's name comes from the Hebrew word *'adam* meaning "human being." God formed him from the ground (*'adama* in Hebrew), so *'adam* comes from the word *'adama*. Although this is a play on words, it also symbolizes humanity's close relationship to, and reliance on, the Earth. In Hebrew, Eve's name *(hawwa)* is related to the Hebrew word for "living" *(hay)*. Eve was given her name "because she was the mother of all the living" (Genesis 3:20).

It's important to remember that the biblical accounts are God's Word. Inspired by the Holy Spirit, the human authors used their skills and talents to express these truths using the literary form of figurative language. The Creation accounts of Genesis uniquely express the truths that God wants us to know for our salvation. Among others, these truths include that there is only one God, that God is all-powerful, and that humans are given the gift of free will. Because these accounts are divinely inspired, we can count on the truth of these powerful stories!

---

figurative language ➤ A literary form that uses symbolic images, stories, and names to point to a deeper truth.

Though the author of the second Creation account refers to the convergence of the Tigris and Euphrates Rivers—shown in this modern-day map of Iraq—the Garden of Eden is not an actual place.

The Garden: United with God

The Garden of Eden is another important symbolic element of the second Creation account. Eden is presented as God's home, and although Genesis locates it near some actual physical landmarks (the Tigris and Euphrates Rivers), it is not a place. Instead, the garden represents the paradise in which humanity was created, united with one another in God's presence.

In Eden, God formed man out of the ground, then planted a garden, put the man in the garden, and entrusted its care to him (see Genesis 2:15). We read that Adam and Eve "heard the sound of the LORD God walking about in the garden" (3:8). God was fully present to them and "from their friendship with God flowed the happiness of their existence in paradise" (*CCC*, number 384).

This was God's plan: humans, all of creation, and God, living in complete peace and harmony with one another. This is what is called the state of **original holiness** and **original justice**. God invited humanity "to intimate communion with himself and clothed them with resplendent grace and justice" (*CCC*, number 54). Knowing why God created us is important because it acts as the target on which we can focus our lives. Ultimately, our goal is to return to the garden: communion with God and with one another.

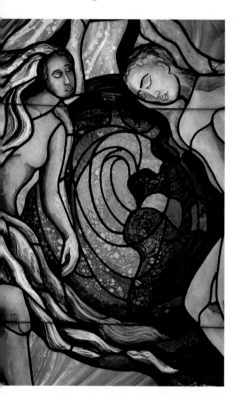

The second Creation account uses figurative language to symbolize the unity between Adam and Eve.

Adam and Eve: United with Each Other

The second Creation account also uses figurative language to describe the unity between Adam and Eve. In this account, God creates Eve from Adam's rib (see Genesis 2:23). Even though Adam was created first and Eve was created as a "helper" to him (2:18), this should not be interpreted to mean that men are in some way superior, or that women should be subservient. On the contrary, though the account might reflect some of the cultural **patriarchy** of the time it was written, Catholic doctrine clearly states that men and women have been created "in perfect equality as human persons" (*CCC*, number 369).

Though both men and women are created in the image and likeness of God and are equal as persons, they are nonetheless different. This is also a good thing. The obvious sexual differences allow for the flourishing of married life and children. A man and a woman complement each other, each

© pixoi / Shutterstock.com

---

original holiness ➤ The original state of human beings in their relationship with God, sharing in the divine life in full communion with him.

original justice ➤ The original state of Adam and Eve before the Fall; sharing in the divine life, they were in a state of complete harmony with God, with themselves, with each other, and with all of creation.

patriarchy ➤ The familial, social, cultural, and political worldview that claims that men are destined to hold positions of power over, and make decisions for, women and children.

providing what the other does not have. What makes each of them distinct is exactly what allows them to "become one body" (2:24).

The human authors of the Bible expressed God's truth using symbolic imagery and literary forms common to their time. The second Creation account of Genesis teaches us that God created us to be happy and to live united with him and with one another. Though each one of us is different, we were made to live in communion with one another. ✳

 of the Book of Genesis

- **Themes:** The goodness of creation, sin and its consequences, covenant, and bringing good out of evil.
- **Important people:** Adam and Eve, Cain and Abel, Noah, Abraham, Sarah, Isaac, Jacob, and Joseph.

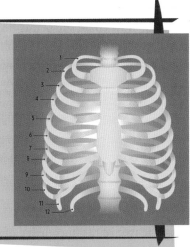

I DIDN'T KNOW THAT!

Do men have fewer ribs than women? Through the centuries, many people have concluded that because God took a rib from Adam to create Eve, men must have one fewer rib than women. Even if you accepted that this element of the account is included to explain why men have fewer ribs, you would be wrong. Men do indeed have twenty-four ribs— the same number that women do.

HMMMMM. . .
What does the second Creation account teach us about how God intended for us to live?

Article 3

You Can't Un-Ring That Bell

It was near the end of their senior year in high school, and Seth was furious at Ava. They had been dating for months, but Seth knew Ava had had a serious crush on Austin before their own romance started. Austin was the popular and burly football star who was recently awarded a scholarship to play at Notre Dame. Nonetheless, late in the summer before senior year, Seth slowly caught Ava's attention, and they soon started dating.

Once Adam and Eve ate the fruit of the tree of knowledge of good and evil, there was no turning back. They had already crossed the line into forbidden territory.

About two months before senior prom, Seth got a text from a friend who heard that Austin had asked Ava to the prom and she had said yes. Seth was enraged. How could she betray him like this? He called her right away (which was a mistake!). Before she even finished saying hello, Seth started yelling. He said every mean and insulting thing he could think of. When he finished, there was silence on the phone. Then Ava calmly said, "Yes, Austin did ask me to the prom, but I said no because I wanted to go with you." More silence. Seth had just finished hurling a barrage of insults at someone he loved, and it was all based on a rumor. Unfortunately, he could not un-ring that bell. He had said awful things to Ava that he could not take back. They worked it out and stayed together, but their relationship was forever changed: they recognized that neither one of them was perfect.

In Genesis, chapter 3, Adam and Eve also chose to believe a lie and ate from the tree of the knowledge of good and evil. This was a bell that humanity could not un-ring. They had crossed a line into a forbidden territory that profoundly affected their experience of the world; the way they related to God and to each other was forever changed.

UNIT 1

Etiology, Another Literary Form

In the previous article, we learned about figurative language and its purpose in the first two chapters of Genesis. Before going further, let's look at another literary form that will help you better understand the Creation accounts and chapters 3–11 in the Book of Genesis.

The accounts in Genesis, chapters 3–11, use the literary form **etiology**. Etiology is the study of the origins or causes of things. For example, ancient cultures around the world have employed folk stories to explain all sorts of things, including death, geological landmarks, the origins of social or natural occurrences, the name of a place, and even why bears have such short tails.

The human authors of Genesis, chapters 1–11, also employed etiologies. They did this to answer perplexing questions about things like why animals exist, why women have pain in childbirth, and why snakes crawl on their bellies. The purpose of these was not to give a scientific or historical explanation. Rather they are creative explanations used by the human authors to convey a religious truth that was inspired by the Holy Spirit: how sin leads to shame and how sin brings isolation, causes pain and suffering, disrupts our harmony with nature, and leads us away from God and life. This is what we'll explore in Genesis, chapter 3.

Genesis, chapter 3, employs an etiology as to why snakes crawl on their bellies.

© phichak / Shutterstock.com

---

etiology ➤ A story that explains something's cause or origin.

Knowing Good and Evil

The tree of the knowledge of good and evil is first introduced in chapter 2 of Genesis, but it is not until chapter 3 that we learn its symbolic element. At the beginning of chapter 3, all is well in the Garden of Eden. Adam and Eve live a life of holiness and justice in communion with God. Everything in the garden is theirs with one exception: God tells them not to eat fruit from the tree of the knowledge of good and evil (see 2:16–17), for reasons the text does not fully explain.

But Adam and Eve are tempted by the serpent, and they eat the forbidden fruit. This event brings a most radical change—Adam and Eve fall into a state of sin which separates them from God and from each other. They immediately recognize their "nakedness," brought on by their shame and feeling of separation. Then they hide from God (see 3:7–8). Now that they know good and evil (see 3:22), they have entered a world of judgment and separation, which keeps one thing from another.

© gldburger / iStock.com

Why is it wrong for humans to separate from one another and from God? Acknowledging differences and separating things in our everyday experience is not necessarily bad. It is good to know right from wrong and to know that it is virtuous to help others and wrong to harm them. Actions have moral consequences, and it is important that we discern what is good from what is evil.

The problem comes when sin distorts our ability to see clearly. Sometimes we see the world through our small self-centered viewpoint. Sin causes us to focus on ourselves, making us feel better or more entitled, creating separations that can be destructive to our relationships with God and one another. For example, when we separate "good" people from "evil" people, we are deciding who is worthy of our attention and love. In some places, a judge and jury can even decide to take away someone's life because of a crime someone committed. We take on the role of God by choosing who lives and who dies. Ironically, this makes us even less like God, for even the worst criminal is not beyond God's love and compassion.

Eating the fruit of the tree of the knowledge of good and evil symbolizes a major shift in the life of humanity. "The account of the fall in Genesis 3 uses figurative language, but affirms a primeval event, a deed that took place *at the beginning of the history of man*"[3] (*CCC*, number 390). Although we do not read chapter 3 as history, it does symbolize something that truly happened. Adam and Eve's act represents the event when our earliest ancestors freely chose to disobey God's Law, and humanity lost its original holiness and justice. **Original Sin** is the sin of the first human beings who disobeyed God's command by choosing to follow their own will. They lost their original holiness and became subject to death. Since then, we have suffered from its consequences.

Adam and Eve's choice to eat the forbidden fruit represents the loss of humanity's original holiness and justice.

Original Sin ➤ From the Latin *origo*, meaning "beginning" or "birth." The term has two meanings: (1) the sin of the first human beings, who disobeyed God's command by choosing to follow their own will and thus lost their original holiness and became subject to death, (2) the fallen state of human nature that affects every person born into the world, except Jesus and Mary.

To See as God Sees

The Fall also illustrates the consequences of placing ourselves apart from God's will. Adam and Eve allowed themselves to be tempted by the serpent to disobey God and chose to place themselves outside of God's plan for them. Whenever we do this, there are consequences, sometimes very serious ones.

Despite the failure of our first parents, God still wants to share his divine life with us so much that he sent his Son, Jesus Christ. By becoming human, the Son of God reminds us that being human is good! The serpent lied to Adam and Eve, telling them they needed to be like gods. The irony is that the first Creation account tells us that Adam and Eve (and us) were already made in God's image and likeness!

Human beings have limitations. We live in a specific place and time and, far from being **omniscient**, our views are often tainted by a culture that is marked by sin. Knowing this, we should be always be cautious of believing we can come to the truth on our own power. We must accept the limitations of who we are as human beings and open ourselves to God's revealed truth, allowing God's grace to direct and fill our lives.

CATHOLICS **MAKING** A DIFFERENCE

Sr. Helen Prejean joined the Congregation of St. Joseph when she was just eighteen years old. After years of working in one of the poorest communities in New Orleans, her life took an unexpected turn after becoming pen pals with two men on Louisiana's death row. She soon became their spiritual director and journeyed with them all the way to their deaths in the electric chair. Her experiences are detailed in her bestselling book *Dead Man Walking* (Vintage, 1994), which eventually was made into an award-winning movie and an opera. Sister Helen has dedicated her life to ending the death penalty and embodies the belief that even for those who have committed terrible sins, nothing "will be able to separate us from the love of God in Christ Jesus our Lord" (Romans 8:39).

© ZUMA Press, Inc. / Alamy Stock Photo

omniscient ▶ From the Latin *omnia*, meaning "all," and *scientia*, meaning "knowledge." Refers to the divine attribute that God is able to know everything, past, present, and future.

God can see the uniqueness of every single human being, yet this does not keep him from seeing all of us as a connected whole. For God, there is no conflict to see us both as many and as one. Saint Paul notes that God is able to overcome any separation that we have devised (see Romans 8:38–39). Though we might separate who is worthy and who is not, in God's eyes no one is beyond the reach of his love and compassion. We are called to see the world similarly.

God can see the uniqueness of every human being and all of humanity as a connected whole.

Despite our limitations, we can rise above our sinful inheritance to share in the divine life that is offered to us. Although we will never be all-knowing, God continually invites us to see things his way and provides guidance for us. Jesus Christ bridges the chasm we created between God and humanity. His very being is the union of God and humanity, and in him we find a role model showing us how to live a good human life.

Saint Paul said, "Have among yourselves the same attitude that is also yours in Christ Jesus" (Philippians 2:5). How do we do that? Love. Love is the key that heals the separation between God and us, and between us and one another. ✳

HMMMMM. . . How did eating from the tree of the knowledge of good and evil change life for Adam and Eve?

Article 4
The Wages of Sin

Jacob was tired of his parents' constant nagging about doing his chores. Take out the trash, make his bed, wash the dishes, feed and give medicine to his dog, Atticus, and so on. If he was just an hour or so late in completing a chore, they jumped on him to do it right away. Jacob began to rebel in little ways. To speed up his morning routine, he sometimes skipped giving the dog his medicine. He had accidentally skipped it before, and it did not seem to make any difference. His parents never knew, so he figured it was no big deal.

Then one morning, Atticus was sick. He was sluggish and tired and did not want to eat. Jacob's parents thought maybe he had eaten something bad in the backyard, so they kept him inside as they all went off to work and school. When they came home, Atticus was worse. They rushed him to the vet, who discovered that Atticus's red blood cell count had dropped significantly, and he was near death. Because the medicine he was supposed to take was combatting a disease that caused his red blood cell count to drop, Jacob had to admit that he was not giving it to him regularly. In the end, Atticus survived and Jacob learned his lesson, but this situation reminded Jacob that failure to do the right thing can have serious consequences.

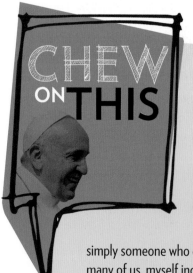

CHEW ON THIS

"Adam, where are you?" This is the first question God asks man after his sin. "Adam, where are you?" Adam lost his bearings, his place in creation, because he thought he could be powerful, able to control everything, to be God. Harmony was lost; man erred and this error occurs over and over again also in relationships with others. "The other" is no longer a brother or sister to be loved, but simply someone who disturbs my life and my comfort. . . . How many of us, myself included, have lost our bearings; we are no longer attentive to the world in which we live; we don't care; we don't protect what God created for everyone, and we end up unable even to care for one another! (Pope Francis, *The Works of Mercy*)

Not all sin leads to a physical death, but it certainly can slowly chip away at our spiritual life. **The Fall** from **Grace**, the biblical Revelation about the origins of sin and evil in the world, shows the consequences of our ancestors' sin. Saint Paul reminds us of the Genesis account when he writes, "For the wages of sin is death" (Romans 6:23). A wage is a payment we receive for something we have done. Sin certainly pays, but the currency is death.

Why do humans have to work to get food? Genesis, chapter 3, provides an etiology as to why.

Fall, the ➤ Also called the Fall from Grace, the biblical Revelation about the origins of sin and evil in the world, expressed figuratively in the account of Adam and Eve in Genesis.

grace ➤ The free and undeserved gift that God gives us to empower us to respond to his call and to live as his adopted sons and daughters. Grace restores our loving communion with the Holy Trinity, lost through sin.

Original Sin

Original Sin refers to the sin of the first human beings who disobeyed God's command, and to the fallen state of human nature. Adam and Eve first rebelled against God, and since then, humanity has experienced the consequences. The first sin was the choice of a self-centered life over a God-centered life. "All subsequent sin would be disobedience toward God and lack of trust in his goodness" (*CCC*, number 397).

The original justice and holiness that characterized God's creation was lost. The grace of living fully in God's presence could no longer be experienced. Genesis, chapter 3, expresses this loss in the consequences that God pronounces at the end of the chapter. Consider Adam and Eve's life before and after the Fall:

Before the Fall	After the Fall
• They lived in perfect union with God.	• They hid from God.
• They were one body.	• They realized they were naked (different).
• They felt no shame.	• They covered themselves with loincloths.
• They lived in the garden.	• They were expelled from the garden.
• They had access to the tree of life.	• They would die.
• They lived in perfect peace and harmony.	• They lived with blame, conflict, and pain.

The consequences of sin, humanity's loss of peace and harmony, are communicated through the etiological elements of the second Creation account. These etiologies offer folk-story-like explanations for natural phenomenon (for example, why snakes crawl on their bellies), but they also communicate the religious truths of the consequences of sin:

Etiology	Religious Truth
• Why humans wear clothing.	• Sin leads to shame.
• Why snakes are cursed among animals and must crawl on the ground.	• Sin brings isolation.
• Why women have pain in childbirth.	• Sin causes pain and suffering.
• Why humans work to get food.	• Sin disrupts our harmony with nature.
• Why humans die.	• Sin leads us away from God and life.

Death

Saint Paul writes, "Just as through one person sin entered the world, and through sin, death, and thus death came to all, inasmuch as all sinned" (Romans 5:12). The "one person" to whom Saint Paul is referring is our first human ancestor, Adam (and Eve). We might have an urge to blame Adam and Eve for the sins in the world, but recall that Adam blamed Eve, and Eve blamed the serpent. By blaming them, we would just be continuing this blame game, avoiding our own responsibility. Yes, we were born and raised in a world tarnished by sin, but our sins are our own, and the consequences are the same: death and separation from God and one another.

When God told Adam that he should not eat from the tree of the knowledge of good and evil, he warned Adam that he would die if he did so. This is true. Instead of living in harmony with God forever, Adam and Eve eventually physically died. But sin is responsible for more than just our physical death. The Church explains that "Adam's sin . . . has transmitted to us a sin with which we are all born afflicted, a sin which is the 'death of the soul'"[4] (*CCC*, number 403). In other words, we experience other types of death and loss due to sin, many of them spiritual in nature.

Sin separates and disrupts the harmony that God intended. Just as a physical death separates body and soul, a spiritual death separates us from God and one another. If you consistently mistreat your friend, she would probably no longer hang around you. Lying to family members can bring about a divisive atmosphere of mistrust and suspicion, which can tear apart the family bond. Racism continuously oppresses groups of people and causes harmful divisions within our society.

Sin is responsible for the separation and disruption of harmony that God originally intended for humanity.

Why Did God Even Let It Happen?

Why evil existed in the first place is a mystery. There is no easy explanation. To gain any insight, we must look at the bigger picture and view the question within the entirety of our faith, including the death and Resurrection of Jesus Christ. "In time we can discover that God in his almighty providence can bring a good from the consequences of an evil, even a moral evil, caused by his creatures" (*CCC*, number 312).

God did not create evil and is not the cause of it. God created humans to love him and one another, and in order to love, we must have the capability to *choose* to love. If you program a robot to hand out food to those in need, the robot did not perform any acts of love. It is just a machine doing what it was programmed to do. Because we were made in God's image, we have the gift of free will. With free will, we have choices and options to do good or evil.

Even when we choose to do wrong, God can make something good come from it. This does not mean that doing something evil is okay, but rather that it can be an experience that we use to learn and grow closer to God and one another. If you have ever insulted or made fun of someone in public, you can see the hurt that it causes. Owning up to the pain you caused can make you a more respectful person in the long run. God never wills evil, but God can use our failures for good—much like fertilizer. Fertilizer is ugly, smelly, and un-

pleasant to work with, but when it is used in the right way, it can create growth and transform a barren place into a beautiful landscape. Although sin has caused unfathomable pain and suffering, it has also allowed us to experience the saving grace of God in his Son, Jesus Christ. ✳

What have you learned, and how did you grow closer to God after you chose to do wrong?

HMMMMM. . . In what way have you seen or experienced sin leading to separation between people, communities, or countries?

Article 5
The Cycle of Sin Begins

As we have learned, the origin of sin is dramatized in the account of Adam and Eve in Genesis, chapter 3, but the story does not end there. Their disobedient act against God sets in motion a cycle of sin. That cycle continues with their children, Cain and Abel, whose sinful inheritance leads to death. And that sinful inheritance, Original Sin, leads to **concupiscence**, the tendency of human beings to be attracted to sin.

Cain and Abel: Our Inheritance

We find the influence of concupiscence in the account of Cain and Abel (see Genesis 4:1–16). Both brothers make offerings, but Cain becomes jealous of Abel, whose offering gains the Lord's favor. Overcome by this jealousy, Cain murders Abel. Beforehand, God tells Cain that "sin lies in wait at the door: its urge is for you, yet you can rule over it" (4:7). This "urge" is the result of concupiscence, and for Cain, it manifests itself as jealousy. The influence of concupiscence does not force Cain to commit this grave sin. God's encouragement to Cain is that he has a choice; he can "rule over it." God has confidence in humanity's innate goodness to overcome temptation.

Because of Original Sin, we all suffer from concupiscence. Certainly, sinful behavior can be learned from others, but concupiscence is much more perplexing than this. Even if you could raise a child without the outside influence of any sinful viewpoint or behavior, the child would still suffer from concupiscence. Ultimately, "the transmission of original sin is a mystery that we cannot fully understand" (*CCC*, number 404).

When Cain became jealous of his brother Abel, God told him that "sin lies in wait at the door: its urge is for you, yet you can rule over it" (Genesis 4:7). This is an example of God's confidence in humanity's ability to overcome temptation.

---

concupiscence ➤ The tendency of all human beings toward sin, as a result of Original Sin.

Racism is an example of communal sin because it results from the collective action of many people. It is up to the community to work together for its end.

In general, it is good to focus on the positive aspects of who we are and what we do. It is important to understand that all of us—without exception—are made in the divine image and are infinitely loved by God. Yet it would be wrong to ignore the source of pain and suffering in our world. Original Sin is not only the act committed by our earliest ancestors; it is also the fallen state into which every person who has ever lived on the planet is born, with the exception of Jesus and his mother, Mary. We are not guilty of our ancestors' personal sin, because we did not commit it. Nonetheless, we have contracted this sinful condition as a result of their sin. We would be foolish to ignore its influence.

MAKE IT SO

It is important to honor and respect parents, teachers, church and civic leaders, and other authorities, but it is also necessary to admit that no one is perfect. Even the best of people in authority can teach sinful viewpoints or habits. Although we maintain respect for their authority, we must measure their morals and deeds against the teachings of Jesus. What have they taught us that fits with Christ's mandate to love our enemies? Do they avoid greed, pride, and envy? How have they influenced us to become more Christlike? It is good to reflect on how those in a position of authority have influenced our own thinking and behavior. Hopefully you will discover that they have been wonderful teachers. And if not, you can learn from that too.

Noah and the Flood: Communal Sin

We tend to think of sin in personal terms because it makes sense that a person can only be responsible for what he or she does. What others do is their own choice. Yet there are sinful situations for which entire communities can be held accountable. These can come in the form of a nation's laws. Slavery and the Jim Crow laws which oppressed African-Americans in the United States are examples of communal sin. Even if an individual were against these laws, each member of the community is responsible for working toward their end. Pollution and other environmental problems are also examples of communal sin because they resulted from the collective actions of many people.

Communal sin is addressed in the account of Noah and the Great Flood (see Genesis 6:5–9:28). Sin had become such a deeply rooted part of society that God dealt with the people as a whole. Only Noah and his family were spared.

To address humanity's sin, this prehistoric account uses a powerful symbol that is common to literature from diverse times and cultures: water. Water is life. We drink it, wash with it, play in it, and fish in it, and over half of the human body consists of H_2O. Though it certainly represents life, water is also a symbol of death. Water is one of the most destructive forces on Earth: it carves out rivers through the landscape; heavy rainfall can create floods that destroy our homes and towns; earthquakes send tsunamis that leave miles of devastation and kill thousands of people. We can find water's symbolism of life and death expressed in the liturgy of the Easter Vigil when the celebrant blesses the baptismal water and says:

> The waters of the great flood
> you made a sign of the waters of Baptism,
> that make an end of sin and a new beginning of goodness.[5]
> (*CCC*, number 1219)

The Great Flood prefigures Christ's Baptism that washes away Original Sin. This is why we baptize children as infants. It is not because they have committed any sin personally but because they were born wounded by Original Sin. Baptism does not cure concupiscence, but it does impart "the life of Christ's grace, erases original sin and turns a man back toward God" (*CCC*, number 405). We are strengthened by God through the sacraments and the Church to resist sin and to do God's will.

Water represents both life and death and is a common symbol found in literature from diverse times and cultures. The account of Noah and the Flood uses water as the means by which God cleanses the Earth of sin.

Déjà Vu: The Tower of Babel

The Tower of Babel (see Genesis 11:1–9) repeats the themes we found in the account of Adam and Eve's sin. The people all over the world live together, and they speak the same language. Like Adam and Eve, they rebel against their human limitations and try to be like God by building a tower to the sky—the place where they believe God resides. They are "united only in [their] perverse ambition to forge [their] own unity"[6] (*CCC*, number 57). Their consequences are also described in the form of etiologies. For example, God scatters them and confuses their language to thwart their ambition and establish the cultural diversity God chooses to work through.

So why would the human authors include this account if they are just repeating the same theme as the stories about Cain and Abel and the Flood? This repetition is no accident. The inclusion of this account shows us that the cycle of sin that began with Adam and Eve is repeated by humanity over and over again. Marked by Original Sin and its accompanying tendency toward evil, humanity's descent into the depths of sin recurs age after age.

But God does not simply leave us to suffer the consequences without any assistance. He repeatedly sends us angels and prophets to speak his Word. He establishes covenants and provides laws to guide us. Ultimately, he sends his Son, Jesus Christ, to reunite God and humanity and show us how to live the life that we were created for: to love God and one another. ✳

The Tower of Babel account shows us that the cycle of sin begun with Adam and Eve continues. The tower itself is most likely modeled after the ziggurat. Pictured here is a restored ziggurat, once a Sumerian temple, in ancient Ur, Iraq.

HMMMMMM. . . How does the cycle of sin described in the Book of Genesis continue today?

1. What does it mean to say that a husband and wife become "one body" (Genesis 2:24)?

2. Explain what Pope Saint John Paul II meant when he said that married couples feel no shame, like Adam and Eve before the Fall.

3. What do we mean when we say the two Creation accounts in Genesis use figurative or symbolic language?

4. What does eating from the tree of the knowledge of good and evil symbolize?

5. What are etiologies, and how are they used in Genesis to explain the consequences of sin?

6. Explain this statement from Saint Paul: "For the wages of sin is death" (Romans 6:23).

7. Explain concupiscence using the account of Cain and Abel.

8. What is communal sin? Explain how the account of Noah and the Flood is an example of communal sin.

UNIT 1

THE CYCLE OF SIN

1. In this painting by William-Adolphe Bougeureau, called *The First Mourning*, Adam and Eve have found the body of their dead son, Abel. Why do you think Adam is holding his left hand over the left side of his body?

2. Consider the way the artist has depicted Adam and Eve. What feelings are portrayed? What is the artist trying to communicate?

3. How does the background scenery give us a clue as to what the future will be like now that violence and murder have entered human history?

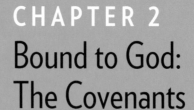

UNIT 1

CHAPTER 2
Bound to God: The Covenants

AFTER THE FALL, WHY DID GOD WANT TO MAKE COVENANTS WITH HUMANITY?

SNAPSHOT

Article 6   Page 41
Ending the Cycle

Article 7   Page 46
The Promise

Article 8   Page 50
Covenant: A Relationship and a Remedy

Article 9   Page 54
The Covenants with Noah and Abraham
• Pre-read: Genesis 9:1–17
• Pre-read: Genesis 12:1–9, 15:1–21

Article 10   Page 60
The Covenants with Moses and David
• Pre-read: Exodus, chapters 19–24
• Pre-read: 2 Samuel, chapter 7

Article 6
Ending the Cycle

Addiction to unhealthy substances can bring untold misery to people regardless of their gender, race, or economic or social status. It affects not only the person with the addiction but others as well, most notably their family members. It has a wide-ranging impact on all of society. Though there seem to be many factors contributing to substance addiction, researchers have learned that people with a parent who is an alcoholic, for example, are three to four times more likely to become alcoholics themselves. Without recovery, alcoholism and other addictions can become cycles of dysfunction with harmful consequences that can be felt generations later.

In 1935, Alcoholics Anonymous, or AA, was founded as a fellowship to help people recover from their addiction to alcohol. Here, they can freely share their stories and struggles with others. By learning about and practicing a spiritual program called the Twelve Step program, they can achieve and maintain sobriety. Those who have stayed sober for many years can offer encouragement and guidance to those who are just starting out in the program.

Occasionally in these meetings, the attendees will hear someone who has been sober for a long time say something like, "I am grateful for my alcoholism." What? How could someone be grateful for a disease that has caused them so much pain? Here's one reason: Having this disease made them put their lives into God's hands, and as a result, they became more reliable, caring, and devoted people. Their recovery from alcoholism helped them find their faith and encouraged them to trust God more and more. Would it surprise you that in a similar way, Christians proclaim their gratitude for Adam and Eve's sin?

The Easter Vigil celebrates the coming of the light of Christ into the world.

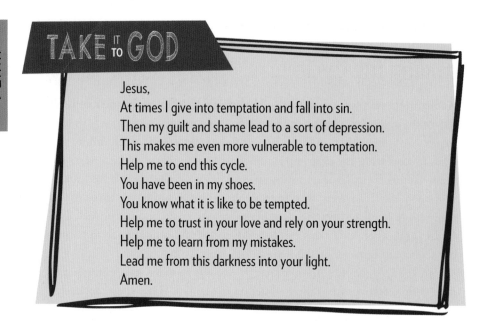

TAKE IT TO GOD

Jesus,
At times I give into temptation and fall into sin.
Then my guilt and shame lead to a sort of depression.
This makes me even more vulnerable to temptation.
Help me to end this cycle.
You have been in my shoes.
You know what it is like to be tempted.
Help me to trust in your love and rely on your strength.
Help me to learn from my mistakes.
Lead me from this darkness into your light.
Amen.

"O Happy Fault"

The **Easter Vigil** is the liturgy celebrated on Holy Saturday, the night before Easter Sunday. It celebrates the coming of the light of Christ into the world. It's also the time when adults and older children are received into the Church through the Sacraments of Baptism, the Eucharist, and Confirmation. The liturgy usually begins outside, then everyone in the congregation processes into a darkened church holding candles lit from the **Paschal candle**. These candles represent Christ's light, which ends the darkness of sin and death.

Easter Vigil ➤ The liturgy celebrated on Holy Saturday night. It celebrates the coming of the light of Christ into the world and is also the time when adults and older children are received into the Church through the Sacraments of Christian Initiation.

Paschal candle ➤ Also called the Easter candle, this is the large, tall candle lit at the Easter Vigil by a flame from the new fire; the symbol of the Risen Christ.

After everyone has entered, the deacon or priest offers up a hymn of praise called the Easter Proclamation, or the **Exsultet**. In this beautiful expression of gratitude to God, we are reminded of his saving activity throughout human history. His saving activity is finally crowned in Christ's death and Resurrection. The Exsultet also highlights the connection between Original Sin and our Savior, Jesus Christ:

> O truly necessary sin of Adam,
> destroyed completely by the Death of Christ!
> O happy fault
> that earned so great, so glorious a Redeemer!
> (*Roman Missal,* page 337)

"Necessary sin of Adam"? "O happy fault"? Calling anything, especially Original Sin, a "happy fault" seems paradoxical. A **paradox** is a statement that seems illogical or contradicts itself. Nonetheless, it expresses a truth. Some of Jesus' teachings are paradoxical; for example: "Thus, the last will be first, and the first will be last" (Matthew 20:16). Taken just as the words are written, they do not make sense, yet they still point to an important truth about human nature and God's will.

"O happy fault" points to an important truth: just as a recovering alcoholic may see his or her addiction as a gift leading to a renewed relationship with God, we as a Church see how Original Sin allowed us to come to know the Son of God Incarnate. Adam's sin was "necessary" because without this "happy fault," we would have never known Jesus Christ, "so glorious a Redeemer!" (You will study the Easter Vigil further in chapter 13.)

The Paschal candle, also called the Easter candle, symbolizes the Risen Christ.

Exsultet ➤ Sung during the Easter Vigil, this triumphant hymn of praise proclaims, "Christ is Risen!" It announces that on this night, humanity and all creation receive the Good News of salvation. Also called the Easter Proclamation.

paradox ➤ A statement that seems contradictory or opposed to common sense and yet is true.

Slowly but Surely

If you put the equation 2 x 2 - 32 = 0 in front of an average second grader, would she or he be able to solve it? If so, this child certainly would not be an *average* second grader! The reason teachers do not assign problems like these to second graders is that their brains have not developed enough to solve them. They must grow, and their ability to think abstractly needs to mature. Until then, they must work their way through addition and subtraction, then multiplication and division, and so on.

Why did God the Father wait to send the Son of God to conquer sin and death? Why did Jesus come roughly two thousand years ago? Why not four thousand years ago? Or better yet, why not right after the first sin was committed? These are good questions to ponder. One thing to keep in mind while you do so is that Sacred Scripture reveals that "God communicates himself to man gradually" (*Catechism of the Catholic Church [CCC]*, number 53). It seems that God gives us only what we can effectively handle. Like second graders who cannot handle algebraic equations, it appears that humans needed to grow in their ability to grasp the fullness of God's truth.

As God revealed more and more to humanity, we can see how our understanding of the cycle of sin and punishment evolved in Scripture. Consider how the understanding of God's punishment for someone's sins develops in these three passages:

Exodus 34:7	Ezekiel 18:20	John 9:1–3
God brings "punishment for their parents' wickedness on children and children's children to the third and fourth generation!"	"Only the one who sins shall die. The son shall not be charged with the guilt of his father."	"As he passed by he saw a man blind from birth. His disciples asked him, 'Rabbi, who sinned, this man or his parents, that he was born blind?' Jesus answered, 'Neither he nor his parents sinned; it is so that the works of God might be made visible through him.'"

In the earliest passage (Exodus 34:7), the understanding is that God not only causes the person to suffer but also causes their children and grandchildren to suffer. Then, generations later, Ezekiel proclaims that God only punishes the sinner—their children do not suffer. Finally, in the New Testament,

Jesus teaches that not all suffering is a punishment for (or a consequence of) sin. In fact, he goes in the opposite direction, implying that the blind man's suffering provides an opportunity for God's healing power and love to be revealed. As humanity grows in understanding and our faith deepens, God slowly but surely makes himself and his will known to us.

Ending the cycle of sin and death has been a gradual process. Throughout salvation history, God progressively reveals himself and his saving plan. We can see this most clearly through the covenants he makes with Abraham, Moses and the Israelites, and King David, for example. Through these covenants, God begins to slowly heal the separation brought about by sin. ✳

In John 9:1–3, Jesus teaches that a blind man's suffering is not a punishment for sin but rather an opportunity for God's healing love to be revealed.

HMMMMM. . .

How can Original Sin be considered a "happy fault"?

UNIT 1

Article 7
The Promise

Stanley hung his head and stared at his shoes as his dad told him, "Sometimes it seems like you are your own worst enemy." After finding out Stanley had not turned in almost half of his homework assignments, his father called his teachers, only to discover he had also been skipping school. "Son, we had high hopes for you, but you've taken a wrecking ball to your academic career." His father shook his head and continued: "I don't think you need any more punishment from your mother and me. The Fs on your transcript are going to be the price you pay."

Usually when Stanley got in trouble, he could focus on the injustice of his parents' punishment, but they did not do anything this time. He was left alone to face the fact that his actions had caused him major problems. It was a giant mess, and even though they had every reason to, his parents did not abandon him. They offered to get him a tutor to help him catch up. When he asked for assistance, they helped right away. Their love for Stanley did not diminish at all.

© Freedom Studio / Shutterstock.com

God's love for us never wavers, no matter what we do.

Like a loving parent, no matter what we do, God's love for us never wavers. Scripture tells us that "God is love" (1 John 4:8). Love is who God is, so for him to quit loving us, he would have to cease being God! Even though our sins bring pain and suffering to us and to one another and certainly do not please him, they still play no role when it comes to his love. There is nothing we can do to make God fall out of love with us.

God's Love Endures

At first glance, much of the third chapter of Genesis seems to be about God's punishment of Adam and Eve. They were exiled from the Garden of Eden, after all. When we read it more closely, however, we see the signs of God's enduring love and continual care for humanity. For example, when Adam and Eve realized they were naked, they immediately sewed together some fig leaves to cover themselves. Like a good parent, God saw that his children were suffering from the mess they had created. The leaves they used were only a quick fix to cover their shame, so God gave them more durable clothing (see Genesis 3:21).

CATHOLICS **MAKING** A DIFFERENCE

Before his conversion experience, Saint Francis of Assisi (c. 1181–1226) loved his extravagant wardrobe. He was a socialite and the son of a wealthy cloth merchant who was expected to take over his father's prosperous business. An injury in battle and a call from God to rebuild his Church changed all that. After a lengthy disagreement with his overbearing father about his life's direction, Francis publicly denounced him by removing his clothing in the court. He returned his money and clothing to his father and announced his mission to serve God. Saint Francis started a religious order known for dedication to the poor. He spent the rest of his life feeding, sheltering, and clothing the poor.

In one verse of this chapter, there is also an announcement that God will be victorious over sin and death. The verse is called the **Protoevangelium**. *Proto* means "the first" or "the earliest form of." *Evangelium* means "good news." So *Protoevangelium* refers to the "first announcement of the good news," or first gospel. It is found in the punishments that God gives to the snake.

> I will put enmity between you and the woman,
> and between your offspring and hers;
> They will strike at your head,
> while you strike at their heel.
>
> (Genesis 3:15)

Consider the symbolism and other elements of this verse:

Literal Sign	Spiritual Meaning
The snake	The snake represents the Devil.
Enmity	*Enmity* means "the state of opposition or being hostile to someone or something."
The woman	Many Church Fathers see the woman as a symbol of the Virgin Mary, the "New Eve."
The woman's offspring	Many Church Fathers see the woman's offspring as Jesus Christ, the "New Adam."
Strike at the heel	This action would cause an injury.
Strike at the head	This action would cause death.

Protoevangelium ➤ From the Greek *protos*, meaning "first," and *euangelion*, meaning "good news." It refers to the passage in the Book of Genesis (see 3:15) that announces the future coming of a messiah and savior: the first announcement of the Good News.

UNIT 1

In the account of God's punishment of the snake, we are allowed a glimpse of the first announcement of the "Good News" of the coming of Jesus Christ. The snake is only able to strike at the heel and inflict injury (sin), whereas the woman's offspring (Jesus Christ) will strike at the snake's head, a more powerful blow that could bring an end to the life of the snake (evil). The Protoevangelium is an early foreshadowing of the Paschal Mystery, that Christ will ultimately conquer sin and death.

There is no doubt that Original Sin has painful consequences, but God did not abandon us. Despite the escalation of sin, his love for us endures, and he is faithful to his promise. ✳

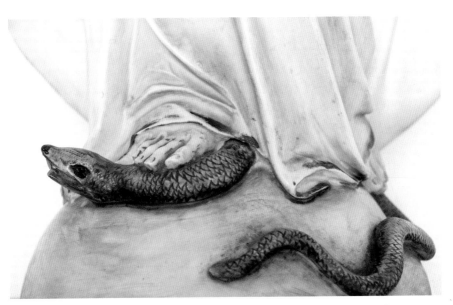

The woman mentioned in Genesis 3:15 is often seen as a symbol of the Virgin Mary, the "new Eve."

HMMMMMM. . .
Which sign of God's love in the second Creation account do you find the most remarkable? Explain.

UNIT 1

Article 8

Covenant: A Relationship and a Remedy

Recall that a **covenant** is a solemn agreement between human beings or between God and human beings in which mutual commitments are made. Through the covenants, God established a special relationship with his people. Even when humanity ignored the commitments they made, God was and is always faithful. Though sin brings about division, the covenants are the ties that bind us to God.

What Is a Covenant?

The English word *covenant* comes from the Latin word *convenire*, meaning "to come together." In the Old Testament, the Hebrew term most often used to express a covenant is *berit*, which originally meant a shackle or a chain. This helps us understand that covenants were a means of binding God with his people.

MAKE IT SO

Have you ever heard "Do I have your word?" or "You better keep your word" when someone was encouraging you to be honest? These phrases connect honesty and relationships by pointing out that trustworthiness is the necessary glue that keeps people together. This applied to the covenants God made with the Israelites, and it also applies in your daily life. Consider the opposite: What does lying do to friendships? Being reliable and honest are essential elements that strengthen your relationships with your family, friends, teachers, coaches, and all of society.

---

covenant ▶ A solemn agreement between human beings or between God and human beings in which mutual commitments are made.

The Hebrew phrase sometimes used for establishing a covenant is *karat berith*, which would mean "to cut a covenant." *Cutting* refers to some physical elements in the rituals used by ancient peoples for establishing a covenant. In one type of ritual, when two people entered into a covenant, they would cut their hands and then bind them together. By doing this, they would mix their blood with each other's. In the minds of the Hebrews, blood contained their lifeforce, so this exchange of blood symbolically united them.

In another type of covenant ritual, the people would cut animals in half, lay the parts on the ground, and walk between them. We see an example of this type of ritual in one of the passages describing the covenant God made with Abraham: "Bring me a three-year-old heifer, a three-year-old female goat, a three-year-old ram, a turtledove, and a young pigeon. [Abraham] brought him all these, split them in two, and placed each half opposite the other" (Genesis 15:9–10).

When Abraham cut a covenant with God, he literally cut animals in half. In ancient times, this was common practice. Most people were illiterate. Writing and signing an actual document wasn't possible.

Covenants Are Relational

Human beings are naturally relational creatures. We need both relationships with individuals and with communities. In our relationships, we have a role and responsibilities. For example, in a friendship there is an agreement (usually unspoken) that those involved will spend time together, treat each other kindly, and be honest with each other. In the case of a student-teacher or student-coach relationship, there is an expectation that the teacher or coach will provide some sort of educational experience in which the student or athlete will learn and grow.

Some relationships, like friendships, begin naturally without any preparation or formal acknowledgement. Like friendships, covenants are rooted in mutual respect and love for each other. On the other hand, covenants also establish formal relationships, with mutually understood and agreed-upon commitments. Like in any relationship, the actions of people in a covenant are guided by their respective roles. When a covenant is established between equals, each person usually makes similar commitments. In the case of a marriage, each spouse promises to love, honor, and serve the other. Sometimes the commitments are different, especially in the case of God's covenants with humanity. In these situations, God takes on the role of leader and provider, while we commit to being faithful and obedient. This is not because God wants to control us, but rather it is because he is all-powerful and loves us. Obedience to God can only help us!

© Sergey Novikov / Shutterstock.com

Covenants, like friendships, are rooted in mutual respect and love.

Covenants Are Remedies to Sin

Just as the marriage covenant binds a husband and wife together, our covenants with God unite us with him. Because sin created a separation from God, covenants are the ties that bind us to God and act as a remedy to sin.

God invited our first ancestors to "intimate communion with himself and clothed them with resplendent grace and justice" (*CCC*, number 54). By committing the first sin of disobedience to God, they disrupted their state of grace and justice. Through covenants, God begins to restore humanity to a state of grace—that is, a proper relationship between humanity and himself. The laws established by some of the covenants aid in this process of restoration. Sin is disobeying God's Law and therefore harming our relationship with God; obeying covenant laws does the opposite. Obeying these laws works as a remedy by restoring our relationship with God. The laws provide the framework and encouragement for us to follow God's will.

God established and renewed covenants throughout salvation history. He started with Adam and Eve and also formed special relationships with Noah, Abraham and Sarah, Moses, and King David. Despite the fact that humans turned away from him, God continued to make himself known to his people. His covenantal relationship was ultimately fulfilled with Jesus Christ, who was the fulfillment of the Old Law and mediator of the New Covenant. ✳

At the Last Supper, Jesus took a cup, gave thanks, and gave it to them, saying, "Drink from it, all of you, for this is my blood of the covenant, which will be shed . . . for the forgiveness of sins" (see Matthew 26:27–28).

HMMMMMM. . . How do God's covenants in the Bible strengthen his relationship with his people?

Article 9

The Covenants with Noah and Abraham

Both the Old and the New

The statement "know thyself," attributed to the philosopher Socrates, points to an important truth: Self-knowledge can help us better understand who we are today. How does one gain that understanding? One way is to look to your past—your family upbringing, your childhood, friendships you made, experiences, and choices you made. Knowing what you were like at a much younger age can help you understand something about yourself. You might even see how those events hinted at the person you would become.

Just as self-knowledge can help us understand who we are today, we look to the Old Testament to fully grasp the Paschal Mystery.

The same can be said about how we understand the mission of our Savior, Jesus Christ. To more fully grasp the Paschal Mystery, we look to the Old Testament, for it is "an indispensable part of Sacred Scripture. Its books are divinely inspired and retain a permanent value"[1] (*CCC*, number 121). The Old Testament offers us the promise of what is to come through the Passion, death, Resurrection, and Ascension of Jesus Christ.

For example, in the Old Testament we can find events and people that seem to foreshadow the work of Jesus Christ. **Typology** is the study of God's work in the Old Testament as a prefiguration of what he accomplished through Jesus Christ. Typology shows us the unity of God's plan in both the Old and New Testaments. Christians read the Old Testament in the light of our faith in Jesus Christ. We recognize that the Old Testament can help us better understand the meaning of the New Testament. Saint Augustine said that "the New Testament lies hidden in the Old and the Old Testament is unveiled in the New"[2] (*CCC*, number 129). The covenants God establishes with his people in the Old Testament point toward Christ's saving work

The Covenant with Noah

Recall reading the story of Noah's family and the Great Flood. How does it end? After forty days of rain, no dry land could be found anywhere, and the clouds obstructed any view of the stars. All points of reference had vanished; Noah and his family were lost in the Flood. Sometimes when we experience a loss, a death, or trauma, we too might feel lost like Noah and his family did. Our world has been turned upside down, and we feel disoriented. There is no place to find comfort or relief.

Sometimes we can feel lost like Noah and his family when we experience great loss. But, even in our darkest moments in life, we too, like Noah, can still find help from God.

typology ➤ The discernment of God's work in the Old Testament as a prefiguration of what he accomplished through Jesus Christ in the fullness of time. Typology illuminates the unity of God's plan in the two Testaments, but does not devalue the Old Covenant or its ongoing relevance and value for the Jewish people.

But even during these times, we can still find help from God—though not always with the speed and manner that we might prefer! Once again we can feel the ground beneath our feet and move forward. After forty days, Noah sent a dove out to search for dry land, but the dove returned bearing no sign that it had found any. On the seventh day, Noah tried again. This time, the dove came back with an olive leaf in its beak (see Genesis 8:11). At last, hope!

Soon enough dry ground appeared amid the waters. When Noah landed, he offered a sacrifice that pleased the Lord. Then God told Noah, "I will establish my covenant with you . . . there shall not be another flood to devastate the earth" (Genesis 9:11). The Lord then established the rainbow as a sign of the covenant with Noah and all his descendants.

This account of the covenant with Noah has similarities to the first account of Creation in Genesis. In both accounts, we have dry land appearing from the water that once covered the Earth. Just as God commanded the man and woman, the Lord tells Noah to populate the earth (see 9:1) and then commands Noah and his family to care for the animals (see 9:2).

I DIDN'T KNOW THAT!

The Jewish people were *and still are* God's Chosen People! Catholics recognize God's enduring relationship with the Jewish people, even as we profess the necessity of recognizing Jesus Christ's work in the plan of salvation. Catholics acknowledge that God's covenants with the Jewish people were the original covenants and remain authentic to this day. For this reason, although we are still called to bear witness to our faith in Jesus "in a humble and sensitive manner," the Church "neither conducts nor supports any specific institutional mission work" to evangelize the Jews ("The Gifts and the Calling of God are Irrevocable," Vatican Commission for Religious Relations with the Jews, 2015).

There are also some important differences between the covenant with Noah and the first Creation account. For example, in the Creation account, the man and woman were vegetarian! God told them that every seed-bearing plant and tree would be their food (see Genesis 1:29). Now God says to Noah that he may eat any living creature that moves (see 9:3). So after the Flood, animals will die to provide humans with food, reminding us that the perfect harmony between all living things that God originally created is not yet restored.

Overall, though, in this covenant with Noah, there is a sense that God is reestablishing the justice and holiness that he originally intended for humanity. There is a universal nature to it. Directly after God makes this covenant, Noah's descendants multiply to become all the nations of the world (see Genesis 10:32). This is a way of saying that God's covenant with Noah now extends to all the nations of the Earth and will remain so as long as the world lasts. This prefigures Christ's outreach to the Gentiles, in which Jesus will "gather into one the dispersed children of God" (John 11:52).

The Covenant with Abraham

The first eleven chapters of Genesis are considered prehistoric accounts. Chapter 12 marks the beginning of Israel's history. Starting with Abraham, God begins a new phase of his plan to restore humanity's holiness and justice. God establishes a covenant with Abraham, promising him three things: (1) to make of him a great nation by providing Abraham with many descendants, (2) to provide Abraham and his descendants a land of their own, and (3) to make Abraham and his descendants a blessing for all the nations.

© jyvart / Shutterstock.com

After Noah, his family, and the animals landed, Noah offered a sacrifice to God. God established a covenant with Noah, promising to never again release the flood waters.

In chapters 12 through 17 of Genesis, God's covenant with Abraham gradually unfolds in three different events. These events are complementary, each one having a slightly different emphasis as clarified in this chart.

Scripture Passage	The Lord's Promise(s)	Abram's Response	Sign Used to Seal the Covenant
Genesis 12:1–9	• He will make Abram a great nation and bless him. • He will make Abram's name great, so that Abram will be a blessing. • He will bless those who bless Abram, and curse those who curse him.	Abram and Sarai leave their homeland, Ur, travel a great distance, and arrive in the land of Canaan as the Lord directed them.	Abram builds two altars, one in Canaan, and one in the hill country, where he also pitches his tent, claiming the land for himself and his descendants.
Genesis, chapter 15	• God reestablishes his covenant with Abram: he will possess the land and his descendants will be many. • Abram will live to a ripe old age.	Abram puts his faith in the Lord.	• Abram takes a heifer, a female goat, a ram, a turtledove, and a pigeon, splits them in two (except for the birds), and places each half opposite the other as the Lord directed. • Abram falls asleep. • A smoking fire pot and flaming torch pass between the animal pieces.
Genesis, chapter 17	God reaffirms the three promises: • Abram will become father of a multitude of nations, and kings will stem from his family line. • He will be Abram's God and the God of his descendants. • Abram and his descendants will possess the land.	Abram and his descendants must keep the covenant throughout the ages.	• Every male must be circumcised, now and throughout the ages, when he is eight days old. • Abram and Sarai are given new names, Abraham and Sarah, to reflect their role in God's plan of salvation.

It is hard for us to really understand the importance of God's covenant with Abraham. To understand its significance, keep two things in mind. First, believers in most of the gods and goddesses worshipped at this time thought they had very little to do with human affairs, unless it was to use and manipulate their human subjects. A god who treated human beings with dignity and even entered into a binding covenant to care for them was unheard of! Second, the exclusive relationship God was establishing with Abraham would eventually lead to the realization that there was only one true God. This is the beginning of **monotheism**, the religious truth that is the foundation of many of the world's great religions today.

God's covenant with Abraham is not so much a legal arrangement to enforce loyalty as it is an ever-deepening relationship of faithfulness and love. This relationship, however, is not just for the good of Abraham and his and Sarah's descendants, but also for all future generations (see Genesis 12:3). God's plan to restore us to perfect union with him continues, with God working through a specific family, just as he did with Noah. God's limitless fidelity and Abraham's faithfulness will become the foundation on which God's relationship with his people continues. ✳

HMMMMM. . .   Explain one way that the covenants with either Noah or Abraham help heal the damage caused by sin.

---

monotheism ➤ The belief in and worship of only one God.

Article 10

The Covenants with Moses and David

For many newly married couples, the first year of marriage can be a challenge. After living on their own for perhaps many years, they now must make room for someone else in their daily routines. Dirty clothes left in a corner of the bedroom frustrate a spouse who likes things neat. Makeup covering the bathroom sink leaves little room for anything else. In their marriage vows, a husband and wife promised to love and honor each other, but the vows never mentioned smelly clothes and nail polish stains in the sink! Taking time to talk and come to mutual agreements about space and daily routines is crucial for concretely expressing their love and care for each other.

Just as mutual agreements between newly married couples can help them express their care for each other, public laws provide boundaries that keep us safe and create a space to live freely. For example, driving laws are meant to keep us free from accidents. In the covenant God establishes with the Israelites through Moses, he also provides laws, not to restrict the Israelites but to help strengthen their relationship with him and with one another.

© Carsten Reisinger / Shutterstock.com

Driving laws provide restrictions to keep us safe
and free from harm. So too do God's covenants.

The Sinai Covenant and Other Ancient Near-East Treaties

To better understand the biblical writings about the covenants that God established with his people, it is helpful to look at the treaties and agreements that people in the ancient Near East created with one another. There were two main types of treaties:

- **Parity treaties** were established between two parties of roughly equal status (for example, a peace treaty between kings at the end of a war).
- **Vassal treaties** were established between unequal parties in which the greater power (for example, a king or a country) forced a less powerful party to cooperate. (A vassal is a person or country that is in a subservient position to another.)

Parity treaties were part of common life and would have been familiar to the Israelites. It's not surprising to find many references to them in the Old Testament. For example, to create peace, Abraham entered into a parity covenant with Abimelech, King of Gerar (see Genesis, chapter 20), and in 1 Kings 5:15–26, King Solomon and King Hiram of Tyre made a covenant to maintain peace as well.

In a vassal treaty, the king of a more powerful country would generally offer protection and a promise of well-being for the smaller nation. Other than this general reassurance, the treaty did not bind the king to do anything. Meanwhile the vassal country had to perform specific duties that were outlined in the treaty.

Ancient Assyrian and Hittite vassal treaties may have had an influence on the writing styles of the biblical authors. The treaties tended to have many of the following elements in their format:

1. *The Preamble* names the powerful king and offers his titles.
2. *The Historical Prologue* identifies the kind acts of the great king and provides the reasoning for the vassal nation to obey.
3. *The Demands* list the specific duties the vassal nation must perform.
4. *The Deposit of the Treaty* explains where the treaty can be found, as well as when public readings will occur.
5. *The List of Witnesses* often consists of the gods of the two countries.
6. *The Curses and Blessings* name the penalties if the treaty is not honored and the promises assured if the treaty is honored.

parity treaty ➤ An agreement made between two equal parties binding them in mutual respect and cooperation.

vassal treaty ➤ An agreement made by two unequal parties. The superior power receives absolute loyalty, service, and submission from the lesser party, the vassal.

We see many of the elements of a vassal treaty in the covenant that God makes with the Israelites through Moses, the **Sinai Covenant** (also called the Mosaic Covenant). At Mount Sinai, God renews his covenant with Abraham's descendants and establishes the Israelites as his Chosen People (see Exodus, chapters 19–24). This chart shows how the parts of the Sinai Covenant match the elements found in vassal treaties:

The Metropolitan Museum of Art, Purchase, 1886

The Succession Treaty of Assyrian King Esarhaddon is a vassal treaty written to secure the reign of the king's two sons after his death.

The Preamble and Historical Prologue	From the mountain, God commanded Moses: "This is what you will say to the house of Jacob; tell the Israelites: You have seen how I treated the Egyptians and how I bore you up on eagles' wings and brought you to myself. Now, if you obey me completely and keep my covenant, you will be my treasured possession among all peoples, though all the earth is mine." (Exodus 19:3-5)
The Demands	The Ten Commandments and other laws and ordinances (Exodus 20:3–23:19)
The Deposit of the Treaty	"Taking the book of the covenant, he read it aloud to the people, who answered, 'All that the LORD has said, we will hear and do.' Then he took the blood and splashed it on the people, saying, 'This is the blood of the covenant which the LORD has made with you according to all these words.'" (Exodus 24:7-8)
The List of Witnesses	The Israelites are monotheistic, so God is the only witness needed.
The Curses and Blessings	"If you obey [the angel] and carry out all I tell you, I will be an enemy to your enemies and a foe to your foes. . . . . You shall serve the LORD, your God; then he will bless [you]" with many good things. (Exodus 23:22,25)

Sinai Covenant ❯ The covenant established with the Israelites at Mount Sinai that renewed God's covenant with Abraham's descendants. The Sinai Covenant established the Israelites as God's Chosen People.

The Sinai Covenant teaches us that Yahweh is clearly the true King of Israel. Like a vassal treaty, the Sinai Covenant is **conditional**, but the benefits of this covenant are unique! God describes the Israelites as his "treasured possession" (Exodus 19:5). They are a Chosen People set aside for himself. God's great love for his people is expressed through the Sinai Covenant.

The Sinai Covenant Expresses God's Love

Forty years after the events at Mount Sinai, before the Israelites cross the Jordan into the Promised Land, the Book of Deuteronomy describes Moses reminding them of the Sinai Covenant and calling on them to recommit themselves to its commandments. He reminds the Israelites that God gave them the Law "so that they would recognize him and serve him as the one living and true God"[3] (*CCC*, number 62).

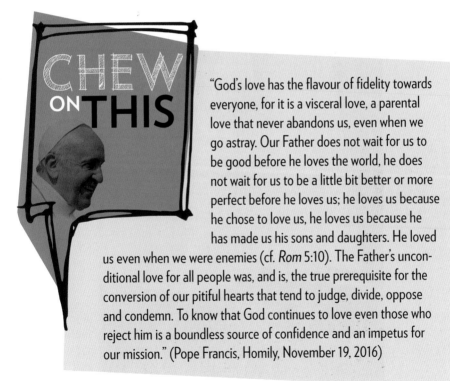

CHEW ON THIS

"God's love has the flavour of fidelity towards everyone, for it is a visceral love, a parental love that never abandons us, even when we go astray. Our Father does not wait for us to be good before he loves the world, he does not wait for us to be a little bit better or more perfect before he loves us; he loves us because he chose to love us, he loves us because he has made us his sons and daughters. He loved us even when we were enemies (cf. *Rom* 5:10). The Father's unconditional love for all people was, and is, the true prerequisite for the conversion of our pitiful hearts that tend to judge, divide, oppose and condemn. To know that God continues to love even those who reject him is a boundless source of confidence and an impetus for our mission." (Pope Francis, Homily, November 19, 2016)

UNIT 1

---

conditional ➤ Used to describe something (such as an agreement) that will happen only if something else will happen.

Sometimes the perception of God's portrayal in the Old Testament is slanted toward an image of an angry and vengeful deity, but this is an incomplete picture. When he reestablishes the covenant with the Israelites through Moses, the Lord characterizes himself as a merciful and loving God (see Exodus 34:6). The Hebrew word *hesed* best characterizes God's role in the covenantal relationship. *Hesed* is usually translated as "love," but it is not as simple as the English term. *Hesed* can also be translated as mercy, compassion, kindness, and faithfulness. It is not just an idea or feeling, but the source of active involvement in a relationship. The Hebrew term also contains an element of endurance in its meaning. So God's *hesed* is an active and involved love that is always faithful, no matter what the circumstances are.

© stevenallan / iStockphoto.com

The Mosaic Law, also called the Law of Moses, primarily refers to the Torah. It was an expression of God's love and encouraged the Israelites to do good and avoid sin.

---

hesed ▶ A Hebrew word for *mercy* that expresses God's loving forgiveness for the Chosen People.

God's love is expressed in the Mosaic Law. The Law encouraged the Israelites to avoid sin, and in doing so, prepared them to receive the one living and true Son of God, Jesus Christ. Embedded in God's covenants were the hopes of uniting God and humanity, so the people of ancient Israel were entrusted with the knowledge of God's promise. Jesus Christ, who was truly human and truly divine, is the fulfillment of those promises. He is the living embodiment of God's Law. In other words, if you want to see how God intended for humanity to live, we just need to look at the life of Jesus Christ.

After Moses' death, God continued his guidance through Moses' successor, Joshua, and later through many other Israelite leaders. The **judges** served the Hebrew people as tribal leaders, military commanders, arbiters of disputes, and enliveners of faith. The **prophets** were God's spokespersons who communicated his message of salvation. Though a patriarchal society, Israel still had many women who lead them on the path to redemption. "Such holy women as Sarah, Rebecca, Rachel, Miriam, Deborah, Hannah, Judith, and Esther kept alive the hope of Israel's salvation" (*CCC*, number 64).

After the Israelites crossed the Red Sea to freedom, Miriam, the prophetess and sister of Moses, took a tambourine and led the women in a triumphal song and dance (Exodus 15:20-21).

judges ➤ The eleven men and one woman who served the Hebrew people as tribal leaders, military commanders, arbiters of disputes, and enliveners of faith.

prophet ➤ A person God chooses to speak his message of salvation. In the Bible, primarily a communicator of a divine message of repentance to the Chosen People, not necessarily a person who predicted the future.

The Davidic Covenant

God's *hesed*, or love, for humanity can be compared to a loving mother's care for her children. Pope Francis said that God is someone "*who is moved and who softens for us* like a mother when she takes her child in her arms, wanting only to love, protect, help, ready to give everything, even herself" ("General Audience," January 13, 2016). Even if her children grew up to be criminals, a faithful mother would still show up to the prison to visit and provide for them in whatever way she could. This does not mean that she approves of their crimes or thinks that there should not be any consequences for their actions; rather, it simply means that her love has no boundaries and is faithful. Similarly, God's love for us is faithful and forgiving (although we can separate ourselves from God's love—even eternally—by our sin). Nowhere is this more clear than in the covenant that God makes with King David.

When God establishes a covenant with King David, it is quite different from the one he made with Moses. God makes a solitary promise to David:

> I will raise up your offspring after you, sprung from your loins, and I will . . .
> establish his royal throne forever. I will be a father to him, and he shall be a
> son to me. If he does wrong, I will reprove him . . . but I will not withdraw
> my favor from him . . . Your house and your kingdom are firm forever
> before me; your throne shall be firmly established forever.
>
> (2 Samuel 7:12–16)

© AF archive / Alamy Stock Photo

Unlike the Mosaic Covenant, the Davidic Covenant is unconditional, promising that God will establish an everlasting kingdom for David and his offspring.

The Mosaic Covenant was a conditional agreement. There were obligations that both God and the Israelites had to obey, and if they did not, there were consequences. Unlike that covenant, God's covenant with King David is one-sided and unconditional. God makes a promise and there is nothing David has to agree to do. God is like the mother who promises to love her children no matter what they do. God simply promises to establish a kingdom from David's offspring that will last forever.

Even though this is an unconditional promise, King David is still bound by Mosaic Law, and there are still consequences for the sinful actions of David and his descendants. But with the **Davidic Covenant**, God chooses to emphasize the unconditional and eternal nature of the covenant—the kingdom he promises is one that will have no end. To firmly establish this kingdom on earth will take the most righteous and obedient of David's descendants—Jesus Christ.

The Jewish people believed that the **Messiah**—the "anointed one" who would come to protect and unite Israel and lead them to freedom—would be a descendant of King David. Jesus Christ is the fulfillment of God's covenant with King David. ✳

OVERVIEW of the Book of Exodus

- **Reason for writing:** To recount the Israelites' escape from slavery in Egypt and their time at Mount Sinai on the way to the Promised Land.
- **Time period:** Sometime between 1500 and 1250 BC.
- **Themes:** God liberates his people from slavery and oppression; God's covenant with Moses provides laws to guide us; God feeds and sustains us in difficult times.

HMMMMM. . .
How is God's covenant with Moses different from his covenant with David? How are the two similar?

Davidic Covenant ➤ The unconditional covenant made between God and David in which God promised David that he would establish an everlasting kingdom through David's descendants, and that the Messiah would come from David's lineage.

Messiah ➤ Hebrew word for "anointed one." The equivalent Greek term is *christos*. Jesus is the Christ and the Messiah because he is the Anointed One who brings salvation through his life, death, and Resurrection.

1. What is meant by the phrase used in the Easter Vigil, "O happy fault"?

2. Why did God the Father wait to send Jesus Christ to save us?

3. After the Fall (see Genesis, chapter 3), what is the sign that shows God still cares about Adam and Eve?

4. What does the word *Protoevangelium* mean, and what is it?

5. What does the Hebrew word *berit* mean? For what kind of relationship was it often used?

6. How do covenants act as a remedy to sin?

7. How is the narrative about Noah similar to the first Creation account?

8. Why was God's covenant with Abraham so significant?

9. Why does the Hebrew word *hesed* best describe God's covenantal relationship with Israel?

10. What purpose did the Mosaic Law fulfill?

11. What does God promise King David?

A SIGN OF GOD'S COVENANTAL LOVE

1. Artist Jen Norton depicts a whimsical folk art-styled Noah's ark as a cuckoo clock at sea. Why do you think she portrays the ark this way? What message is she trying to convey?

2. What other symbols does the artist use, and what do they mean?

3. What elements from God's covenant with Noah does the artist capture in this painting?

CHAPTER 3
Pointing toward Christ's Sacrifice

HOW ARE THE OLD TESTAMENT SACRIFICES CONNECTED TO JESUS' SACRIFICE?

SNAPSHOT

Article 11   Page 71
The Past: A Glimpse into the Future
• Pre-read: Genesis, chapter 22

Article 12   Page 76
The Lamb of God
• Pre-read: Exodus, chapters 11–15

Article 13   Page 81
Carrying the Sins of Others
• Pre-read: Leviticus 16:1–28

Article 14   Page 87
Love Requires Sacrifice
• Pre-read: Leviticus, chapter 1

Article 15   Page 91
The Prophets: Hints of the Coming Messiah
• Pre-read: Isaiah 42:1–7, 49:1–6, 50:4–9, 52:13–53:12

Article 11
The Past: A Glimpse into the Future

In 1963, Jean Vanier visited one of the many psychiatric hospitals that housed people with severe developmental disabilities. As he was leaving, he heard one of them shout, "Will you be my friend?" Vanier's response to that question changed his life. He later wrote, "I wanted to create a place where they could find inner freedom, develop their personhood and abilities, and be fulfilled" (in *The Paradox of Disability*, edited by Hans S. Reinders).

Encouraged by his mentor and friends, Jean took a leap of faith and invited two developmentally disabled men to live with him in the town of Trosly, France. Despite the difficulties they faced, the men forged a bond and created a relationship in which all three of them thrived. This became the foundation of L'Arche ("The Ark"), a community whose aims include to "welcome people who have intellectual disabilities . . . to respond to the distress of those who are too often rejected, and to give them a valid place in society" (L'Arche, USA). Today, there are 147 L'Arche communities worldwide in which over eight thousand people, with and without disabilities, make their homes together.

TAKE IT TO GOD

God the Father,
I don't get it sometimes.
Why does faith involve having to trust in someone I cannot see?
Why does faith require me to do things that are difficult, or even painful?
Why can't you just make things easier for us?
Yet, there is something deep in my heart that draws me to you.
Awaken courage within me so that I can trust you.
Remind me of all the others who have listened to your voice
    and found your gifts while following your holy will.
Amen.

Jean Vanier's dedication to those on the margins of society is not completely a surprise if you know a little about his family history. He was the son of Georges and Pauline Vanier, a Canadian couple who were deeply invested in their Catholic faith and service to others. During World War I, Pauline served as a nurse, while Georges lost his right leg in battle and was appointed to the Distinguished Service Order. At the end of World War II, they helped arrange food and shelter for refugees from the Nazi concentration camps. In 1965, they founded the Vanier Institute of the Family to "promote the spiritual and material well-being of Canadian families." There is even a cause to ask the Church to recognize Georges and Pauline Vanier as saints. In the Vaniers' heartfelt commitment to help those in need, we can get a glimpse of what would come in the life of their son, Jean.

Jean Vanier created an organization called L'Arche after his experience with people with mental disabilities forever changed his life.

The Paschal Mystery Prefigured in the Old Testament

Just as Jean Vanier's family history gives a glimpse of what would come in his life, the Old Testament prefigures what will be fully revealed in the New Testament: the Paschal Mystery. The Paschal Mystery refers to the work of salvation accomplished by Jesus Christ through his Passion, death, Resurrection, and Ascension. The only Son of God took on our human nature to free us all from the slavery of sin. He lived a sinless life yet was willing to sacrifice himself for sinners.

Events described in the Old Testament often offer us previews of the events that occur in the New Testament. There's an account of a father's willingness to sacrifice a son, a death that opens a path to freedom, an innocent victim, and hints of a savior prepared to give his life so that others may live. Let's look at these Old Testament events and discuss how they are signposts pointing toward the sacrifice made by Jesus Christ.

A Father's Only Son

One of the first prefigurings of the Paschal Mystery is the account of the testing of Abraham (see Genesis 22:1–19). To fully appreciate this story, recall the situation. As part of God's covenant with Abraham, God promises Abraham many descendants. Time passes, and Abraham and Sarah are getting quite old and are still childless. God renews his covenant with Abraham and again promises him many descendants, but still no son. Finally, the miraculous happens. Sarah, who is well past her childbearing years, gives birth to a beloved son, Isaac. God is faithful in keeping his promise!

Years pass, and everything seems good. Then, unexpectedly, another test is required. God asks Abraham to do something that does not make sense: offer up his son as a sacrifice to the Lord. God had assured Abraham that he would have many descendants, and Isaac is his only son. In order to follow God's will, Abraham is prepared to lose what God has promised him. He trusts God enough to give up the son he loves.

The near sacrifice of Isaac is one of many Old Testament signposts that points toward Jesus' sacrifice.

The account of Abraham preparing to sacrifice Isaac is a signpost that points toward the sacrifice of Jesus Christ. Consider the similarities of the two events in this chart. It is easy to see how the sacrifice of Isaac offers a preview of the events of the Paschal Mystery when Jesus Christ, the beloved Son of the Father, freely accepts his own sacrificial death.

Sacrifice of Isaac	Similarities	Jesus' Sacrifice
"Take your son Isaac . . ." (Genesis 22:2)	Both were "sons of Abraham."	"The book of the genealogy of Jesus Christ, the son of David, the son of Abraham." (Matthew 1:1)
". . . your only one, whom you love . . ." (Genesis 22:2)	Both were beloved.	"And a voice came from the heavens, 'You are my beloved Son.'" (Mark 1:11)
". . . and go to the land of Moriah." (Genesis 22:2)	Their sacrifice was to be offered in the land of Moriah (where Jerusalem is located).	"Behold, we are going up to Jerusalem, and the Son of Man will be handed over to the chief priests and the scribes, and they will condemn him to death." (Matthew 20:18)
"There offer him up as a burnt offering on one of the heights that I will point out to you." (Genesis 22:2)	The fathers were willing to sacrifice their sons.	"For God so loved the world that he gave his only Son." (John 3:16)

Sacrifice of Isaac	Similarities	Jesus' Sacrifice
"So Abraham took the wood for the burnt offering and laid it on his son Isaac." (Genesis 22:6)	Both sons carried the wood for their own sacrifice.	"So they took Jesus, and carrying the cross himself he went out to what is called the Place of the Skull." (John 19:16–17)
"Next he bound his son Isaac, and put him on top of the wood on the altar." (Genesis 22:9)	Both were placed on top of the wood.	"There they crucified him." (John 19:18)
"On the third day . . . 'Do not lay your hand on the boy,' said the angel." (Genesis 22:4,12)	Both sons were freed from death on the third day.	"Christ died for our sins in accordance with the scriptures; that he was buried; that he was raised on the third day." (1 Corinthians 15:3–4)

Sometimes trusting God means that we allow ourselves to be guided by God. Jean Vanier had no plans to create a worldwide organization; he only followed God's call to move into a home with two severely disabled men. Only later was he able to see where God was leading him. God does not always reveal the entire road he wants us to travel. Sometimes he just shows us the next single step. ✳

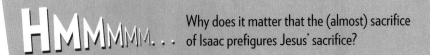

HMMMMMM. . . Why does it matter that the (almost) sacrifice of Isaac prefigures Jesus' sacrifice?

Article 12
The Lamb of God

Most years, as Christians are celebrating the Resurrection of Jesus Christ in their Easter liturgies, Jewish people around the world are celebrating **Passover**. As told in the Book of Exodus, Passover is the night the angel of death passed over the houses of the Israelites, which were marked by the blood of a sacrificial lamb. The angel killed all the firstborn Egyptian males—human and animal—but spared the Israelites' firstborn sons. Passover celebrates the deliverance of the Chosen People from bondage in Egypt, paving the way for the Exodus from Egypt to the Promised Land.

© Imhild B / Shutterstock.com

The death of the Passover lamb saved the Israelites' firstborn sons from the angel of death. The Blood of Christ frees us from the slavery of sin.

Passover ➤ The night the Lord passed over the houses of the Israelites marked by the blood of the lamb, and spared the firstborn sons from death. It also is the feast that celebrates the deliverance of the Chosen People from bondage in Egypt and the Exodus from Egypt to the Promised Land.

UNIT 1

In the Jewish Passover celebration, we can find the roots of our own liturgical celebrations. The Passover incorporates the reading of sacred texts, remembers difficult times, and honors those sent by God to save his people. Significantly, there is a meal that includes unleavened bread and wine. Many of the words, gestures, and symbols of this ancient Jewish ritual are the roots of the Mass.

In the **synoptic Gospels**—Matthew, Mark, and Luke—Jesus celebrates a meal called the Last Supper just before his death. The Last Supper takes place during a Passover meal with his Apostles. During this meal, Jesus establishes a new covenant by offering his own Body and Blood in **the Eucharist**. In the Gospel of John, the Last Supper occurs *before* the Passover celebrations. Jesus is sentenced to death at the same time the Passover lambs are being slaughtered, making an even more powerful connection between Jesus' sacrifice on the cross and the sacrifice of the Passover lamb.

I DIDN'T KNOW THAT!

Are Christians cannibals?! That is what some people thought about the early Christians! In the celebration of the Eucharist, we eat and drink the Body and Blood of Christ, just as the early Christians did. At that time, the Jewish People believed that touching a dead body or blood made you unclean, so eating and drinking them would be utterly detestable. Though we truly eat and drink the Body and Blood of Christ, Catholics are not cannibals. When the bread and wine are consecrated, the substance (*what it is*) changes into Christ, but its texture and appearance remain the same—it does not look, feel, or taste like flesh and blood. In the Eucharist, we share in the life of Christ, but that does not make us cannibals!

© Adam Jan Figel / Shutterstock.com

synoptic Gospels ➤ From the Greek for "seeing the whole together," the name given to the Gospels of Matthew, Mark, and Luke, because they are similar in style and content.

Eucharist, the ➤ The celebration of the entire Mass. The term can also refer specifically to the consecrated bread and wine that have become the Body and Blood of Christ.

Salvation from Slavery

The Passover events lead the Israelites to freedom from physical slavery. It took the death of the Egyptians' firstborn sons to convince Pharaoh to release the Israelites from their captivity. And another death, the substitute death of the Passover lamb, saved the Israelites' firstborn sons from the angel of death. These events prepare us to better understand the way Christ's death and Resurrection save us from slavery and death. Since the first sin of Adam and Eve, humanity has been enslaved by temptation and evil. Through their disobedience, sin enslaved us and separated us from God and one another. Now Jesus' obedient sacrifice unites God and humanity and frees us from the slavery of sin.

What does it mean to say that sin enslaves us? Jesus explained this notion by using an analogy of a slave's obedience to his master: "Everyone who commits sin is a slave of sin" (John 8:34). The type of sin Jesus is talking about is habitual sin, sin we keep repeating. Sin has become our master and we are unable to resist it.

We call this tendency toward sin concupiscence. As a result of Original Sin, all humanity is afflicted with this tendency, even after our Baptism. Compulsions like greed, lust, or even a desire for others' approval can cause tremendous harm to ourselves and others. But Saint Paul reminds us that through the Paschal Mystery, Jesus conquered sin and death; we are saved and freed from the slavery of sin: "As to his death, he died to sin once and for all; as to his life, he lives for God. Consequently, you too must think of yourselves as [being] dead to sin and living for God in Christ Jesus" (Romans 6:10–11). Knowing and believing that we are united in the death and Resurrection of

Jesus Christ, we are freed from the slavery of sin. Living in light of that union, and making a strong effort to resist harmful behavior, is our way to overcome sin.

© Sophia Hilmar / Pixabay

Through the Paschal Mystery, we are no longer held bound by sin, because Jesus conquered sin and death once and for all.

The Passover and the Eucharist

In his directions for the Passover meal, God tells the Israelites to eat unleavened bread (see Exodus 12:20). Why unleavened? Leaven is the ingredient, usually yeast, that makes dough rise. Without any leaven, you get a flatbread. It takes less time to make an unleavened bread because you don't have to wait for the dough to rise. By commanding them to eat unleavened bread, God prepared the Israelites for a quick escape from slavery.

Fast forward to Luke's Gospel. "When the day of the feast of Unleavened Bread arrived, the day for sacrificing the Passover lamb, [Jesus] sent out Peter and John, instructing them, 'Go and make preparations for us to eat the Passover'" (Luke 22:7–8). At the Last Supper, a new type of Passover meal, Jesus institutes the Eucharist. He asks that we "do this in memory of [him]" (22:19). And that is what we do every Sunday when we participate in the Mass. During the Mass, the unleavened bread and wine that was used in the original Passover now become the true Body and Blood of Christ.

When we consume the Eucharist, we are accepting God into our bodies and into our lives. The Eucharist strengthens us against concupiscence, against the slavery of sin. It prepares us for our own entry into the Kingdom of God where each of us will experience the freedom of eternal salvation.

The Paschal Lamb

This brings us to another way the Passover account in Exodus prefigures the Paschal Mystery: the sacrifice of the Passover lamb. We read in Exodus that if the Israelites put the blood on the doorposts their houses, the Lord would pass over and not strike down their firstborn children (see 12:23). The blood came from the **Paschal Lamb** shared at the Passover meal. There were specific requirements for choosing this lamb and how it was to be sacrificed. In the Gospel of John, the author compares these requirements to Jesus' Passion and death, showing that Jesus is the Paschal Lamb. This chart shows these comparisons: ✱

Paschal Lamb ➤ In the Old Testament, the sacrificial lamb shared at the Seder meal of the Passover on the night the Israelites escaped from Egypt; in the New Testament, the Paschal Lamb is Jesus, the Incarnate Son of God who dies on a cross to take away "the sin of the world" (John 1:29).

The Paschal Lamb	Jesus' Passion and Death in the Gospel of John
• The lamb chosen to be sacrificed had to be unblemished, with no imperfections (see Exodus 12:5).	• John the Baptist declared Jesus as the Lamb of God (see 1:29); the one who can take away sin must also be the one who is sinless, unblemished. • At Jesus' trial, Pontius Pilate, the one who will sentence him to death, found no guilt in him (see 18:38).
• When sacrificing and eating the lamb, none of its bones were to be broken (see 12:46).	• At the Crucifixion, the soldiers broke the legs of the two criminals crucified with Jesus, but did not break Jesus' legs because he was already dead (see 19:32–33).
• The blood of the lamb protected Israel from death (see 12:23).	• The blood of Jesus saves us from death (see 3:16).

© Akabei / iStockphoto.com

The Passover lamb had to be unblemished, with no imperfections (see Exodus 12:5).

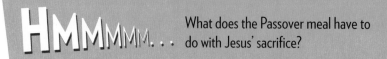

HMMMMM. . .

What does the Passover meal have to do with Jesus' sacrifice?

Article 13
Carrying the Sins of Others

Though she was only joking, Rachel had said something awful to Jorge. She made a comment about the shape of his body that was terribly inappropriate. She hurt his feelings and felt terrible about it. She did not see Jorge for about a week. She called to apologize, but he did not answer the phone. She texted him, but did not get a response. She had a sick feeling in the pit of her stomach, and there was nothing she could do except wait for him to talk to her. Forgiveness was his to give.

Jorge suffered because of Rachel's sin. He carried that pain, but over time decided to put it aside to heal their relationship. He talked to Rachel, and she begged for his forgiveness. He accepted her apology and forgave her, and their

friendship soon got back on track. Rachel was so relieved. Their reconciliation felt like a gift she did not deserve. She knew she had to honor this gift by becoming better, by never making a crude comment like that to Jorge or anyone else again.

Take Rachel and Jorge's story of healing and extend it to our relationship with God. Original Sin and our personal sin have damaged our relationship with God. When we recognize our part in causing this damage, it is natural to feel guilt and shame. The Good News is that Jesus Christ's sacrifice offers us the forgiveness and reconciliation needed to restore our relationship. He has carried the burden of sin for all of humanity.

© JackF / iStockphoto.com

When have you hurt someone, later recognized your guilt, and then asked for forgiveness?

UNIT 1

Letting Go of Guilt

Guilt is not a bad thing, but it doesn't feel good. Still, it is an essential element of the human experience—it is our conscience's way of telling us that we have done something wrong. On the other hand, an overabundance of guilt can lead to shame, which is not healthy. What is the difference between the two?

Someone experiencing guilt says, "I did something bad."

Someone experiencing shame says, "I am a bad person."

It is never good for someone to believe they are a bad person. No human being is bad. Our actions might be evil, but even then, we are still, at our core, made in the image of God. Everyone. Nothing can ever change that.

It is important for everyone to have an opportunity to be unburdened of their guilt. The Sacrament of Penance and Reconciliation offers us the opportunity to admit our guilt and receive God's forgiveness. And long before Catholics ever went to confession, the Israelites had a yearly ritual in which the community was able to purge their guilt, called Yom Kippur, or the Day of Atonement.

© WP Wittman Images

How do you feel after receiving the Sacrament of Penance and Reconciliation?

Yom Kippur: The Day of Atonement

Yom Kippur is the holiest day of the year, a day when Jewish people fast, pray, and repent for their sins. The Hebrew term *Yom Kippur* means "Day of **Atonement**." Atonement refers to reparation or payment for wrongdoing or sin, and reconciliation with God. The word *atone* is a combination of the words *at* and *one*. It means to bring together what is separated, or to bring into harmony.

During the centuries when the Israelites had a Temple in Jerusalem, Yom Kippur was the only day the high priest could enter the sanctuary that contained the Ark of the Covenant, called the Holy of Holies. There he would sprinkle goat's blood on the Ark and on the people as part of a purification ritual. It might seem somewhat gross to have blood sprinkled on you. This is why it is important to remember that in their minds, blood was life. Sprinkling both the altar and the people with blood was a sign that God and his people were united in life.

The Book of Leviticus contains another ritual the high priest performs on this holy day:

> Laying both hands on its head, he shall confess over it all the iniquities of the
> Israelites and their trespasses, including all their sins, and so put them on the
> goat's head. He shall then have it led into the wilderness by an attendant.
> The goat will carry off all their iniquities to an isolated region. (16:21-22)

In this holy ritual, the community acknowledges and takes responsibility for their sins. Their sins are ritually placed on the head of a goat, which is then led into the wilderness to die. This is the origin of the word **scapegoat**. This ritual was the means that God provided for the Israelites to be freed of their guilt.

Yom Kippur ➤ This Hebrew term refers to the Day of Atonement, a Jewish holy day that is observed with prayer and fasting in accordance with Leviticus, chapter 16.

atonement ➤ Reparation for wrongdoing or sin and reconciliation with God, accomplished for mankind by Christ's sacrifice.

scapegoat ➤ This term refers to the ritual in the Old Testament of symbolically placing the sins of the Chosen People on a goat and then driving the goat into the desert (see Leviticus, chapter 16).

Today, people sometimes use the word *scapegoat* to describe a person who takes the blame for something that he or she isn't fully responsible for. For example, you might hear about a professional basketball team who comes in last place in their division. The coach did his best to provide leadership and guidance, but the players missed too many shots, played poor defense, and turned over the ball too many times. The players complained about the coach, and the owners fired him at the end of the year. The coach might have played some role in the team's lackluster season, but the players and owners blamed it all on him, and so made him the scapegoat.

On Yom Kippur, the scapegoat took on the sins of the people. What do you find most interesting about this ancient ritual?

This type of scapegoating is not the same as what the Israelites were doing on Yom Kippur. In their ceremonial ritual, the Israelites are not blaming the goat for their sins. On the contrary, they are accepting responsibility and admitting guilt for their wrongdoing. The ritual of placing their sins on the goat is the symbolic way that members of the community are released from their guilt and have a fresh start.

The Scapegoat

In the New Testament, you can find references to Yom Kippur in the Book of Hebrews, which describes Jesus as the high priest (see 9:11), yet also as the scapegoat. The role the goat plays in the celebration of Yom Kippur prefigures the way that Christ is our scapegoat. Through Christ's sacrifice on the cross, he "entered once for all into the sanctuary, not with the blood of goats and calves but with his own blood, thus obtaining eternal redemption" (9:12). Jesus Christ's sacrifice atoned for, or carried, the guilt of our sins so that we could be reconciled with God. Through his blood, we attain eternal life.

© Thoom / Shutterstock.com

In his Letter to the Hebrews, Saint Paul describes
Jesus as the scapegoat who takes away our sins.

God is not a bloodthirsty deity who demands the death of an innocent human being before he offers forgiveness. To understand the idea of Christ's atonement, let us look at someone who modeled his life after Jesus. Martin Luther King Jr. was an innocent (though not sinless) person who willingly carried the burden of our nation's sins of racism. King was ridiculed; he regularly received death threats; he was arrested and jailed; his home was bombed; and ultimately, he gave his life so that others could be free.

God did not demand or even want his death. King himself did not *want* to die, but he was *willing* to do so. The night before he was assassinated he said: "Like anybody, I would like to live a long life—longevity has its place. But I'm not concerned about that now. I just want to do God's will" ("I've Been to the Mountaintop," April 3, 1968). King was willing to carry the burden so that our community could become free from the sin of racism, a freedom we have yet to fully attain.

UNIT 1

Martin Luther King Jr. would most likely be the first to admit that his sacrifice is only a participation in the sacrifice of Christ, because Christ's death "restores man to communion with God by reconciling him to God"[1] (*CCC*, number 613). Furthermore, "this sacrifice of Christ is unique; it completes and surpasses all other sacrifices"[2] (number 614). Neither Jesus nor his heavenly Father *wanted* Jesus to suffer and die, but he was *willing* to pay the price so that we could be free from the slavery of sin.

The Jewish holy day of Yom Kippur foreshadowed the sacrifice of Jesus Christ. Like the scapegoat who carried the sins of the community so they could be free, the Son of God bore the burden of our sins so that humanity could find the freedom of eternal salvation. ✳

Throughout the history of the United States, immigrant groups like Jews, Germans, Chinese, Japanese, Hispanics, Muslims, and even Catholics have been blamed for social ills like unemployment and crime. For example, in the mid-1800s, Irish immigrants, most of whom were Catholic, became the target of many people's anger and hatred for those very reasons. The Church condemns this type of scapegoating: "Every form of social or cultural discrimination in fundamental personal rights . . . must be curbed and eradicated as incompatible with God's design"[3] (*CCC*, number 1935). When you hear someone blame a single group for the ills of society, speak out against it. Your silence can be mistaken as approval. Do not let someone scapegoat a group of people without hearing your opposition to it.

© Everett Historical / Shutterstock.com

A NEVER-FAILING IRISH INDUSTRY.

HMMMMMM. . .   How is Jesus' saving work similar to the role of the scapegoat on Yom Kippur?

Article 14
Love Requires Sacrifice

The Book of Genesis notes that Cain brought a mere "offering to the Lord," while Abel offered "the firstlings of his flock" (4:3–4). This implies that Cain did not offer the best of what he had. While his jealousy led him to murder his brother, it seems that Cain's first sin might have been greed. He did not want to give up his best. It seems that there was something he loved more than God.

Love requires sacrifice, so much so that we can confidently say that there is no love without sacrifice. Love, also called "charity," is the virtue by which we love God above all things. Out of that love of God, we also love our neighbors as ourselves. In this sense, love is not an emotion but rather the source of the ways in which we put others' needs ahead of our own. Love requires that we give of ourselves. It could be as simple as holding a door to allow someone to enter before you, or as demanding as a firefighter giving up her life to save the life of another person.

The sacrifices that the Israelites offered at the Temple prefigured the ultimate and definitive sacrifice that Jesus Christ made on the cross. His sacrificial act of selfless love was a gift to us "from God the Father himself, for the Father handed his Son over to sinners in order to reconcile us with himself" (*CCC*, number 614).

When have you showed love by putting the needs of someone else ahead of your own?

---

love ➤ Also called "charity," the Theological Virtue by which we love God above all things and, out of that love of God, love our neighbors as ourselves.

Temple Sacrifices

The instructions for the different types of ritual sacrifices the Israelites made at the Temple are detailed in the Book of Leviticus. There are directions for both communal and individual sacrifices, as well as for different types of situations such as daily sacrifices and sin offerings. It was important that what they sacrificed was worthy—or worth something. It might have been tempting to offer a sick goat who was near death. Instead you had to offer the best of your flock.

Some types of Temple sacrifices required a goat or lamb, but there were provisions in case you were too poor to own or purchase one. For example, for a woman's purification ritual it states that she may use two turtledoves or two pigeons if she cannot afford a lamb (see Leviticus 12:8). After Jesus' birth, you get a hint of the Holy Family's financial situation when you read that Mary offered "a pair of turtledoves" for her purification ritual (Luke 2:24).

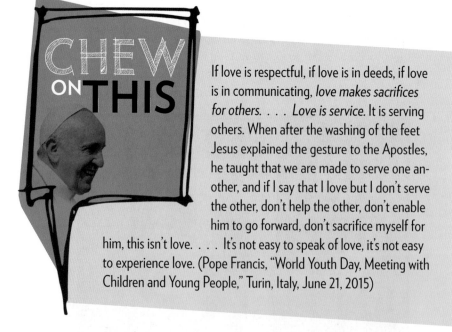

CHEW ON THIS

If love is respectful, if love is in deeds, if love is in communicating, *love makes sacrifices for others. . . . Love is service.* It is serving others. When after the washing of the feet Jesus explained the gesture to the Apostles, he taught that we are made to serve one another, and if I say that I love but I don't serve the other, don't help the other, don't enable him to go forward, don't sacrifice myself for him, this isn't love. . . . It's not easy to speak of love, it's not easy to experience love. (Pope Francis, "World Youth Day, Meeting with Children and Young People," Turin, Italy, June 21, 2015)

Love Requires Our Best

Most important, sacrifices were signs of love and devotion to God. This love requires that we give the best that we can, as illustrated by Abel's sacrifice. What that actual gift is will depend on the giver. Jesus notes that the poor widow's gift is greater than anyone else's:

> "When he looked up he saw some wealthy people putting their offerings into the treasury and he noticed a poor widow putting in two small coins. He said, 'I tell you truly, this poor widow put in more than all the rest; for those others have all made offerings from their surplus wealth, but she, from her poverty, has offered her whole livelihood.'" (Luke 21:1–4)

In terms of the amount of money given, the widow's offering probably did not come close to what the others gave, but that did not matter to Jesus. Love is not a contest. It is offering *your* best to God and others.

© Bridgeman Images

While at the Temple, Jesus noted that the poor widow gave her best gift to the Temple treasury (see Luke 21:1–4). When have you given your best to God and to others?

Christ's Sacrifice

Just as the sacrifices offered in the Temple were made as signs of love and devotion to God, Christ's sacrifice on the cross was a sign of God's love and devotion to us. The Temple sacrifices prefigured the ultimate sacrifice of Jesus Christ.

Jesus is the "New Adam" who lived as God had originally intended for all of humanity to live. His complete obedience to the Father modelled for us dedication to following God's will. Rather than disobey God's will, he chose to sacrifice his life, atoning for all sin ever committed. Jesus did not want to die, but he was dedicated to something more important than himself (see Luke 22:42).

Adam and Eve's sin was their disobedience of God; essentially, sin is just that—disobedience of God. In contrast, Saint Paul declares Jesus is the New Adam who is completely obedient to God. He writes, "For just as through the disobedience of one person the many were made sinners, so through the obedience of one the many will be made righteous" (Romans 5:19).

Jesus is the Son of God Incarnate—God Made Flesh. And because God is love, Jesus is the perfection of love (see 1 John 4:16–17). Again, in this sense, love is not an emotion but rather our selfless devotion to God and others. Because love is not an emotion, we can still love someone we really don't like. It is not necessary to have warm positive feelings about others to love them. Jesus' sacrifice is a sign of his love as the Son of God, love that is expressed through his obedience to the Father. ✳

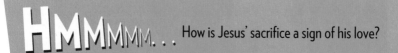

HMMMMM. . . How is Jesus' sacrifice a sign of his love?

Article 15

The Prophets: Hints of the Coming Messiah

Chau had a group of friends she really liked. The new semester brought them all together in a class that also included a new student named Mariel. The new girl was shy and often dressed in old baggy clothes. For some reason, Chau's friends started picking on her and calling her "the bag lady." At first Chau said nothing, and she felt guilty being part of this group of bullies. Chau also knew that as long as she did nothing, she really was a bully.

After a couple of weeks of this, Chau had enough. Before class she confronted her friends and asked them to stop mistreating Mariel. "She hasn't done anything to us. Let's just leave her alone." Immediately, her friends turned on Chau. "Oh! So you like the bag lady now, huh?" They laughed and walked past her into the classroom. They told Mariel: "Hey bag lady! I think you finally found a friend." They pointed at Chau who was entering the room with her head down, obviously embarrassed. As Chau passed by, Mariel scowled at her and angrily whispered: "Don't make it worse! Just leave me alone!"

Doing what is right does not mean it will change the situation or that it will even be appreciated. You do the right thing simply because it is the right thing to do. In the Old Testament, the prophets were often mistreated and sometimes even killed for doing the right thing. Their words and lives pointed toward the coming Messiah, Jesus Christ, who suffered a similar fate.

© nicolesy / iStockphoto.com

When have you done the right thing—not because you wanted a reward or to be noticed—but simply because it was the right thing to do?

The Messages

The Old Testament prophets' call to be faithful to God and act justly hints at what God had planned for the mission of Jesus Christ. For example, Hosea called people to quit worshipping false gods and to return to an intimate and close relationship with the Lord (see Hosea 6:6). Ezekiel condemned the people for ignoring the Law (see Ezekiel 9:9). Amos condemned those who neglected the poor and oppressed (see Amos 4:1). Unless the people changed, their offerings to God were merely superficial and meaningless rituals.

Jesus fit very comfortably into the tradition of the Jewish prophets, but there was one major difference. The prophets were messengers of God's Word, and Jesus *was* God's Word—in the flesh. Like the prophets, he encouraged people to restore their faith in God and to "seek first the kingdom [of God] and his righteousness" (Matthew 6:33). Jesus called his followers to not simply follow God's Law, but to fulfill its purpose. The scribes and Pharisees focused on the letter of the law, but Jesus commanded, "I tell you, unless your righteousness surpasses that of the scribes and Pharisees, you will not enter into the kingdom of heaven" (5:20). His quest for justice prompted his critics to complain that he welcomed and dined with sinners (see Luke 15:2). Jesus offered a deeper understanding of justice that emphasized reconciliation over retribution and repayment (see 15:11–32).

CATHOLICS MAKING A DIFFERENCE

Fr. Daniel Berrigan was a Jesuit priest who in many ways was a modern-day prophet. Like the prophets of the Old Testament, Father Berrigan used outrageous shock tactics to draw people's attention to the injustices of the war in Vietnam, the violence of the nuclear arms race, and the devastating toll abortion has taken. He poured blood on draft records, hammered the nosecone of a nuclear warhead, and trespassed onto facilities that provided abortions. He was arrested numerous times for his protests and spent time in prison as a consequence for his efforts to encourage respect for the dignity of all human life.

© Frances M. Roberts / Newscom

Some prophets performed outrageous symbolic gestures to get people's attention so that they might hear God's message. Recall that Hosea married a prostitute; Jeremiah compared God's people to a rotten loincloth (see Jeremiah 13:1–11); and Ezekiel baked bread on cow manure (see Ezekiel 4:15). In his prophetic role, Jesus also carried out a few tactics aimed at shocking the people to their senses. He condemned hypocritical religious leaders and declared that tax collectors and prostitutes would enter heaven before them (see Matthew 21:31). He condemned a fig tree to death to point out the fruitless faith of the people (see Mark 11:12–14,20–25). In perhaps his most powerful symbolic gesture, Jesus flipped over the tables of the money changers and drove them out of the Temple to reclaim it as God's (see Matthew 21:12–13).

Jesus shocked a lot of people when he ate meals with sinners.

The Fate of the Messengers

Not only did the prophets' messages prefigure the work of Christ, but their lives did too. Convincing others to change their ways to live a life that is pleasing to God is not easy. When the Lord called Jeremiah, he warned him that his life would be difficult (see Jeremiah 1:19). Jeremiah later complained that he was often mocked (see 20:7) and that even his friends were quick to point out his missteps (see 20:10). Elijah complained to God that the prophets before him were even murdered by the Israelites (see 1 Kings 19:10).

Why did they kill God's messengers? Consider this analogy: What would it be like if everyone wore pink-shaded contact lenses? Over time, everyone would see the world in shades of pink. When someone who sees the world as it truly is declares it to be a beautiful, multicolored creation, everyone will think that person is crazy. Then consider what it would be like if seeing a pink world was the foundation for everyone's livelihood, relationships, and beliefs. Everyone believes in a pink god, and they make a living by producing items in shades of pink. They will think someone who claims that the world is multicolored is not only crazy but is also a threat to their way of life.

God's prophets were threatening because they spoke the truth, and the truth meant that people had to let go of their current comfortable way of life. The prophets called people to live the way that God intended. Calling for change angered people because change can be difficult and painful. Instead of changing, they chose to silence the ones calling for change. The same was true for Jesus.

I DIDN'T KNOW THAT!

Don't blame the messenger!" Have you ever heard this phrase or something similar to it? It's often used to describe the act of lashing out at the blameless bearer of bad news. The supposed origin of the phrase dates back to the fifth century BC. In his play *Antigone,* Sophocles included a similar sentiment: "No one loves the messenger who brings bad news." Even Shakespeare used it in *Antony and Cleopatra* when Cleopatra threatens to treat the messenger's eyes as balls after he delivers the news that her Antony has married another. The prophets, on the other hand, spoke God's truth despite the fact that it put their lives in danger.

Jesus was a Jewish man who challenged inadequate interpretations of the Mosaic Law (Torah.) This greatly displeased many of the Jewish leaders (see Matthew 15:1–3). He preached a New Law that valued love and compassion over ritual purity (see Mark 2:23–28). Jesus often criticized the leaders for their hypocrisy and treatment of the poor and outcasts (see Matthew 23:1–36). His final act of driving the money changers out of the Temple upset these leaders so much that they began to call for his death (see Mark 11:15–18). They probably also harbored a good deal of jealousy considering the crowds Jesus attracted (see, for example, John 7:31–32). Ultimately, Jesus was accused of blasphemy by the **Sanhedrin**, the Jewish supreme council, and sentenced to death (see Matthew 26:65–66).

© Album / Alamy Stock Photo

The Sanhedrin was an assembly of Jewish leaders who often criticized Jesus for putting a new Law of Love above ritual purity laws.

Sanhedrin ➤ The highest council of the ancient Jews, consisting of seventy-one members exercising authority in religious matters.

Despite this sentence, the Jewish leaders could not legally put someone to death. Only the Roman authorities had that right. Jesus' popularity and his teachings about the growing kingdom of God (see Luke 13:18–19) would also have been considered a threat to Roman rule. The Romans were dedicated to keeping their kingdom free from anyone who even appeared to be rebellious. Like many of the prophets before him, Jesus was perceived as a threatening figure who endangered the way of life of many powerful people.

Pointing toward the Messiah

The message of the prophets was not only about condemnation and punishment. Many also proclaimed hope for the future. They told of a coming messiah, a Hebrew word meaning "anointed one." This **messianic hope** was their belief that a leader, sent by God, would come to protect and unite Israel, and lead the nation to freedom. The common expectation was that this person would be a military and political leader, much like King David. However, the prophet Isaiah offered some insight into a need for a different kind of leader.

Second Isaiah (chapters 40–55 of the Book of Isaiah) was most likely written during the Babylonian Exile, the fifty-year period when Jewish People were taken from their homes and held in captivity in Babylon. During this time, they yearned for a savior to release them from bondage. Second Isaiah gave them reason to hope by describing a servant who, through his suffering, does the will of God and provides justice for the people. There are four different passages about this suffering messiah called the Servant Songs (Isaiah 42:1–7, 49:1–6, 50:4–9, 52:13–53:12). They act as sort of a job description identifying the kind of person who will offer the people salvation.

Compare these passages from the Servant Songs with the corresponding New Testament passages in this chart. Can you see why Jesus' earliest followers identified him as the Messiah, or Christ (the Greek term for "anointed one")?

---

messianic hope ➤ The Jewish belief and expectation that a messiah would come to protect and unite Israel and lead the people to freedom.

Second Isaiah's Suffering Servant	New Testament Fulfillment

Here is my servant whom I uphold,
    my chosen one with whom I am pleased.
Upon him I have put my spirit;
    he shall bring forth justice to the nations.
(42:1)
	On coming up out of the water he saw the heavens being torn open and the Spirit, like a dove, descending upon him. And a voice came from the heavens, "You are my beloved Son; with you I am well pleased."
	(Mark 1:10–11, see also Matthew 12:18–21)

I, the LORD, have called you for justice,
    I have grasped you by the hand;
I formed you, and set you
    as a covenant for the people,
    a light for the nations,
To open the eyes of the blind,
    to bring out prisoners from confinement,
    and from the dungeon, those who
        live in darkness.
(42:6–7)
	[Jesus] unrolled the scroll and found the passage where it was written:
	"The Spirit of the Lord is upon me,
	    because he has anointed me
	        to bring glad tidings to the poor.
	He has sent me to proclaim liberty to captives
	    and recovery of sight to the blind,
	        to let the oppressed go free,
	and to proclaim a year acceptable to the Lord."
	(Luke 4:17–19)

It is too little, he says, for you to be my servant,
    to raise up the tribes of Jacob,
    and restore the survivors of Israel;
I will make you a light to the nations,
    that my salvation may reach to
        the ends of the earth.
(49:6)
	He took [Jesus] into his arms and blessed God, saying:
	"Now, Master, you may let your servant go
	    in peace, according to your word,
	for my eyes have seen your salvation,
	    which you prepared in sight of all
	        the peoples,
	a light for revelation to the Gentiles,
	    and glory for your people Israel."
	(Luke 2:28–32)

The Lord GOD opened my ear;
    I did not refuse,
    did not turn away.
I gave my back to those who beat me,
    my cheeks to those who tore out my beard;
My face I did not hide
    from insults and spitting.
(50:5–6)
	After he had Jesus scourged, he handed him over to be crucified. Then the soldiers . . . stripped off his clothes and threw a scarlet military cloak about him. Weaving a crown out of thorns, they placed it on his head, and a reed in his right hand. And kneeling before him, they mocked him, saying, "Hail, King of the Jews!" They spat upon him and took the reed and kept striking him on the head.
	(Matthew 27:26–30)

UNIT 1

Second Isaiah's Suffering Servant	New Testament Fulfillment

See, my servant shall prosper,
   he shall be raised high and greatly exalted.
                            (52:13)
	God greatly exalted him
	   and bestowed on him the name
	   that is above every name,
	   that at the name of Jesus
	   every knee should bend,
	   of those in heaven and on earth and
	      under the earth,
	   and every tongue confess that
	   Jesus Christ is Lord.
	               (Philippians 2:9–11)

He was spurned and avoided by men,
   a man of suffering, knowing pain.
                      (53:3)
	[Jesus] said, "The Son of Man must suffer greatly and be rejected by the elders, the chief priests, and the scribes." (Luke 9:22)

Yet it was our pain that he bore,
   our sufferings he endured.
We thought of him as stricken,
   struck down by God and afflicted,
But he was pierced for our sins,
   crushed for our iniquity.
He bore the punishment that makes us whole,
   by his wounds we were healed.
                  (53:4–5)
	He himself bore our sins in his body upon the cross, so that, free from sin, we might live for righteousness. By his wounds you have been healed. (1 Peter 2:24)

Though harshly treated, he submitted
   and did not open his mouth;
Like a lamb led to slaughter
   or a sheep silent before shearers,
   he did not open his mouth.
                  (53:7)
	As soon as morning came, the chief priests with the elders and the scribes, that is, the whole Sanhedrin, held a council. They bound Jesus, led him away, and handed him over to Pilate. Pilate questioned him, "Are you the king of the Jews?" He said to him in reply, "You say so." The chief priests accused him of many things. Again Pilate questioned him, "Have you no answer? See how many things they accuse you of." Jesus gave him no further answer, so that Pilate was amazed. (Mark 15:1–5)

Second Isaiah's Suffering Servant	New Testament Fulfillment
Because he surrendered himself to death, was counted among the transgressors, Bore the sins of many, and interceded for the transgressors. (53:12)	Then he took a cup, gave thanks, and gave it to them, saying, "Drink from it, all of you, for this is my blood of the covenant, which will be shed on behalf of many for the forgiveness of sins." (Matthew 26:27–28)

UNIT 1

Through their words, deeds, and sacrifices, the prophets prefigured the coming of the Messiah. God's messengers conveyed his wishes to the people, called the people to be faithful and act justly, and often suffered terrible consequences for following God's will. Through their lives, they gave God's people a vision for the saving work of Jesus Christ. ✳

 **of the Book of Isaiah**

- **Time period:** Between 742 and 500 BC.
- **Author:** The three Isaiahs or their followers.
- **Themes:** Faithfulness to God, justice for the poor, hope for the future, messianic prophecies, God as lord over all nations.
- **Important people:** Isaiah, and the last kings of Judah: Uzziah, Jotham, Ahaz, and Hezekiah.

HMMMMM...

Who is a prophet today who shares Jesus' mission to bring justice to the poor and hope to the oppressed?

1. What is the Paschal Mystery?

2. How was Abraham's plan to sacrifice Isaac similar to Jesus' Crucifixion?

3. How do the synoptic Gospels portray the Last Supper differently than the Gospel of John does?

4. What details in John's account of Jesus' Crucifixion were meant to portray him as the Paschal Lamb of God?

5. What is Yom Kippur?

6. The Israelites yearned for a savior to release them from bondage. What kind of savior were they expecting, and what kind of savior did Second Isaiah describe?

7. Why does love require sacrifice?

8. How was the fate of the prophets similar to Jesus' fate?

9. Why were the prophets and Jesus threatening to so many people?

THE SCAPEGOAT

1. What mood does this painting convey?

2. The artist, William Holman Hunt, chose to paint the goat near a certain body of water in Israel. What clues might help you name that body of water?

3. How does the artist capture the role of the scapegoat?

UNIT 1 HIGHLIGHTS

CHAPTER 1 God's Original Plan

Event 1

Creation: Union with God and One Another

God creates humanity to be in union with him and one another. God created everything in a state of original holiness and justice.

Genesis, chapters 1–2

Event 2

The Fall: Sin Separates

Humanity's sin of disobedience separates us from God and one another, resulting in pain and suffering.

Genesis, chapter 3

Event 3

The Cycle of Sin

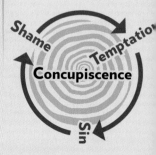

Shame
Temptation
Concupiscence
Sin

Because of Original Sin, all human beings are born with concupiscence, or the tendency toward sin and its continuing cycle.

Genesis, chapters 4–11

CHAPTER 2 Bound to God: The Covenants

Ending the Cycle of Sin

The Cycle of Sin Begins

Original Sin

The Cycle of Sin Ends

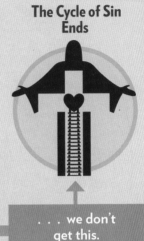

This is the "necessary sin" and "happy fault" because without this . . .

. . . we don't get this.

The Promise

The Bad News

Original Sin:
Evil Makes its Entrance

(Genesis 3:1–13)

The Good News

The *Protoevangelium:*
God Promises to Conquer Evil

(Genesis 3:14–15)

Covenants

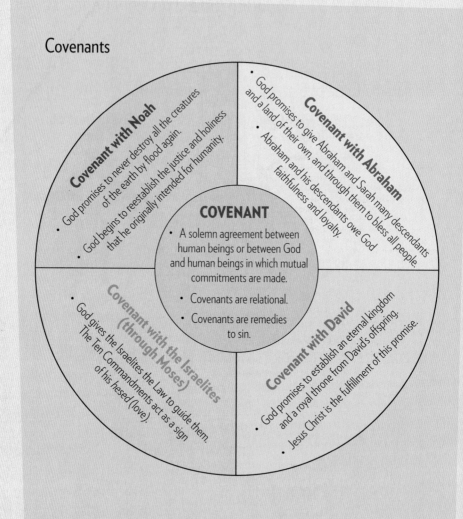

COVENANT

- A solemn agreement between human beings or between God and human beings in which mutual commitments are made.
- Covenants are relational.
- Covenants are remedies to sin.

Covenant with Noah

- God promises to never destroy all the creatures of the earth by flood again.
- God begins to reestablish the justice and holiness that he originally intended for humanity.

Covenant with Abraham

- God promises to give Abraham and Sarah many descendants and a land of their own, and through them to bless all people.
- Abraham and his descendants owe God faithfulness and loyalty.

Covenant with the Israelites (through Moses)

- God gives the Israelites the Law to guide them. The Ten Commandments act as a sign of his hesed (love).

Covenant with David

- God promises to establish an eternal kingdom and a royal throne from David's offspring.
- Jesus Christ is the fulfillment of this promise.

CHAPTER 3   Pointing toward Christ's Sacrifice

Old Testament Events Point toward Christ's Sacrifice

The Scapegoat (Yom Kippur)

The scapegoat that frees the community from their sins

The Near-Sacrifice of Isaac

A father's willingness to sacrifice his only son

Temple Sacrifices

Offering the best of what we have to God

The Paschal Lamb

The Passover lamb sacrificed to free people from the bondage of slavery

The Prophets

Those who suffered and were sometimes killed for preaching God's Word and for calling his people to be faithful and to practice justice

UNIT 1
BRING IT HOME

WHAT DIVIDED GOD AND HUMANITY? WHAT UNITED US AGAIN?

FOCUS QUESTIONS

CHAPTER 1   If God made everything good, how did things get so bad?

CHAPTER 2   After the Fall, why did God want to make covenants with humanity?

CHAPTER 3   How are the Old Testament sacrifices connected to Jesus' sacrifice?

COLIN
Father Judge High School

This unit explains sin and consequence in a different way than I learned about it when I was younger. What I got from this unit was that the first chapters of Genesis aren't really meant to be a scientific or historic explanation for how we became separated from God. The more I read about the story of Adam and Eve and the serpent, the more I realized the story is about a cycle of sinful behavior, shame and loneliness, consequences, and God's love. This Original Sin was so outrageous that it set in motion a cycle of sin that affected everyone . . . even me. We all have free will, but our separation from God distorts our ability to see clearly the right thing to do.

REFLECT

Take some time to read and reflect on the unit and chapter focus questions listed on the facing page.

- What question or section did you identify most closely with?

- What did you find within the unit that was comforting or challenging?

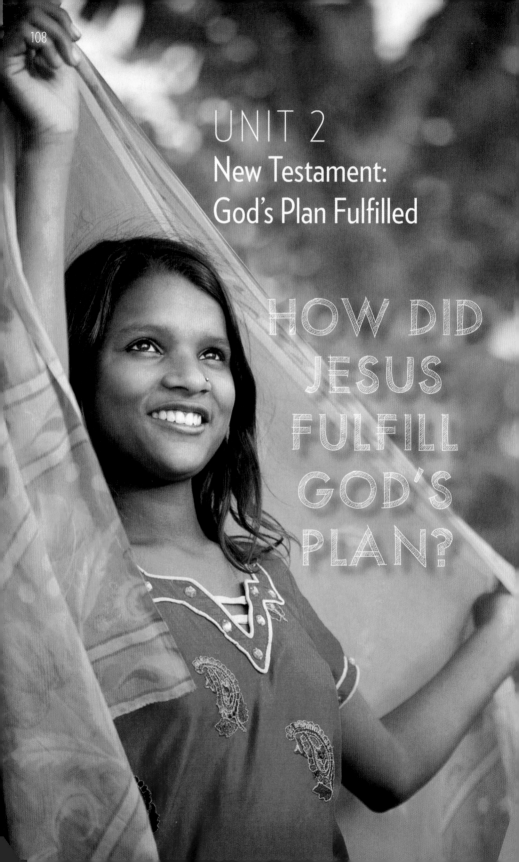

UNIT 2
New Testament: God's Plan Fulfilled

HOW DID JESUS FULFILL GOD'S PLAN?

LOOKING AHEAD

CHAPTER 4   Page 110

The Life and Teachings of Jesus

CHAPTER 5   Page 140

Jesus' Death: Four Perspectives

CHAPTER 6   Page 172

Resurrection and Ascension

UNIT 2

God gave humans free will and, unfortunately, many of us chose to sin. God worked through the prophets to guide people back to the right path, but they were often rejected. We know the right things to do, but we often reject them and do what pleases us. God took drastic measures to bring us back to him, allowing his only Son, Jesus, to be sacrificed. He was a living example of what the fulfillment of God's plan meant.

ROSA
Totino-Grace High School

CHAPTER 4
The Life and Teachings of Jesus

HOW DOES JESUS' LIFE SHOW HE IS THE MESSIAH?

SNAPSHOT

Article 16   Page 111
The Birth of Christ
- Pre-read: Matthew 1:1–2:23
- Pre-read: Luke 1:1–2:40, 3:23–38

Article 17   Page 119
In the Flesh
- Pre-read: Romans 5:12–14
- Pre-read: 1 Corinthians 15:21–22,45–49

Article 18   Page 125
Bearing the Burden
- Pre-read: Mark 8:34–38
- Pre-read: Matthew 10:16–33

Article 19   Page 132
Grabbed from the Grave
- Pre-read: Mark 5:21–43
- Pre-read: Matthew 9:18–26
- Pre-read: John 11:1–44

Article 16
The Birth of Christ

Imagine living in a place where you go to school in the dark, and while you are at school, the sun peeks over the horizon for just a few hours before it sets again. By the time the bell rings at the end of the school day, the cold darkness of night has already arrived. This is what it's like for people who live in the far north, like Fairbanks, Alaska, whose citizens see fewer than four hours of sun on some winter days.

Due to the lack of exposure to sunlight, some people struggle in the winter months with a condition called seasonal affective disorder, also known by its appropriately titled acronym "SAD." SAD can bring on symptoms of depression, low energy, a sense of hopelessness, or even suicidal thoughts at its worst. For these people, when springtime and summer arrive, the cold darkness disappears, and the heat and light of the sun return, the depression begins to fade away.

The human authors of the Bible intuitively knew that light was an essential element for human health and happiness, and they used this imagery to describe the coming of the Messiah. Quoting the Old Testament prophet Isaiah, the Gospel of Matthew says:

> The people who sit in darkness
>   have seen a great light,
>   on those dwelling in a land
>   overshadowed by death
>   light has arisen.
>   (4:16)

"The people who sit in darkness / have seen a great light" (Matthew 4:16). The Gospels recognize Jesus as this great light, the Messiah, who brings hope and new life.

Matthew and the other Gospels recognize Jesus as this great light, the Messiah who brings happiness, hope, and new life to those living in darkness. They recognize Jesus Christ as the fulfillment of the promises of the Old Testament.

The Infancy Narratives

Although the four Gospels share commonalities, it is their differences that make each one unique. One such difference is how they begin. John starts his Gospel with a poetic reflection on the divinity of Christ. Mark mentions nothing about Jesus' childhood and heads straight into his Baptism and healing ministry. Only in Matthew and Luke do you find the **infancy narratives**—the accounts of Jesus' birth and early childhood. Even then, their accounts focus on different events and themes.

The infancy narratives are certainly rooted in history, but their main purpose is not to provide historical records. The infancy narratives of Matthew and Luke are primarily theological statements about the person and mission of Jesus Christ. In other words, the accounts of Jesus' birth and early life focus on explaining *who Jesus is*, rather than *what happened*. This does not mean that these events never occurred, because the oral traditions certainly passed down historically accurate information; rather, it means that the focus of our attention should be on what God is revealing through these accounts.

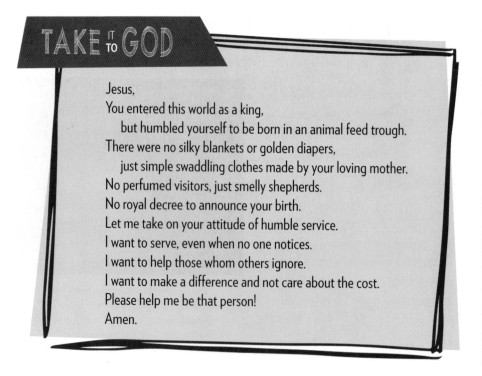

TAKE IT TO GOD

Jesus,
You entered this world as a king,
    but humbled yourself to be born in an animal feed trough.
There were no silky blankets or golden diapers,
    just simple swaddling clothes made by your loving mother.
No perfumed visitors, just smelly shepherds.
No royal decree to announce your birth.
Let me take on your attitude of humble service.
I want to serve, even when no one notices.
I want to help those whom others ignore.
I want to make a difference and not care about the cost.
Please help me be that person!
Amen.

---

infancy narratives ➤ The accounts of Jesus' birth and early childhood.

Matthew's and Luke's Communities

Although both Matthew and Luke include an infancy narrative in their respective Gospels, they did not write to and for the same audience. The Gospel of Matthew was written around the year AD 85 and is addressed to a community of mostly Jewish people who were followers of Christ. Luke's Gospel was written around AD 80–90 and addressed a mainly Gentile community that appears to have been quite diverse. To meet the needs of their audiences, the Gospel writers focused on and emphasized different aspects of Jesus' birth. This chart shows some of these differences.

UNIT 2

COMPARING MATTHEW'S AND LUKE'S INFANCY NARRATIVES		
	Matthew 1:1–2:23	Luke 1:1–2:40, 3:23–38
To whom does God announce the news of Jesus' birth?	Joseph	Mary
How do Mary and Joseph end up in Bethlehem?	This account isn't included.	They obey the decree to enroll in the census; Bethlehem is the traditional home of Joseph's family.
What are Joseph and Mary's experiences before Jesus' birth?	Joseph finds out that Mary is pregnant and decides to divorce her quietly, but an angel appears to him in a dream and tells him not to.	An angel appears to Mary with the news that she will be the mother of Jesus. Mary visits her pregnant cousin Elizabeth, who will be the mother of John the Baptist.
Who comes to visit the baby Jesus?	Magi from the east come to visit.	Shepherds come to visit.

COMPARING MATTHEW'S AND LUKE'S INFANCY NARRATIVES

	Matthew 1:1–2:23	Luke 1:1–2:40, 3:23–38
When Jesus is circumcised, why does Simeon say Jesus came?	This account isn't included.	"To be a light for revelation to the Gentiles, and glory for [God's] people Israel." (2:32)
Are there any similarities to Old Testament stories?	Joseph has dreams like the Joseph in the Book of Genesis. The account of Jesus' escape from the massacre of the innocent children is reminiscent of Moses.	Zechariah and Elizabeth are old and unable to have children. Abraham and Sarah (Genesis), and Elkanah and Hannah (First Samuel), had the same problem.
On whom does the Gospel focus more—Mary or Joseph?	The Gospel focuses more on Joseph.	The Gospel focuses more on Mary.
Who is the oldest ancestor in the genealogy?	Abraham, the father of all the Jewish people, is the oldest.	Adam, the father of all humanity, is the oldest.

Matthew's Infancy Narrative

Matthew's infancy narrative is told through the viewpoint of Joseph, a man we know little about. After the accounts of Jesus' youth, Matthew says nothing more about Joseph other than that he was a carpenter (see 13:55). So what can we learn about him from Matthew's infancy narrative?

Joseph was a man of great faith. Put yourself in his shoes: you are a man engaged to a young woman who suddenly becomes pregnant and claims that God is the Father! What makes Joseph so special is that he believes that God can and does speak to him. It was natural for him to act upon what God told him in his dreams.

Matthew also writes that Joseph was a good, righteous man (see 1:19). By calling him "righteous," Matthew shows that Joseph followed the Law and knew he had to cut off his engagement because of her pregnancy. But he still cared for Mary, and he knew that being an unwed pregnant woman could put her in an extremely difficult situation. Joseph was a selfless man whose faith led him to take Mary as his wife and assume the role of father to Jesus.

© Theorm / Shutterstock.com

Joseph, a man of great faith, figures prominently in Matthew's infancy narrative.

The Gospel of Matthew begins with a genealogy traced through Joseph's family. Notice that it begins with Abraham, the father of the Jewish faith. The Gospel's Jewish audience would have felt an immediate connection to Jesus when the Gospel identifies him as a "son of Abraham" (1:1).

The genealogy is split into three groups of fourteen generations each. These groups are divided at significant people or pivotal events in Jewish history, the most prominent being King David, whose descendant was expected to be the Messiah. This tells Matthew's audience that not only will Jesus play a monumental role in their history, but he is also the Messiah, or Christ, for whom they have waited.

Although Jewish genealogy was traced through the fathers, there are four women, besides Jesus' mother, Mary, mentioned: Tamar, Rahab, Ruth, and "the wife of Uriah" (Bathsheba). Three of these women would have been embarrassing to the Jewish People for various reasons, but the one thing they

UNIT 2

all have in common is that they were Gentiles. Matthew's genealogy makes a point of recognizing the important role that Gentiles played in Jewish history and their necessary continuing presence in the Christian community.

> In Joseph's dream, he is told that Isaiah's prophecy was to be fulfilled:
>   Behold, the virgin shall be with child and bear a son,
>   and they shall name him Emmanuel.
>
> (Matthew 1:23)

Emmanuel is a Hebrew word meaning "God is with us." For the Jewish community, the presence of God was found in the Ark of the Covenant, which was kept in the Holy of Holies in the Temple. Calling Jesus "Emmanuel" would have been comforting for the Jewish Christian community following the destruction of the Temple, which happened about the time the Gospel of Matthew was written. Through Jesus, God was truly with them.

Other images in Matthew's infancy narrative would have been familiar to his Jewish audience as well. Joseph's dreams would likely have reminded them of the Joseph from Genesis who also had dreams that were fulfilled (see 37:5–11, 42:8–9). This Joseph also saved his family and all Egypt from the famine. Jesus' escape from the massacre of baby boys recalled another savior—Moses, who eluded the murder of all infant Hebrew boys ordered by the pharaoh (see Exodus 1:15–2:10).

The Magi who come to pay homage to Jesus are foreigners "from the east" (Matthew 2:1). It would have been notable to the Gospel's Jewish audience that Gentiles were the first to recognize Jesus as a king, a prefiguring that Gentiles are also part of Jesus' faithful followers. Gold, frankincense, and myrrh might seem odd gifts for a baby, but they tell us important things about Jesus. Gold was a fitting gift for a king, and frankincense was used by the priests in sacred rituals (see Exodus 30:34–36). Myrrh was used as incense, but it was also used to embalm dead bodies. The gifts of the Magi point to Jesus' role as priest and king, and foreshadow his death.

The inclusion of Jesus' genealogy (starting with Abraham), the visit of the Magi, and the emphasis on Joseph would have reminded Matthew's audience of God's saving hand throughout their history. These elements offer a glimpse of what the Gospel of Matthew will offer: the account of another Savior, Jesus, the Messiah, who came for all of humanity—Jews and Gentiles alike. He is Emmanuel and the fulfillment of their history and God's saving work.

Emmanuel ➤ A Hebrew word meaning "God is with us."

Mary and her cousin Elizabeth play a significant role in Luke's infancy narrative.

Luke's Infancy Narrative

In contrast to the Gospel of Matthew, the Gospel of Luke's infancy narrative emphasizes Jesus' humble beginnings and breaks down social barriers:

- **Women:** The narrative doesn't revolve around men, but rather Mary and Elizabeth, who play a significant role in salvation history.
- **Poor travelers:** The Holy Family is temporarily homeless, so Mary gives birth to Jesus in a stable and lays him in a manger (a trough from which farm animals are fed).
- **Presentation at the Temple:** When Mary and Joseph present Jesus at the Temple, it is the custom to offer a lamb up as a sacrifice. But Luke notes that they offer two turtle doves (see 2:24), which is the requirement for those who cannot afford a lamb.
- **Shepherds:** Shepherding is a lowly occupation at the time, but it is they who are told that a savior has been born (see 2:11) and are the first to pay homage to Jesus.

The humble circumstances of Jesus' birth, the recognition of the poor shepherds, and the Gospel's emphasis on women must have made an impression on Luke's diverse audience. His infancy narrative, and much of the rest of his Gospel, places no importance on economic or social status.

The Gospel of Luke does not actually begin with the birth of Jesus, but rather the announcement of John the Baptist's birth. Despite his mainly Gentile audience, the author of Luke uses some imagery from Jewish history in this account:

- Mary's relative, Elizabeth, and her husband, Zechariah, are old and have not been able to have children. Their story is much like that of Elkanah and Hannah, who were the parents of Samuel, Israel's last judge as well as one of its greatest prophets (see 1 Samuel 1:1–23). Zechariah and Elizabeth's son, John the Baptist, is also a great prophet, who paves the way for Jesus' ministry. By pointing out Jesus' relationship to John, Luke places Jesus in the line of Jewish prophets.

- When they present Jesus in the Temple, Mary and Joseph encounter a devout man named Simeon. The Holy Spirit promised Simeon that he would meet the Messiah before he dies. He takes the baby into his arms and declares that Jesus came to be "a light for revelation to the Gentiles, / and glory for [God's] people Israel" (2:32). Jesus came to save everyone, Israelites and Gentiles (non-Israelites).

- Luke's genealogy also has some details that reveal Jesus' identity. Like Matthew's, it traces Jesus back to Abraham, but it does not end there. Luke takes Jesus' ancestry all the way back to Adam. It is his way of telling his Gentile audience that, yes, Jesus is a son of Abraham, but he is also a descendant of our very first parents. That points to a truth that will be fully revealed later in Jesus' ministry, that both Jews and Gentiles are included in God's plan of salvation. ✳

HMMMMMM. . . How do concerns about race and status affect religion today?

Article 17
In the Flesh

Have you ever wondered why God doesn't stop the terrible events in the world? Do you sometimes ask God what you could do to help relieve some of that suffering? In a frustrated moment, have you ever asked God why he doesn't just come down to Earth and explain the meaning of your life to you? The Good News is that this has already happened! God came to us in the flesh and showed us the meaning and purpose of our lives.

UNIT 2

The term **Incarnation** comes from a Latin word meaning "to become flesh." It refers to the mystery of Jesus Christ, the Divine Son of God, becoming human. Through the Incarnation, Jesus Christ became truly man while remaining truly God. He is the New Adam who heals the sin of our first ancestors and the divide that came about as a result. Jesus embodies the union of God and humanity. Through him, we come to know God's will for our own lives.

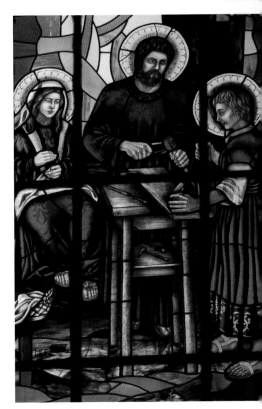

© Jorisvo / iStockphoto.com

Human and Divine

Jesus Christ is the Incarnate Son of God, the Second Person of the Trinity, who took on our human nature. That is, the Son of God "worked with human hands; he thought with a human mind. He acted with a human will, and with a human heart he loved. Born of the Virgin Mary, he has truly been made one of us, like to us in all things except sin"[1] (*Catechism of the Catholic Church [CCC]*, number 470).

As a boy, Jesus apprenticed with Joseph to become a carpenter. Some biblical scholars believe he learned masonry work as well.

Incarnation ➤ From the Latin, meaning "to become flesh," referring to the mystery of Jesus Christ, the Divine Son of God, becoming man. In the Incarnation, Jesus Christ became truly man while remaining truly God.

It is important to note that Jesus is not half-human and half-God. In a similar way, you are not half of your mother and half of your father. Even though you have genetically inherited features from your parents, you are one unique individual human being. Jesus is also not half and half; he is a unique person, a divine Person with two natures: truly human and truly divine.

The Middle Man

Because Jesus is both truly human and truly divine, he is the perfect **mediator** between humanity and God. A mediator is a person who acts as a "middle man" or a "go-between" between two or more parties to help bridge gaps of misunderstandings or language barriers, or bring about reconciliation. We have lots of different types of mediators in our world: teachers help students decipher the subject matter they are trying to learn; counselors help couples resolve problems in their marriage; translators help us communicate with people who don't speak the same language.

When it comes to our relationship with God, Jesus is our middle man. Saint Paul writes:

> For there is one God.
> There is also one mediator between God and the human race,
> Christ Jesus.
>
> (1 Timothy 2:5)

Through Christ's sacrificial death and glorious Resurrection, he has restored our communion with God and gained access for us to God's saving grace. Like a translator, Jesus can take the infinite and incomprehensible wisdom of God and make it understandable for humans. Like a counselor, Jesus helped humanity restore our relationship with God and heal the separation caused by sin. Like a teacher, Jesus helps us to learn how God wants us to live.

The New Adam

Another way the New Testament describes the reconciling work of Christ is by giving him the title the New Adam (or "the last Adam"). Paul give Jesus this title in his First Letter to the Corinthians and in his Letter to the Romans (see 1 Corinthians 15:45). God created Adam to live in union with him in a state of original

---

mediator ➤ Someone who acts as a go-between between separate or opposing parties in order to connect or reconcile them. Jesus Christ is the unique mediator between God and humanity; through his death and Resurrection we have gained access to God's saving grace.

holiness and justice, but Adam chose to sin. Jesus Christ became the New Adam; he embodied the union of God and humanity that was intended for the first Adam. In doing so, Jesus allowed the grace of salvation to become available to us all.

Adam (Our First Human Ancestors)	The New Adam (Jesus Christ)
Created to live in God's presence	God's presence in human flesh
Had free will to choose between right and wrong	Had free will to choose between right and wrong
Chose to sin by disobeying God	Never sinned, was fully obedient to God
Allowed sin to enter the world	Brought grace into the world
Arrogantly attempted to be like God which brought death	Humbly accepted a human death which brought eternal life

UNIT 2

I DIDN'T KNOW THAT!

For centuries, the Rosary has been an enduring form of prayer for Catholics all over the world. Meditation on the three sets of Mysteries of the Rosary mainly focused on the events surrounding Jesus' birth, Passion, death, and Resurrection. In 2002, Pope Saint John Paul II found it "fitting to add . . . a meditation on certain particularly significant moments in his public ministry" and added the Luminous Mysteries ("On the Most Holy Rosary," October 16, 2002). The Luminous Mysteries include the following:

- the Baptism of Jesus
- the miracle at the wedding feast of Cana
- the announcement of the Kingdom through parables and miracles
- Jesus' Transfiguration at Mount Tabor
- the institution of the Eucharist

Mysteries of the Rosary ➤ The sacred events in the lives of Jesus and Mary that are meditated on when praying the Rosary. They are called mysteries because they are beyond our understanding. There are four groups of mysteries: Joyful, Sorrowful, Glorious, and Luminous.

UNIT 2

Why the Word Became Flesh

The remedy for darkness is light. The cure for evil is goodness. The remedy for slavery is freedom. The remedy for separation is union. The remedy for sin is grace. In Jesus Christ, we find all of these remedies. Saint Gregory of Nyssa said, "Closed in the darkness, it was necessary to bring us the light; captives, we awaited a Savior; prisoners, help; slaves, a liberator"[2] (*CCC*, number 457). Because God loved us, he sent his only Son to be the expiation—the atonement—for all our sins and to heal this division. Christ came to destroy the power of the Devil. The sin of Adam and Eve brought about the separation between God and humans, so humans needed the union of Christ's divinity and humanity.

Put another way, Christ's saving work is all about love. Sin harms our ability to give and receive love as God intends for us. But through Christ's saving work, our ability to truly love is restored. Christ demonstrated that

© Bernardo Ramonfaur / Shutterstock.com

God's love is rooted in a selfless care and concern that put others' needs ahead of his own. Jesus was a model of human love and holiness who showed us the way to be fully human and live the way God intended us to live.

Saint Athanasius explained the need for the Incarnation by saying, "For the Son of God became man so that we might become God"[3] (*CCC*, number 460). How are we going to "become God"? He certainly does not mean that we are going to take God's place, but rather that we will enjoy a union with God that is infinitely intimate. The *Catechism of the Catholic Church* describes Heaven as the "communion of life and love with the Trinity" (number 1024). In other words, the Son of God became man so that we could enjoy this intimate heavenly union with God, making us "sharers in his divinity"[4] (number 460).

Saint Paul describes Jesus as the "New Adam"—God's presence in human form. Through his complete obedience to his Father, Jesus accepted a human death in order to bring salvation.

Mary: God-Bearer, Model of Humility

It might seem that doing God's will would be easy. If you do what God wants, everything should be smooth sailing, right? That may be so if God only asked us to do easy things, but God sometimes asks us to do difficult things. What God asked Mary, the mother of Jesus, to do was not easy.

Mary was most likely a young teenager when she was visited by the angel Gabriel. Gabriel announces that Mary is going to bear a son who will be called "Son of the Most High," whom God will give "the throne of David his father" (Luke 1:32). Imagine how Mary must have felt! Luke describes her as being "greatly troubled" (1:29) and "afraid" (1:30). Who wouldn't be? Mary wondered how this was even possible since she was a virgin.

To add to her dilemma, Mary was betrothed to a very good, righteous man, Joseph. How was she going to explain her pregnancy to him? Surely, he would not marry her now. She knew that to be a pregnant woman without a husband in her culture would be a shameful and possibly even a perilous situation. Still, knowing the consequences, Mary said yes.

Mary's response is an astonishing testament of her faith in God. By the power of the Holy Spirit, Jesus was conceived in her womb. Mary did not ask for time to assess the pros and cons, nor did she decide on a plan of action before she responded. She trusted God; the rest she would work out with God's assistance.

Mary is given the title *Theotokos,* a Greek word meaning "God bearer," because she carried and gave birth to the Son of God.

UNIT 2

Mary is Jesus' mother, so "what the Catholic faith believes about Mary is based on what it believes about Christ" (*CCC*, number 487). Mary is the Mother of God because she is the mother of Jesus Christ, who is one Person with two natures, divine and human. Because she carried the Son of God in her womb, she is given the title of *Theotokos*, a Greek word meaning "God-bearer."

Mary's yes to God not only included giving birth to Jesus, but it also meant a life of motherhood and discipleship. Scripture recalls her active presence at important moments in Jesus' ministry. For example, she and Joseph presented the infant Jesus in the Temple as was required by Mosaic Law. At the Temple, a righteous man named Simeon blessed the Holy Family and told Mary, "you yourself a sword will pierce" (Luke 2:35). This prophecy pointed to pain Mary would experience in witnessing Jesus' Passion and death. Later, Mary was not just present at, but also prompted, Jesus' first miracle in the Gospel of John (see John 2:1–12). Mary's faith in her Son's compassion and power comes through clearly in this account.

Mary stayed devoted to Jesus as both his mother and his disciple to the very end. Having to watch her Son suffer a gruesome and painful death on the cross must have felt like a sword piercing her heart. We honor Mary as the greatest saint for her humility and faithfulness to God, for her devotion to Christ, her Immaculate Conception, and for bringing the Son of God into the world. ✳

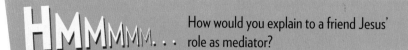

HMMMMMM. . .   How would you explain to a friend Jesus' role as mediator?

Theotokos ➤ A Greek title for Mary meaning "God-bearer."

Article 18
Bearing the Burden

If you want your muscles to grow stronger, you have to tear them. This doesn't seem to make any sense. It is counterintuitive, going against what someone would normally or logically expect. Tearing muscle would seem to be more likely to destroy muscle, rather than make it grow. Yet muscle growth is exactly what happens! When you exercise and feel sore afterward, it is because you created a bunch of microtears in your muscles. When your body senses these microtears, it starts the process of repairing them. Regular exercise will continue this process past the point of simply repairing them. It keeps building your muscles, making them grow stronger.

Like the idea of tearing muscle to make it grow, Jesus' teachings are often counterintuitive, such as "the last will be first, and the first will be last" (Matthew 20:16). At face value, his words do not make sense—how can you really be first if you are last? The beauty of a saying like this is that it can reveal multiple truths about the nature of greed, humility, or even eternal life. It challenges us to rethink cultural "truths" we might accept without question. To harvest the fruit of these sayings requires prayer, patience, and an open heart. Sometimes, a little life experience can help too. Let's look at some of Jesus' counterintuitive teachings, in the belief that they will lead us to hope, true happiness, and eternal life.

The idea of tearing your muscles to make them grow is counterintuitive, just like some of Jesus' teachings, such as "The last will be first, and the first will be last" (Matthew 20:16).

The Wealth of Giving It Away

It might seem wonderful to get everything you ever wanted. Dreams like this usually center around having a huge bank account that would enable you to travel the world and buy anything you want. But getting everything you want is not necessarily a good thing. There are many true stories about lottery winners whose lives are less happy after winning the lottery than before! Wealth is not a cure for broken and dysfunctional relationships or attitudes of greed and selfishness. In fact, it just tends to make these issues even worse.

Intentionally letting go of the things you really want can be an act of self-denial. Sometimes it can be very painful. But it can also lead you to become more selfless, more empathetic to other people's losses, and more generous. Jesus embraced poverty and encouraged his followers to do so.

But Christians must be careful to distinguish between voluntary poverty and involuntary poverty. It can be a wonderful blessing to take on poverty as a free choice, but being victimized by poverty is a completely different situation. Involuntary poverty is a terribly sinful societal disease that we must always seek to end. Jesus never glorified this kind of poverty as a spiritual discipline, but rather encouraged his followers to alleviate the troubles of those in need (see Matthew 25:31–46).

© addkm / Shutterstock.com

As disciples of Jesus, we are called to help those in need (see Matthew 25:31–46).

Speaking of our responsibility to help people living in poverty, some of Jesus' most brutal condemnations were directed at the wealthy. Just consider a few of the many statements Jesus made about wealth:

> Take care to guard against all greed, for though one may be rich, one's life does not consist of possessions. (Luke 12:15)

> No servant can serve two masters. He will either hate one and love the other, or be devoted to one and despise the other. You cannot serve God and mammon. (Luke 16:13) (*Mammon* is an Aramaic term meaning "wealth.")

These might seem like harsh words, but there are two things to remember. First, Jesus is not saying that all wealthy people will be excluded from Heaven. Second, if we look carefully at Jesus' teachings on wealth, it becomes clearer that the problem isn't having wealth but in keeping it only for ourselves. It is interesting that all four Gospels identify the name of the disciple, Joseph of Arimathea, a wealthy man, who recovered Jesus' body and buried him (see Matthew 27:57). The problem of wealth is not the money itself, but the ease in which it can distract us from doing God's will. By giving it away, sharing it with others, we free ourselves to focus on what is of lasting value: the building up God's Kingdom.

> As for you, do not seek what you are to eat and what you are to drink, and do not worry anymore. All the nations of the world seek for these things, and your Father knows that you need them. Instead, seek his kingdom, and these other things will be given you besides. Do not be afraid any longer, little flock, for your Father is pleased to give you the kingdom. Sell your belongings and give alms. Provide money bags for yourselves that do not wear out, an inexhaustible treasure in heaven that no thief can reach nor moth destroy. For where your treasure is, there also will your heart be.
>
> (Luke 12:29–34)

When we share our treasure—and our time and talent—we free ourselves from unhealthy distractions and are able to put full attention into doing God's will.

UNIT 2

Take Up Your Cross

Once, when his disciples were discussing the rumors about Jesus' identity, Jesus asked them who they thought he was. Peter boldly announced, "You are the Messiah" (Mark 8:29). After acknowledging this, Jesus predicted his own Passion and death, and Peter rebuked him for it. He obviously did not see what purpose Jesus' death would serve. Jesus' response to Peter was swift, direct, and seemingly harsh. Instead of quietly correcting him, he made an example of Peter by calling him "Satan" (8:33) when everyone else could hear it! Ouch!

Did Jesus really believe that Peter was "Satan"? Nothing else in the Gospels leads us to think that. Recall that Jesus sometimes used **hyperbole**, or exaggerations, to make a point. He wanted his disciples to know that his Passion and death were essential elements of his mission. Someone who is intent on avoiding his or her own suffering cannot love, because love requires selflessness and sacrifice. By calling Peter "Satan," Jesus emphasized that those who avoid making loving sacrifices are not doing God's work.

MAKE IT SO

Taking up your cross does not necessarily mean something as drastic as losing your life. It could simply mean that you help carry the burden of others. You can do this in a number of ways:

- Spend an hour on the weekend volunteering at a food bank.
- Ask a teacher in one of the younger grades if any students need help, then tutor them for thirty minutes once a week.
- Sit in the school cafeteria next to someone who looks lonely.
- Take the time to listen to a friend express their sadness over a loss.
- Once a month, give your weekly allowance to your favorite charity.

At first, doing these things might feel like a sacrifice of your time, your comfort, or maybe even your popularity. But as you keep doing them, they will feel less like a sacrifice and more like a truly fulfilling way to live!

---

hyperbole ➤ Exaggerated statements or claims not meant to be taken literally.

Christ also wanted them to know that sharing in his sacrifice is part of a disciple's mission as well. Right after this incident, Jesus made it clear that there is a cost for being his follower: "Whoever wishes to come after me must deny himself, take up his cross, and follow me" (Mark 8:34). This is the cost we must pay if we are true followers of Christ. When asked to name the Great Commandment, Jesus responded that we should love God and our neighbor (see Matthew 22:34–40). Through his life and teachings, Jesus purified our consciences and showed us that love is intimately tied up with sacrifice. Each of us is called to bear a cross that is unique to our lives, but it is also a sharing in Jesus' cross: through our suffering, we are led to a new life that fulfills our every hope and brings infinite joy.

UNIT 2

© iStock.com / fstop123

Acting on your religious beliefs can be risky. For example, standing up for someone who is being bullied might put you in a position of being bullied as well. Still, Jesus encourages us to do the right thing.

Suffering Persecution

It is difficult enough hearing that being a follower of Jesus Christ requires sacrifice in order to help others. On top of that, Jesus informs his disciples that they might also be persecuted as well.

When the Gospels were written—some forty to seventy years after Jesus' death and Resurrection—Christians were increasingly persecuted by the Roman authorities. The rapidly growing number of Christians was perceived more and more as a threat in Palestine, as well as in other places in the Roman Empire. Becoming a Christian might mean being ostracized by friends and family or even arrested for refusing to acknowledge the Roman emperor as a god. If the Roman authorities thought you were a threat to the status quo, they could even put you to death. Persecution was a real and serious threat for many early Christians. Saint Peter's letter encouraged them: "But if you are patient when you suffer for doing what is good, this is a grace before God. For to this you have been called, because Christ also suffered for you, leaving you an example that you should follow in his footsteps" (1 Peter 2:20–21).

Is this true for modern-day followers of Jesus? The answer is yes and no. In the Western world, many people are Christians, and proclaiming yourself a follower of Christ is rarely a threat. However, there are numerous places where Christians have experienced terrible waves of persecution. In some parts of the world today, merely identifying yourself as a Christian requires great bravery.

CATHOLICS **MAKING** A DIFFERENCE

During World War II, many Catholic priests in Germany and other countries risked their lives by preaching against Hitler and his Nazis. Because they were not Jewish, they could have remained silent without fear of any harm, but their faith outweighed any sense of self-preservation. Because they spoke out against this great evil, thousands of Catholic priests were rounded up and imprisoned at the concentration camp Dachau. Like many of the other victims, they were forced into labor, starved, tortured, and used as human guinea pigs for sadistic experiments. Of the more than 2,500 Catholic priests held at the "priest barracks" of Dachau, almost a thousand died there.

For most of us, identifying ourselves as Christians is not a problem. On the other hand, if we live in accordance with Christ's teachings, we could find ourselves victims of persecution. Even in the West, where Christians can make up the majority of the population, doing what Christ asks of us can challenge the status quo and infuriate those who feel threatened by change. When we oppose them, we open ourselves up to the possibility of persecution.

Even as a young person, you might find yourself ridiculed for acting on your religious beliefs. When you confront bullies for harassing a classmate, you might find yourself getting bullied. When you speak out against abortion or the death penalty, you might get accused of not caring for women or the murdered victims and their families. When you demand that those suffering from racism or poverty be supported and offered the same opportunities as others, you may get called rude and insulting names. Christ encourages his followers to do what is right despite persecution because there is something greater at stake.

Christ's entire life was a work of redemption that revealed the Father's love for us. His poverty, his sacrifice, his willingness to endure persecution, and his selfless love show us how we are to live our lives. We are justified, and our relationship with God is restored through Jesus' Passion and death on the cross and his Resurrection into a new life. ✳

UNIT 2

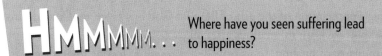

HMMMMM. . . Where have you seen suffering lead to happiness?

Article 19

Grabbed from the Grave

Jennifer nervously repeated the Lord's Prayer over and over as her best friend since third grade, Sara, was in the hospital room fighting for her life. They had been in a car accident. Jennifer walked with only a few bruises, but Sara had not fastened her seatbelt and was ejected from the car. Jennifer heard the terrible sound of the heart monitor alarm and could see the doctors and nurses run frantically into Sara's room. All the good times she and Sara had had together rushed through Jennifer's mind and tears streamed down her face. She felt helpless, but she trusted that Sara was in God's hands no matter what happened. Minutes later, the alarm quieted, and the doctors and nurses seemed like they were working normally again. Later, a doctor visited and told Jennifer that Sara was going to be fine. Jennifer was flooded with feelings of gratitude and appreciation for the gift of life in a way she had never experienced before.

When a person survives after his or her heart stops beating on the operating table, it is often a result of the wonderful advances of medical science, not the result of a miracle like we read about in the Bible. **Miracles** are signs or wonders, such as healing or the control of nature, that can only be attributed to divine power. Jesus performed miracles, which is different than what a doctor does. What they do have in common is that they bring all those involved into a deeper appreciation of the gift of life that God has given us. Considering this, maybe they are both miraculous after all!

In his ministry of healing, Jesus travelled through Palestine giving sight to the blind (see John, chapter 9), curing the sick (see Mark 1:29–31), and driving out demons (see Luke 11:14). He compassionately took on the burden of our illnesses and restored people to both physical and spiritual health. Before his Resurrection from the dead, the Son of God also offered hints to his power over death, as in these three accounts of raising people from the dead.

---

miracles ➤ Signs or wonders, such as healing or the control of nature, that can be attributed to divine power only.

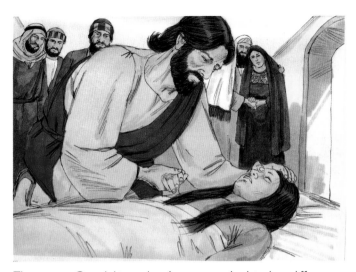

The synoptic Gospels hint at Jesus' power over death in three different miracles. The raising of Jairus's daughter is one of them.

Jairus's Daughter

A few important historical and cultural details in the account of Jesus raising Jairus's daughter (see Mark 5:21–24,35–43) can enlighten our interpretation and our understanding of the meaning of these events:

- The events of this account take place near the Sea of Galilee, not far from Nazareth where Jesus grew up.
- Synagogue officials like Jairus would most likely look at Jesus suspiciously and consider him an outsider or, even worse, a blasphemer.
- Mark notes that the girl was twelve years old, which at that time was considered the beginning of her womanhood.
- In the middle of this narrative, Mark includes the account of Jesus healing the woman who had been hemorrhaging for twelve years.

Just as he had recently brought peace to a stormy sea (see Mark 4:35–41), Jesus brings faith to a doubting congregation of people waiting for him at Jairus's home. When he and his disciples arrived, the crowd had already accepted the girl's death and remarked that there was no need for Jesus. As in the disciples' boat tossed about by the storm, in Jairus's home there was "a commotion, people weeping and wailing loudly" (5:38). Jesus was unperturbed by the doubt and ridicule, and similar to his comments to the disciples at sea, he told Jairus, "Do not be afraid; just have faith" (5:36). Jesus teaches us that faith is an essential element to how God impacts our lives. We are not passive objects that God changes, but rather we are called to be active recipients of God's gifts.

Mark's Gospel sometimes has stories "sandwiched" within other stories to make certain points or highlight a theme. Like putting the meat in between two pieces of bread, he will start one story, then move to a second story, and then finish the original story. He uses this technique here by combining the account of Jairus's daughter with the healing of the woman with a hemorrhage (5:25–34). Hemorrhaging, in this context, most likely means that she has an illness causing her to continually have her menstrual period. There are some significant similarities between the two accounts that highlight a theme in Mark's writing.

Jairus's Daughter	Woman with a Hemorrhage
She is twelve years old.	She has had a hemorrhage for twelve years.
Her father is desperate to find a cure.	She is desperate to find a cure.
She has reached an age when she can get pregnant.	Her illness prevented her from becoming pregnant.
Contact with her (a dead body) would make Jesus ritually unclean by Jewish Law.	Contact with her (a woman having her menstrual period) would make Jesus ritually unclean by Jewish Law.
She is healed by physical contact with Jesus.	She is healed by physical contact with Jesus.
Faith was a key element in the miracle.	Faith was a key element in the miracle.

For both Jairus's daughter and the woman with the hemorrhage, Jesus brings healing and life to a desperate situation. The woman had been suffering for as long as the girl had been alive. Jewish purity laws would caution Jesus against any physical contact with the woman or the girl, but Jesus' compassion for both outweighs any concern he has for the letter of the Law. His actions fulfill the purpose of all of God's Laws: love. The faith of Jairus and the woman also plays an essential role: God's presence is always there for us, but we must actively reach out and participate with God to change our lives. Most importantly, the passage points to Jesus' power over death and his gift of life. The twelve-year-old girl is raised and presumably will go on to become a mother. This possibility is open to the healed woman as well. Their new beginnings foreshadow Jesus' Resurrection into new life that is to come later in the Gospel.

An ill woman's great faith in Jesus played an essential role in her healing.

The Official's Daughter

Many scholars attribute the similar accounts in Matthew, Mark, and Luke to Luke's and Matthew's use of Mark's Gospel as a source for their writings. Matthew's description of Jesus healing the official's daughter (see 9:18–19,23–26) is an example of this, as it closely mirrors the events in Mark's account of Jairus's daughter, including the healing of the hemorrhaging woman.

There are a few differences between the two Gospels, though. It might seem odd to us that Matthew mentions the presence of flute players at the home when Jesus arrives. However, knowing about the cultural practices of the time helps us understand. In this case, Jewish families followed a set of customs when someone died. They made sure there were wailing women whose loud cries announced the death to other members of the community. They also ensured that flute players were employed, as the flute was often associated with death in that time. With these details Matthew makes it clear to his Jewish readers that there was no doubt that the young girl was dead.

While Mark notes that Jesus told his disciples to not tell everyone about what just took place (see Mark 5:43), Matthew points out that eventually the news spread (see Matthew 9:26). Mark is emphasizing that Jesus was honorable and humble, while Matthew emphasizes that good news like this is hard to keep contained! Both of these accounts are true, and the different details Mark and Matthew include help us more fully understand God's revealed truth.

Lazarus

The Gospel of John is the only Gospel that tells the account of Jesus raising Lazarus from the dead (see 11:1–44). Lazarus and his sisters, Martha and Mary, are close friends of and deeply loved by Jesus (see 11:5).

The raising of Lazarus is the climax of the section called The Book of Signs (see 1:19–12:50), in which Jesus performs miracles, or "signs," that point to his divinity. As with much of John's Gospel, the events described are often written in a way that provides his readers with a deeper understanding of Jesus' identity and mission. The raising of Lazarus also foreshadows Jesus' own death and Resurrection.

© rudall30 / Shutterstock.com

Jesus' raising of his friend Lazarus to life is the breaking point that ironically leads to Jesus' death.

In John's Gospel, Jesus encourages his faithful friend Martha to an even deeper faith in him. When he arrives, she expresses her trust that Jesus would have healed her brother if he had arrived before Lazarus died (see 11:21). She again declares her faith by proclaiming, "Yes, Lord. I have come to believe that you are the Messiah, the Son of God" (11:27). Despite her great faith in Jesus, Martha's limitations are revealed when Jesus orders the removal of the stone covering Lazarus's tomb, and she complains that there will be a stench. For Martha, Jesus is the Lord, but she does not see him as the Lord over life and death. Jesus leads her toward a deeper faith and understanding of who he is.

UNIT 2

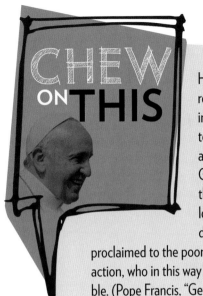

CHEW ON THIS

Here Jesus' intent becomes clear: He responds by saying that he is the real instrument of the Father's mercy, who goes to encounter everyone, bringing consolation and salvation, and, in doing so, he manifests God's justice. The blind, the lame, the lepers, the deaf, regain their dignity and are no longer excluded because of their disease, the dead return to life, while the Good News is proclaimed to the poor. And this becomes the summary of Jesus' action, who in this way makes God's own actions visible and tangible. (Pope Francis, "General Audience," September 7, 2016)

Like Martha, we are sometimes confronted with the limitations of our faith. Sure, we believe in God, but when times get tough we sometimes would rather not be disappointed by having unfulfilled expectations. Jesus wants our faith to be bold and deep. Though our will is not always his will, we still can expect great things from God.

The most striking and terribly ironic aspect of the raising of Lazarus is that it acts as the breaking point that leads to Jesus' death. Immediately after this account, John describes a meeting of the Sanhedrin, the supreme council of Jewish religious leaders who begin to plot his death (see 11:53). The irony is that Jesus' gift of life to Lazarus is what leads to his own death. John uses these events not only to describe the miraculous raising of Lazarus but also to highlight a theological truth: Jesus Christ is the Son of God who gave his life so that we could have life, both in this world and in the next. ✴

HMMMMMM. . . Why is faith in Jesus a key element in each of these miracles?

1. Other than Jesus' mother, who are the four women that the Gospel of Matthew identifies in Jesus' genealogy? Why are these women singled out?

2. What details does the Gospel of Luke use to highlight the value and worthiness of those who are poor?

3. Why do we call Jesus the New Adam?

4. What does the term *Theotokos* mean? Why do we use this title for Mary, the Mother of Jesus, the Son of God?

5. What was Jesus' attitude toward poverty?

6. What did Jesus mean when he commanded his followers to "take up [your] cross, and follow me" (Mark 8:34)?

7. Name the three accounts of Jesus raising someone from the dead discussed in this chapter and the Gospel in which each can be found. What do these accounts foreshadow?

8. What occurred after Jesus raised Lazarus from the dead? Why is this an ironic twist?

© Milind Arvind Ketkar / Shutterstock.com

ART STUDY

In Saint Peter's Basilica at the Vatican, you can find Michelangelo's sculpture *The Pietà*, one of the masterpieces of Renaissance art. It shows the body of Jesus being held by his mother, Mary, after he was taken down from the cross.

1. What does this artwork express about the motherhood of Mary?

2. What elements learned in this chapter do you see reflected in this sculpture?

CHAPTER 5
Jesus' Death: Four Perspectives

WHY DID JESUS HAVE TO DIE TO SAVE US?

SNAPSHOT

Article 20   Page 141
One Threat in Five Events
- Pre-read: Mark 11:15–19
- Pre-read: Luke 7:36–50
- Pre-read: Matthew 26:26–30, John 13:1–17:26
- Pre-read: Luke 22:21–23,47–53
- Pre-read: Mark 14:32–42

Article 21   Page 148
Why They Killed Jesus
- Pre-read: Mark 15:6–15, Luke 23:1–25
- Pre-read: Matthew 27:15–26

Article 22   Page 155
Carrying the Cross
- Pre-read: Mark 15:15–20
- Pre-read: Luke 23:26–32

Article 23   Page 159
Crucifixion and Death
- Pre-read: Luke 23:33–49
- Pre-read: Mark 15:34–35, Psalm 22
- Pre-read: Matthew 27:51–53
- Pre-read: John 19:18–37

Article 20
One Threat in Five Events

When someone makes an act of heroic self-sacrifice, we are often curious about the reason. Looking at the decisions and actions a person like this takes earlier in life can give us insight into the final events of that person's life. Take for example, Chief Peter Ganci Jr. of the New York City Fire Department, who was killed on 9-11. He became a volunteer firefighter in high school, and after he graduated, he joined the Army and served in Vietnam. He later joined the New York City Fire Department where he was awarded for bravery and was respected by his fellow firefighters. His life of service made it no surprise that even after the first tower collapsed, he remained at his post at the World Trade Center, guiding the rescue efforts. Chief Ganci was killed when the second tower collapsed.

In a similar way, looking at Jesus' life just before his arrest can give us insight into the meaning of his sacrifice. We will look at five events leading up to his Passion to understand why he was considered a threat to Jewish and Roman authorities, gain some insight into his identity and mission, and learn about our own mission as we follow the footsteps of Christ.

UNIT 2

© FDNY

New York City firefighter Chief Peter Ganci Jr. was killed on 9-11 in an act of heroic self-sacrifice. He chose to remain at his post at the World Trade Center to help with rescue efforts rather than flee the scene.

One: Cleansing the Temple

Matthew 21:12–17, Mark 11:15–19, Luke 19:45–48, John 2:13–22

The cleansing of the Temple is a pivotal moment in Jesus' ministry, leading up to his Passion. All four of the Gospels include this event, but some have added additional details to emphasize Jesus' mission and the threat he posed. Here are some examples:

- The Gospel of John highlights the cleansing of the Temple by placing it at the beginning of Jesus' ministry rather than at the end.
- The three synoptic Gospels include Jesus quoting the prophet Isaiah, noting that God's intention is for the Temple to be "a house of prayer for all peoples" (Isaiah 56:7).
- The three synoptic Gospels include Jesus quoting the prophet Jeremiah, through whom the Lord said, "Has this house which bears my name become in your eyes a den of thieves?" (Jeremiah 7:11). By repeating this quote, Jesus is condemning the leaders of his time for refusing to care for the aliens, orphans, and widows, as well as for their greed.
- Matthew's version includes Jesus healing the blind and the lame, who, according to the Law, were not allowed to enter the Temple (see 2 Samuel 5:8).
- Mark and Luke end this scene with the Jewish leaders plotting Jesus' death, while Matthew waits until later in the Gospel for this to occur. In the cleansing of the Temple, Jesus publicly challenges their authority and questions their integrity. It is not surprising that they see him as a very dangerous threat. (See more on their motivations in article 21.)

© rudall30 / Shutterstock.com

Jesus doesn't hold back when he expresses God's will for the Temple to be a house of prayer for everyone, including those who are poor, orphaned, widowed, blind, and lame.

TAKE IT TO GOD

Jesus,
You showed courage in doing the right thing,
    no matter what the risk was.
Help me to do what is right and
    to have the courage to stand up for what is right.
Help me to gather the courage to choose your will and
    to inspire others to do the same.
Help me to stand up straight and to be who you made me to be—
    strong, confident, and unafraid.
Amen.

Two: The Anointing at Bethany

Matthew 26:6–13, Mark 14:3–9, Luke 7:36–50, John 12:1–8

All four Gospels report that Jesus was anointed with oil by a woman, but in Luke, it occurs much earlier in the Gospel and is not a part of the immediate events leading up to the Passover feast. John's Gospel names the woman as Lazarus's sister, Mary, but in the other three, the woman is anonymous.

In the ancient world, anointing was sometimes used as a ritual to invest someone with power. Royalty, like King David, were anointed by a prophet or **chief priest** when they took power (see 2 Samuel 2:4). Men were also anointed by the chief priest when they were consecrated for a holy purpose, such as priestly service (see Exodus 29:1–9). At the time of Christ, many Jewish People were expecting an "anointed one" (*Messiah* in Hebrew) to be the savior of their nation.

Jesus' anointing fits these categories. It is an initiation for his role as king—not "King of the Jews," as will be the accusation affixed to his cross—but rather his Kingdom in Heaven. By including this anointing account just before Jesus' death, the Gospel authors are making the point that Jesus is the Messiah who saves us from sin. It also foreshadows his role as the high priest who offers the sacrificial lamb—himself (see Hebrews 5:1–10).

---

chief priests ➤ These were Jewish priests of high rank in the Temple. They had administrative authority and presided over important Temple functions and were probably leaders in the Sanhedrin.

It is significant that all four Gospels note a woman anoints Jesus. Recall that the society in which Jesus lived was patriarchal. Women had little status in society, were considered inferior to men, and were under men's authority. Yet it is a woman, not the chief priest, who anoints Jesus. Jesus' acceptance of women's equal participation in public and religious life and his promotion of their dignity is another way he is a threat to the Jewish leaders. As people who benefitted from patriarchal culture, again it is no surprise that the chief priests are plotting Jesus' execution.

Three: Judas Betrays Jesus

Matthew 26:14–16,20–25,47–50; Mark 14:10–11,17–21,43–46;
Luke 22:21–23,47–48; John 13:21–30, 18:1–14

All four Gospels identify the Apostle who betrayed Jesus as Judas Iscariot. The meaning of the title Iscariot is unclear. Some scholars believe that it is a Hebrew word meaning "man from Kerioth," a town west of the Dead Sea. If that's the case, this would have made him the only Apostle from the south. Others believe it comes from the Greek word *sikarios*, meaning "assassin." We are not sure if the name Iscariot highlights Judas's position as an outsider in the group or his role in Jesus' arrest and death, but both meanings seem to be appropriate.

MAKE IT SO

Does your temple need to be cleansed? When Jesus cleansed the Temple, he challenged a religious system that had grown corrupt. Saint Paul really brings it home when he asks, "Do you not know that you are the temple of God, and that the Spirit of God dwells in you?" (1 Corinthians 3:16). Think about that, and consider what gets in the way of your faith in God. Do you place too much importance on things like success, money, or popularity? If so, let Christ crack the whip and drive them out of your temple! One way you could try to do that is by keeping a journal for a month. Divide the pages into two columns, and each day write the things you did to focus on God in the first column, and in the second column, write the things that took your focus off God. At the end of the month, reflect on what you have learned about yourself.

Why did Judas betray Jesus? It is not exactly clear, but Judas's involvement with money is noted in all of the Gospels. The three synoptic Gospels describe the chief priests offering a payment to Judas, with Matthew even noting the amount: thirty pieces of silver. John's Gospel points out that Judas was the treasurer in the group (see 13:29), and when Jesus is anointed, Judas voices his concern that the oil could have been sold and the money used to feed the poor (see 12:4–5). John's Gospel does not mention Judas meeting with the chief priests, but he does mention the influence of the Devil (see 13:2), as does Luke (Luke 22:3). Judas is a warning to Christians not to assume that just because we follow Christ we are above temptation. We must be attuned to the negative influences and temptations that can lead us astray from God.

Four: The Last Supper

Matthew 26:26–30, Mark 14:22–26, Luke 22:14–20, John 13:1–17:26

In the synoptic Gospels, the Last Supper is a Passover meal in which Jesus institutes the Eucharist. Recall that the Gospel of Mark was most likely the first to be written. Mark establishes the life of Jesus in narrative form. Both the Gospels of Matthew and Luke borrow from Mark, but Luke offers some minor differences. Take a look at this chart:

Mark	Matthew	Luke
• Jesus begins by taking bread, blessing it, breaking it, giving it to his disciples, and telling them, "Take it; this is my body" (14:22).	• Jesus begins by taking bread, blessing it, breaking it, giving it to his disciples, and telling them, "Take and eat; this is my body" (26:26).	• Jesus begins by saying, "I shall not eat it [again] until there is fulfillment in the kingdom of God" (22:16).
• Jesus says that his blood will be shed "for many" (14:24).	• Jesus says that his blood will be shed "for the forgiveness of sins" (26:28).	• Jesus commands his disciples to "do this in memory of me" (22:19).
• Jesus ends by saying that the next time he drinks wine will be "in the kingdom of God" (14:25).	• Jesus ends by saying that the next time he drinks wine will be "in the kingdom of my Father" (26:29).	• Jesus predicts Judas's betrayal and Peter's denial before going to the Mount of Olives (see 22:21–23,31–34).
• Jesus predicts Judas's betrayal before the meal and Peter's denial on the way to the Mount of Olives (see 14:17–20,27–30).	• Jesus predicts Judas's betrayal before the meal and Peter's denial on the way to the Mount of Olives (see 26:21–25,31–34).	

Why the differences? One reason is that Matthew was written to a community that consisted mainly of Jewish followers of Jesus. By adding the "forgiveness of sins," Matthew connects Jesus with his audience's understanding of the sin offerings made at the Temple. It also foreshadows Jesus' sacrifice on the cross to save all humanity from sin. Luke has been traditionally known as a student of Saint Paul. His inclusion of "Do this in memory of me" may have been the result of Paul's influence. Paul also includes this phrase in his account of the Last Supper (see 1 Corinthians 11:23–25).

The Gospel of John's account of the Last Supper is quite different from the synoptics' accounts. First, it is not a Passover meal, but one that takes place the day before. Recall that John places Jesus' Crucifixion on Passover to symbolize his role as the slaughtered lamb. Second, the Last Supper meal in John does not include Jesus establishing the Eucharist; there is no mention of bread and wine. Instead, John records a set of speeches by Jesus in which he prepares the Apostles to continue his work after his death and Resurrection.

© 2018 www.TheGloryStory.com

Jesus' sacrifice was a difficult choice he freely made.

Five: The Agony in the Garden

Matthew 26:36–46, Mark 14:32–42, Luke 22:39–46, John 18:1
As can be expected, the synoptic Gospels offer a similar telling of what happens after the Last Supper. John, on the other hand, provides very little information.

Matthew, Mark, Luke	John

• Jesus and his disciples go to the Mount of Olives (Matthew and Mark name Gethsemane as the specific location).
 	
• Jesus' humanity is highlighted:
 	
   ◦ He struggles with his mission.
 	
   ◦ He feels sad and lonely when his friends fall asleep.
 	
   ◦ He expresses his anxiety to his Father about the future he is facing.
 	
   ◦ He clearly does not want to die, but his desire to do his Father's will far outweighs any sense of self-preservation.
 	
   ◦ His sacrifice on the cross is a difficult choice that he freely makes.
	• Jesus and his disciples go to a garden across the Kidron Valley.
	
	• Nothing is said about Jesus experiencing agony.

UNIT 2

Why such a big difference? The Gospel of John focuses on Christ's divinity and consistently portrays Jesus as someone who was fully in control of his destiny. If John had included Jesus' struggle and agony in the garden, then it would not have made this point as effectively and communicated the truths the author was inspired to express.

When we compare the synoptic accounts of Jesus' Passion with the account from the Gospel of John, his identity as true God and true man becomes clear. Jesus is both fully human and fully divine, the perfect mediator between God and humanity. He is both perfect priest and perfect sacrifice, whose willing obedience to his heavenly Father restores our communion with God. ✳

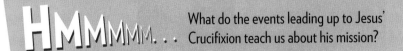

HMMMMMM. . . What do the events leading up to Jesus' Crucifixion teach us about his mission?

Article 21
Why They Killed Jesus

The Gospels are clear about this: following God's will does not mean that your life will become easier or be without conflict. In fact, living a Christian life will likely mean the opposite (see Matthew 24:9). Doing good for others is probably the most earth-shattering thing you can do in the world. Think about it! Simple kindness can be life-changing, especially when it's done for an enemy. Demanding justice usually challenges the status quo, which makes those in power feel threatened. Jesus' life is a testament to this. Jesus' teachings and ministry confronted both the religious and the political establishment of his time.

Private Collection Photo © Ken Welsh / Bridgeman Images

The Pharisees and Jesus often clashed over what they
considered Jesus' neglect in following the Law.

The Religious Leaders

Recall that at this time, Palestine was under the rule of the Roman Empire. The Jewish People were an oppressed people governed by a powerful and sometimes ruthless foreign power. High-ranking local leaders, including religious leaders such as the chief priests, were approved by and loyal to the Romans. Because of this, many of the Jewish People considered the Temple leadership to be corrupt. The chief priests were assisted by wealthy and powerful Jewish business and political leaders referred to as the elders, and by religious teachers and record keepers called **scribes**.

Interestingly, all four Gospels point to the same groups of religious leaders as the ones primarily responsible for Jesus' death: the chief priests, elders, and scribes. In the synoptic Gospels, there are no reports of Jesus having conflicts with the chief priests until he makes his final entrance into Jerusalem, but consider the events that happen during this time:

- Jesus enters Jerusalem with crowds who yell, "Hosanna to the Son of David!" (Matthew 21:9).
- Jesus runs the money changers out of the Temple.
- Jesus teaches in the Temple area, praising the poor and condemning those who ignore them.
- Jesus predicts the destruction of the Temple.
- Jesus denounces the scribes and **Pharisees**.

Given these events, it is easy to see how Jesus' presence and teachings threaten the very livelihood of all those associated with the Temple, particularly the chief priests. As we saw in the previous article, Mark and Luke describe the chief priests and scribes conspiring to kill Jesus after he cleanses the Temple (see Mark 11:18 and Luke 19:47). Matthew places their conspiracy right after Jesus' judgment of the nations (see 26:3–4).

UNIT 2

Pharisees ➤ This group of Jews was well-known for its strict interpretations of all the laws of the Old Testament. The Pharisees believed in the resurrection of the dead.

scribes ➤ These people were scholars and teachers of the Jewish Law and Scripture. They were associated with both the chief priests and the Pharisees.

UNIT 2

The chief priests were the Jewish religious leaders in charge
of the Temple in Jerusalem. They offered sacrifices and
oversaw the general operations of the Temple.

John's Gospel focuses on the theological meaning of Jesus' death and
highlights the irony in the events that led to it. Right after Jesus raised Lazarus
from the dead, John describes a session of the Sanhedrin—composed primarily
of the chief priests, elders, and scribes—in which they plot to kill Jesus (see
11:53). Jesus' death comes about because of his gift of life.

Though these issues certainly played a role, the specific charge that is brought against Jesus when he faces the Sanhedrin is **blasphemy**. Blasphemy refers to disrespect for God, claiming to have the powers of God, or claiming to be God. Matthew and Mark explicitly say that the Sanhedrin found Jesus guilty of blasphemy (see Matthew 26:65 and Mark 14:64). Luke and John don't use that word but certainly imply it. In Luke, the Sanhedrin's line of questioning focuses on whether Jesus calls himself the Messiah or the Son of God (see 22:66–71). In John's Gospel, when Jesus is arrested, the soldiers ask if he is Jesus the Nazorean, and he responds by saying, "I AM." The soldiers then "turned away and fell to the ground" (18:6) because "I AM" is God's holy name (see Exodus 3:14).

Under Jewish Law, blasphemy was a crime punishable by death. The Book of Leviticus stipulates that a blasphemer was to be taken outside the camp and stoned to death by the whole community (see 24:14–16). The Jewish leadership could not order this punishment, though, because only the Romans had the authority to sentence someone to death (see John 18:31). The problem was that the Romans generally would not be bothered by the charge of blasphemy. They were not overly concerned about someone showing disrespect for the Jewish People's God. Roman leaders were mainly concerned about keeping law and order. To put Jesus to death, the Jewish leaders needed to convince the Roman governor of Judea that Jesus was a threat to public order.

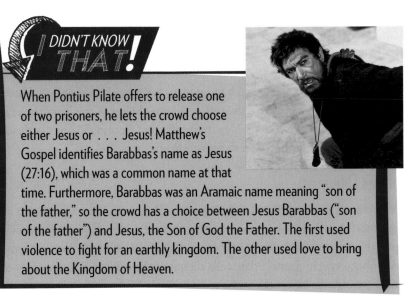

I DIDN'T KNOW THAT!

When Pontius Pilate offers to release one of two prisoners, he lets the crowd choose either Jesus or . . . Jesus! Matthew's Gospel identifies Barabbas's name as Jesus (27:16), which was a common name at that time. Furthermore, Barabbas was an Aramaic name meaning "son of the father," so the crowd has a choice between Jesus Barabbas ("son of the father") and Jesus, the Son of God the Father. The first used violence to fight for an earthly kingdom. The other used love to bring about the Kingdom of Heaven.

blasphemy ➤ Speaking, acting, or thinking about God in a way that is irreverent, mocking, or offensive. It is a sin against the Second Commandment.

UNIT 2

The Political Leaders

During the time when Jesus' trial occurred, Pontius Pilate was the Roman governor of all Judea, and Herod Antipas (son of Herod the Great) was the Jewish leader who oversaw Galilee, the area where Jesus was raised. Pontius Pilate was notorious for being a ruthless and abusive ruler to the Jewish People. He stole from the Temple treasury and murdered many defenseless Jews. Herod Antipas was only allowed to stay in power as long as he collaborated with the Roman Empire. He was considered a traitor by his fellow Jews and is also the one who ordered the beheading of John the Baptist.

Luke's Gospel describes the charges against Jesus with the most detail. "We found this man misleading our people; he opposes the payment of taxes to Caesar and maintains that he is the Messiah, a king" (23:2). The chief priests also claim that Jesus was "inciting the people to revolt" (23:14). In all four Gospels, Pilate addresses the accusation that Jesus is "the king of the Jews."

To understand the impact of these charges, we must understand the role of Roman leaders in occupied nations, especially the Roman governor. Among their priorities, the Roman leaders had the job of collecting the taxes and keeping the peace. They had to do their utmost to make sure a rebellion did not break out, because rebellions were not good for collecting taxes. So, if there was any hint of rebellion against Roman rule, it was firmly crushed without hesitation.

Given all of this, many of the Jewish People expected the promised Messiah to be like King David—a powerful military leader who would overthrow Roman rule and restore the kingdom of Israel. Jesus was not that kind of Messiah; we know his mission was quite different. He established the Kingdom of God, a spiritual Kingdom, and had no plans for a worldly kingdom. However, by calling Jesus the Messiah, the self-proclaimed king of the Jews, the chief priests and elders planted the idea in the mind of Pontius Pilate that Jesus was the leader of a rebellion and a danger to Rome.

Pilate's Dilemma

In varying degrees, all four Gospels portray Pontius Pilate somewhat sympathetically, and describe him as having a moral dilemma when sentencing Jesus. He even defends Jesus' innocence at various points. When the crowd cries out to crucify Jesus, Pilate tells them that he can't find Jesus guilty of a crime punishable by crucifixion (see Luke 23:22). The crowd does not relent and demands that Barabbas be released instead, which is what Pilate does.

Luke's Gospel even includes a passage in which Pilate tries to completely avoid judging Jesus. Because Jesus was from Nazareth in Galilee, Pilate sends him to Herod Antipas, the Jewish governor who rules there, but Herod just mocks Jesus and returns him to Pilate.

Outside of the Gospels, historical records paint a slightly different picture of Pontius Pilate. They point to what we might call today the human rights abuses of Pontius Pilate. He was a terribly ruthless governor. Given these stories, it is hard to see why Pilate would hesitate putting Jesus to death. Perhaps it is possible that he had a moment of insight about Jesus and realized he was not the threat the Jewish leaders made him out to be. In any case, the Gospels are unanimous in recording that Pilate ultimately makes the decision to have Christ executed. In today's language, we might say that Pilate is persuaded that Jesus is an "enemy of the state."

Pontius Pilate was the Roman governor of Judea, well known for being a heartless, callous ruler.

UNIT 2

A Social and Religious Threat

Jesus teaches that love of God and your neighbor is the sign of true holiness. The chief priests and scribes would have agreed with this statement. But then Jesus goes on to show what this love really looks like, and this threatens the Jewish leaders' understanding of what true faith looks like. Jesus loves beggars and lepers and sinners and even his enemies! He talks to them, spends time with them, and even touches them. This is too much for leaders who take great pains not to get near anyone considered "unclean." But it is exactly the way Jesus loves these "unlovable" people that makes him so popular with many of the people.

Even though the chief priests and scribes criticize Jesus' supposed lack of attention to the Law, Jesus is not ignoring it. Instead, he brings a new vision and understanding of God's Law: it is meant to be a Law of Love. His life is truly a fulfillment of the Law of Love. Like the prophets before him, Jesus demands just treatment of those in need, and he unwaveringly confronts the religious hypocrisy of the Jewish leadership of his time. All the while Jesus' true identity as the Son of God goes unrecognized by these religious leaders.

To the Romans, Jesus seems to be a threat to the peace needed to continue their oppressive hold over the country. The Jewish religious leaders are telling Pilate that Jesus is declaring himself a king, implying that he might lead a revolt against the Romans. Influenced by these claims, Pontius Pilate has Jesus arrested and charged with rebellion.

Jesus is a threat to the Roman Empire only in the sense that goodness is a threat to evil. Living by the Law of Love is a great threat to people who maintain their wealth and power by abusing other people's basic human rights. Jesus seems quite aware that his actions will cause the conflict they do. He tells his disciples, "I have come to bring not peace but the sword" (Matthew 10:34). The irony of course, is that Jesus truly is a man of peace, as the only weapon Jesus ever touches is the one that pierces his side. ✳

HMMMMM. . .
Explain how Jesus' life and teachings can create conflict, both in his time and in ours.

Article 22

Carrying the Cross

Have you ever lived through a very difficult, painful experience that turned out to be one of the most important and transformative times in your life? The good times are fun to remember, but they may not push us toward growth. Consider the happy times in your life. There is no urgency to change and grow in these times. In fact, you probably experience the opposite and struggle to keep everything as it is. When we encounter a painful situation that we cannot change, it forces *us* to change—and to grow. This is how we develop and mature as human beings throughout our lifetime. It is as true for a fifteen-year-old as it is for a fifty-year-old.

Maybe the painful situation is the death of a person, the end of a relationship, or moving to a new place. Or it might be the disappointment that comes when a friend or family member seriously lets you down. When you face difficult moments like these, don't ignore them or run away from them. Ask yourself what you can learn from the experience that could change your life for the better. Perhaps the experience made you realize that you are not as smart or strong as you thought you were. Or it made you realize that you are smarter and stronger than you ever imagined!

Jesus' path to his Crucifixion was a sorrowful, humiliating, and extremely painful collection of events that forever changed the lives of humanity for the better. His Cruci-fixion was the path to his Resurrection and our salvation. As we study the passages about the last hours of his life, let's consider what can be learned from these painful events.

© tommaso79 / Shutterstock.com

Difficult, painful life experiences can change your life for the better. What difficult event in your life pushed you to change and grow?

The Scourging and Mockery

Matthew 27:26–31, Mark 15:15–20, Luke 23:11,16, John 19:1–5

All four Gospels mention Jesus being scourged, which was a punishment that often preceded crucifixion. Scourging was a terrible form of torture in which the victim was stripped and then beaten with a leather whip that had bone or other objects woven into it. The beating alone would rip the flesh from the victim's back and could cause injury and blood loss severe enough to kill a person.

Because Jesus is convicted as the leader of a rebellion and for being called "king of the Jews," the soldiers then begin to mock him. Matthew and Mark both point out that Jesus is brought into the praetorium, the residence of the governor, Pontius Pilate. He is surrounded by the whole cohort, which is made up of six hundred soldiers, and is forced to wear a cloak and a crown of thorns. They humiliate Jesus by hailing him as "King of the Jews," spitting on him, and beating him even more—a description much like the treatment of the suffering servant prophesied by Isaiah:

> I gave my back to those who beat me,
>> my cheeks to those who tore out my beard;
> My face I did not hide
>> from insults and spitting.
>
> (Isaiah 50:6)

Let's hope that none of us will ever go through an experience anywhere near as painful and drastic as Jesus did. However, it is quite possible that you, or someone you know, has been mocked or humiliated for doing the right thing. When something like this happens, remember that we are following in Jesus' footsteps and sharing in his saving work. We can feel assured by his teaching:

> Blessed are they who are persecuted for the sake of righteousness,
>> for theirs is the kingdom of heaven.
>
> (Matthew 5:10)

Simon: Carrying the Cross with Jesus

Matthew 27:32, Mark 15:21, Luke 23:26

The Gospels of Matthew, Mark, and Luke all note the assistance Jesus receives in carrying the cross from Simon the Cyrenian. Not only does John not include Simon in his narrative, but he notes that Jesus carries his cross himself (see 19:17). Compared to the other Gospels, John tends to focus more on Jesus' divinity and portrays him as all-powerful and in control of his destiny.

Like Simon, we are also called to follow in the footsteps of Jesus and help carry his cross, to participate in his mission. That is why Christians display crosses on our necklaces, t-shirts, and the walls of our homes, so that we never lose sight of Jesus' mission. Of course, our actions reflect our Christian faith more than any symbol ever could. Jesus reminds his followers what true discipleship is when he says, "Whoever wishes to come after me must deny himself, take up his cross, and follow me" (Matthew 16:24).

UNIT 2

© Skylines / Shutterstock.com

What religious symbol do you wear, or have hanging on a wall of your home, that identifies you as a follower of Jesus?

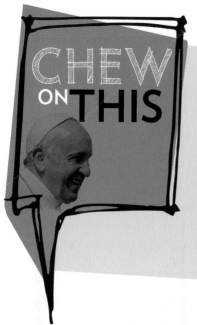

Love, charity is service, helping others, serving others. There are many people who go through life like this, in service to others. . . . When you can forget yourself and think of others, this is love! And with the washing of feet the Lord teaches us to be servants, and more: to serve as he has served us, each and every one of us. (Pope Francis, "Extraordinary Jubilee of Mercy, Jubilee Audience," March 12, 2016)

Tradition: The Stations of the Cross

One of the best ways to reflect on Jesus' Passion and death is to pray the Stations of the Cross. Recall that this Catholic devotion is rooted in Scripture and commemorates Jesus' last hours on Earth, beginning with his condemnation and ending with the placement of his body in the tomb. As a Catholic, you've probably had some experience of praying the Stations of the Cross, especially on Fridays during Lent. It can be prayed by an individual or in a group.

The Stations of the Cross consists of fourteen events and is commonly used as a mini-pilgrimage as the individual or group moves from station to station. Participants stop at each of the fourteen stations and recite prayers while meditating on a specific event from Christ's last day. In praying the Stations of the Cross, we can enrich our own spiritual lives by experiencing Jesus' Passion and death in a unique way. ✱

In what ways are we called to imitate Jesus' Way of the Cross?

Article 23
Crucifixion and Death

Imagine coming home in the evening after your school wins the state basketball championship. You explain to your family what happened, who the important players were, the major turning points, and the final shot that won the game. Now imagine hearing a classmate telling the same story to his parents. He would probably name most of the same highlights but might describe it a little differently or include the contributions of different players. It is the same story, just a different version.

When the four canonical Gospels of the New Testament cover the events surrounding Jesus' Crucifixion and death, they all present the same basic narrative. However, each of the four Gospels focuses on aspects of the events that address the needs of their original audiences. By studying these differences, we can come to an even greater understanding of the meaning of Jesus' death.

We should always remember that even with these minor differences, there is an amazing agreement between the four Gospels about the events surrounding Jesus' Passion, death, Resurrection, and Ascension.

The four Gospels in the New Testament provide the same basic accounts, but each has its own unique aspects of the events.

UNIT 2

Death by Crucifixion

At the time of Jesus, crucifixion was the Roman death penalty that was usually reserved for those in the lower classes who committed the worst of crimes. After the trial, the convicted criminal would usually carry the wooden crossbeam to the place where they were to be crucified. They normally would not carry the entire cross, just the horizontal beam to which their hands were tied or nailed. There would already be a post stuck in the ground, or sometimes they might attach the crossbeam to a tree. Saint Peter is recorded to have said that Jesus was nailed to a tree (see Acts 5:30), though it could just be a reference to the wooden post.

Crucifixion was a very cruel form of execution.

To crucify someone, soldiers would attach the victim's arms to the crossbeam using rope, nails, or both. They would raise up the beam and fasten it to the post or tree, then nail or tie down the victim's legs. Depending on how it was done, death by crucifixion could come in hours, or it could be sadistically drawn out to last days. If they wanted the person to suffer longer, they might attach a block of wood beneath the buttocks, so the victim could support his weight. Otherwise, the weight of the body pulling down on the arms made it increasingly difficult to breathe. If they wanted a victim to die faster, they might break his legs so that he could not support himself. In that case he would soon die of suffocation. Others could die of thirst, hunger, exhaustion, exposure to the elements, heart failure, or any combination of these factors.

Crucifixion was intended to be a humiliating and painful death and was purposefully done in public view so that many people would see it. A sign was hung around the neck or placed above the victim to identify the person's crime. All of this was done to deter others from committing the same crime. It was a Roman form of terrorism used to frighten the population into submission.

JESUS' CRUCIFIXION: COMPARING THE FOUR GOSPELS

Event	Matthew, Chapter 27	Mark, Chapter 15	Luke, Chapter 23	John, Chapter 19
Where Jesus is crucified	"Golgotha (which means Place of the Skull)" (verse 33)	"Golgotha (which is translated Place of the Skull)" (verse 22)	"the place called the Skull" (verse 33)	"the Place of the Skull, in Hebrew, Golgotha" (verse 17)
Casting lots for his clothes	"After they had crucified him, they divided his garments by casting lots" (verse 35).	"Then they crucified him and divided his garments by casting lots for them" (verse 24).	"They divided his garments by casting lots" (verse 34).	"So they said to one another, 'Let's not tear it, but cast lots for it to see whose it will be'" (verse 24).
Others crucified with Jesus	"Two revolutionaries" who were "abusing" Jesus (verses 38,44)	"two revolutionaries" who "kept abusing him" (verses 27,32)	"Criminals," one of whom "reviled Jesus" while the other declared him innocent (verses 33,39,41)	"two others" (verse 18)
The placard placed above Jesus' head	"This is Jesus, the King of the Jews" (verse 37).	"The King of the Jews" (verse 26)	"This is the King of the Jews" (verse 38).	"Jesus the Nazorean, the King of the Jews" (verse 19)

UNIT 2

Golgotha ➤ A Hebrew word meaning "place of the skull," referring to the place where Jesus was crucified.

JESUS' CRUCIFIXION: COMPARING THE FOUR GOSPELS

Event	Matthew, Chapter 27	Mark, Chapter 15	Luke, Chapter 23	John, Chapter 19
Spectators	• "Those passing by" as well as "the chief priests with the scribes and elders" mocked Jesus (verses 39,41). • "many women . . . who had followed Jesus from Galilee" (verses 55-56)	• "Those passing by" as well as "the chief priests, with the scribes" mocked Jesus (verses 29,31). • "women who had followed him when he was in Galilee" (verses 40-41)	• "The people stood by and watched" while "the rulers" mocked Jesus (verse 35) • "all his acquaintances stood at a distance, including the women who had followed him from Galilee" (verse 49)	• "many of the Jews" (verse 20) • "his mother and his mother's sister . . . and the disciple there whom he loved" (verses 25–26)

At crucifixions, the Romans would sometimes put a sign on the victim's cross, naming their crime. All four Gospels mention the sign over Jesus' head. This inscription was meant to make fun of him, as much as it was to name the crime for which he was convicted: "Jesus the Nazorean, the King of the Jews" (John 19:19). You might sometimes see the letters "INRI" at the top of crucifixes, which form an acronym for the Latin translation of the sign: *Iesus Nazarenus Rex Iudaeorum.*

Some of the other details in the Gospel accounts are connected to Old Testament foreshadowing. For example, all four Gospels include the scene in which the soldiers cast lots to divide Jesus' garments among themselves. John's Gospel makes it clear that this is a reference to Psalm 22 in which the speaker laments the abuse he suffers at the hands of his enemies: "they divide my garments among them; / for my clothing they cast lots" (verse 19; see John 19:24). Because Psalm 22 is ultimately a prayer of trust in God, John uses this imagery to remind his audience that God's work can be accomplished even through the most dire circumstances.

The synoptic Gospels also mention spectators making fun of Jesus and challenging him to get down off the cross and save himself. This detail is another foreshadowing from Psalm 22:

> All who see me mock me;
>> they curl their lips and jeer;
>> they shake their heads at me:
> "He relied on the LORD—let him deliver him;
>> if he loves him, let him rescue him."
>> (Verses 8-9)

Jesus had already faced a similar temptation from the Devil when he began his ministry (see Matthew 4:6). It is helpful to consider what did *not* happen here. Jesus did not succumb to any temptation and engage his divine power to jump off the cross, beat up the soldiers, release the criminals, and get away. Like Isaiah's suffering servant, he willingly accepted an unjust punishment to fulfill God's plan for our salvation (see Isaiah 50:4–7).

At some point in history, artists began using the acronym INRI because it was difficult to include the entire Latin phrase in a painting or sculpture.

CATHOLICS **MAKING** A DIFFERENCE

In 1993, after John Sage's beloved sister Marilyn was brutally murdered, he became overwhelmed with anger and sank into a dark depression. A lifelong Catholic, he decided to get involved in a Bible study group, which inspired him to do something positive. He started Bridges to Life, a faith-based prison program in which victims of crime share their stories, and offenders reflect on their lives in order to accept responsibility and cease committing crimes. Since 1998, over twenty-five thousand inmates have participated in Bridges to Life, and studies have shown that its graduates are far less likely to repeat their offenses. John Sage continues to guide Bridges to Life, whose mission is to share "the transforming power of God's love and forgiveness" (History and Mission, *www.bridgestolife.org*).

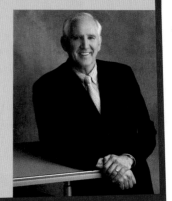

© Bridges To Life

They Know Not What They Do

In Luke's Gospel, Jesus forgives those who are crucifying him (see 23:34). The soldiers are nailing his hands and feet to a cross! How could they *not* know what they are doing? Certainly they are not aware that they are crucifying the Son of God, but doing this to any human being is disturbing. Jesus' forgiveness shows an awareness of how the effects of Original Sin weaken our will and cloud our understanding and judgment:

- Occasionally we are just weak. We know that something is wrong to do, but the temptation is strong and we do it anyway.
- Other times we do things that might seem to be okay but actually are not.
- Sometimes we are unaware that our actions have terrible unintended consequences.
- There are times when we justify doing a sinful act in order to accomplish what we think is a greater good.

We are sometimes weak, deluded, misled, ignorant, or all of the above. Jesus refuses to condemn us because he sees who we truly are: beloved children of God. He does not get trapped by a desire for retaliation, but rather he simply loves us and offers something to help us grow: forgiveness.

Jesus lived what he preached. Not only did Jesus save all humanity from sin, in a very practical way the forgiveness he offered to his executioners showed us how to face injustice and hatred and respond with love (see Matthew 5:44). By imitating Christ, we can also do our part to end the cycle of sin not only in our own lives but also in the lives of those around us.

Why Have You Forsaken Me?

Matthew's and Mark's Gospels record that shortly before he dies, Jesus cries out, "*'Eloi, Eloi, lema sabachthani?'* which is translated, 'My God, my God, why have you forsaken me?'" (Mark 15:34; see also Matthew 27:46). At first glance, it appears that in a moment of despair Jesus doubts his divine Father, but by using good Bible interpretation principles, we discover the opposite is true.

Then, as we sometimes do now, simply citing the beginning of a poem or song could prompt someone to recall the entire reading. For example, simply hearing the line "I have a dream" can bring to mind the entirety of Martin Luther King Jr.'s speech and its call for justice for all people, regardless of the color of their skin. This is what Jesus was doing on the cross: he was reciting the beginning of Psalm 22.

Psalm 22 begins "My God, my God, why have you abandoned me?" (verse 2), but when we read the entire psalm, it is ultimately a psalm about trust in God. The psalm is the prayer of someone who *feels* abandoned by God. Despite this feeling, the psalmist ends by declaring trust in the Lord:

> For he has not spurned or disdained
>> the misery of this poor wretch,
> Did not turn away from me,
>> but heard me when I cried out. . . .
> And I will live for the LORD;
>> my descendants will serve you.
> The generation to come will be told of the Lord,
>> that they may proclaim to a people yet unborn
>> the deliverance you have brought.
>
> (Verses 25,31–32)

UNIT 2

UNIT 2

The Veil Is Torn

The author of the Gospel of Mark notes that when Jesus died, the veil in the Temple was torn in half (see 15:38). The tearing of the veil in the sanctuary is a significant event. Recall that the sanctuary was an area of the Jewish Temple called the Holy of Holies, where the Ark of the Covenant, the place in which God symbolically resided, was kept. The Temple was modeled after the tabernacle, the tent that sheltered the Ark of the Covenant when the Israelites were in the desert. In both the tent and the Temple, a veil separated the Holy of Holies from the other areas in the tabernacle. Only the high priest could pass behind that veil, and only once a year on the Day of Atonement. When Jesus died, he atoned for all our sins, so the veil was torn and

The Ark of the Covenant was kept in the Holy of Holies behind a veil that separated it from the rest of the Temple interior. It was only accessed by the priests. After Jesus' death, the veil was torn, exposing God's presence for all to see.

the presence of God was laid bare for all to see. With no veil to cover it, all of humanity had access to God's presence.

Matthew also notes that the Earth quaked, tombs were opened, and that the bodies of many saints were raised. As Jesus promised, "The hour is coming in which all who are in the tombs will hear [the Son of God's] voice and will come out" (John 5:28–29). Because of this, we have hope in our own resurrection from the dead when God's presence will be laid bare for us to see.

Events Particular to John's Gospel

By now it will not be a surprise to you that the Gospel of John addresses a few events not covered in the synoptic Gospels. The following chart highlights some of the events unique to the Gospel of John.

Event	Scripture Verses	Explanation
Jesus presents John to his mother Mary and asks her to accept John as her son.	"When Jesus saw his mother and the disciple there whom he loved, he said to his mother, 'Woman, behold, your son.' Then he said to the disciple, 'Behold, your mother.' And from that hour the disciple took her into his home" (19:26–27).	The passage about John and Mary can be interpreted both literally and symbolically. On one level, Jesus is providing for the safety and care of his mother. Symbolically, John the disciple represents all Christians, making Mary the Mother of the Church.
The soldiers do not break Jesus' bones.	"The Jews asked Pilate that their legs be broken and they be taken down. So the soldiers came and broke the legs of the first and then of the other one who was crucified with Jesus. But when they came to Jesus and saw that he was already dead, they did not break his legs" (19:31–33).	John's Gospel focuses on the symbolism of Jesus as the Paschal Lamb. When God gave Moses the directions to prepare the lamb for the Passover meal, he commanded, "You shall not break any of its bones" (Exodus 12:46). John highlights this detail to emphasize Jesus' role as the sacrificial lamb who saves God's people.
A soldier pierced Jesus' side with a spear.	"One soldier thrust his lance into his side, and immediately blood and water flowed out" (19:34). "For this happened so that the scripture passage might be fulfilled: . . . 'They will look upon him whom they have pierced.'" (19:36–37)	Besides the important symbolic imagery of the blood and water (see below), John also uses this event to focus on Jesus as the fulfillment of Zechariah's prophecy: "I will pour out on the house of David and on the inhabitants of Jerusalem a spirit of mercy and supplication, so that when they look on him whom they have thrust through, they will mourn for him as one mourns for an only child, and they will grieve for him as one grieves over a firstborn" (Zechariah 12:10).

UNIT 2

John reports that instead of breaking Jesus' legs, as they did with the others crucified with him, the soldiers pierced Jesus' side with a spear, and blood and water flowed from the wound. This passage can also be interpreted literally and symbolically. Considering the kind of trauma that Jesus experienced, it is quite possible that fluids had built up in his lungs or around his heart—an indication of being in the throes of heart failure. When the soldier thrust the spear into Jesus, it could be that "water" or clear fluid came out of his body mixed with his blood.

Blood and water both carry symbolic weight as well. Water is a sign of cleansing, such as the Flood that God used to wipe away the wickedness of human beings (see Genesis 6:5–7). Water also recalls the freedom from slavery that the Israelites experienced when they escaped through the parting of the Red Sea (see Exodus 14:29–30). Most important, water is the primary symbol of the Sacrament of Baptism. Being covered by the waters of Baptism is our entry into our new life with God, a life made possible by Jesus' death.

Blood also plays a role in our salvation. Recall when the angel of death passed over the Israelite homes marked by the blood of the Paschal lamb (see Exodus 12:22–23). At the Last Supper, Jesus gave us his body and blood, as a new covenant for the forgiveness of sins (see Matthew 26:27–28). We now receive his Body and Blood in the Sacrament of the Eucharist. In the Eucharist, we celebrate Jesus' death and Resurrection and are nourished to live out his mission in the world today.

I DIDN'T KNOW THAT!

In the Gospels, the Jewish leadership plays a significant role in Jesus' death. In Matthew, Mark, and Luke, they place responsibility on the crowd too, but John more specifically identifies those crying out for Jesus' death as "the Jews" (see 19:12). John's emphasis on the Jewish People's responsibility for Jesus' death probably reflects the tensions between Christians and Jews *when his Gospel was written*. It is important to remember that Jesus, his mother Mary, and most of his earliest followers were Jewish. Although certain Jewish individuals played a role, it must be emphasized that the Church declared at the Second Vatican Council that "neither all Jews indiscriminately at that time, nor Jews today, can be charged with the crimes committed during [Jesus'] Passion"[1] (*CCC*, number 597).

He Emptied Himself

You may have heard someone describe a person with a big ego by saying, "He is so full of himself!" Selflessness is the opposite. Jesus' Crucifixion and death were a sign of his love for all humankind, and a model of selflessness for us to follow. In his Letter to the Philippians, Saint Paul describes Jesus as having "emptied himself." He also sets that as the goal for all of Jesus' followers:

> Jesus, . . . he emptied himself,
>> taking the form of a slave,
>> coming in human likeness;
>> and found human in appearance,
>> he humbled himself,
>>> becoming obedient to death,
>>> even death on a cross.
>>>> (Philippians 2:7–8)

UNIT 2

HMMMM. . . Saint Paul says that we, like Jesus, must empty ourselves. What does that mean? What do you need to let go of in order to serve others?

1. What point was Jesus making when he cleansed the Temple?

2. How was Jesus' anointing an initiation for him?

3. How is John's account of the Last Supper different from that of the synoptic Gospels?

4. With what charge did the Sanhedrin ultimately accuse Jesus and why?

5. What accusations did Jesus face in front of Pontius Pilate?

6. What actually caused someone to die when he or she was crucified?

7. Why did the Romans use crucifixion as their form of the death penalty?

8. What does the torn veil symbolize?

9. What details about Jesus' death are unique to the Gospel of John?

The Passion of Jesus Christ

UNIT 2

Jesus is condemned to die

Jesus accepts his cross

Jesus falls

Jesus meets his mother

Simon helps carry cross

Veronica wipes Jesus' face

Jesus falls second time

Jesus meets the women

Jesus falls third time

Jesus is stripped

Jesus is nailed to cross

Jesus dies

Jesus is taken down from cross

Jesus is laid in tomb

Images: Shutterstock.com

1. Which stage do you think was the most emotionally difficult for Jesus and why?

2. How did others express their love for Jesus during his Passion?

3. Which stage of Jesus' Passion best represents the kinds of difficulties you most often face and why?

CHAPTER 6
Resurrection and Ascension

WHY IS BELIEVING IN JESUS' RESURRECTION SO IMPORTANT?

SNAPSHOT

Article 24   Page 173
Nothing in the Dark?
• Pre-read: Matthew 28:1–15
• Pre-read: Luke 24:1–12

Article 25   Page 178
What Is Resurrection?
• Pre-read: 1 Corinthians 15:1–34

Article 26   Page 184
Resurrection Appearances
• Pre-read: Luke 24:13–35
• Pre-read: John 20:1–29
• Pre-read: John 21:15–19

Article 27   Page 191
The Ascension
• Pre-read: Matthew 28:16–20
• Pre-read: Mark 16:19–20
• Pre-read: Acts of the Apostles 1:6–12, 2:1–13

Article 24
Nothing in the Dark?

Jesus referred to his coming Resurrection as the "sign of Jonah" (Matthew 12:39). Why? Just as the prophet Jonah was hidden for three days in the belly of a fish, so too was Jesus hidden for three days in the "belly" of the Earth. In these three days, between Christ's death and his Resurrection, the disciples were afraid and hopeless and had no idea what the next days might bring. They were also left in the dark, metaphorically speaking.

The darkness and stillness of the tomb highlight the mysterious nature of the Resurrection. Just because Jesus was in the tomb for several days doesn't mean nothing was happening in the dark. God's plan of salvation was still at work, for "God ordained that his Son should not only 'die for our sins' but should also . . . experience the condition of death"[1] (*CCC*, number 624). Before going further in understanding Jesus' time in the tomb, let's first understand the burial practices at the time, and who was responsible for burying Jesus.

A typical tomb in first-century Palestine was hewn from rock. Its "door" was a round stone that could be rolled to open and close the tomb.

UNIT 2

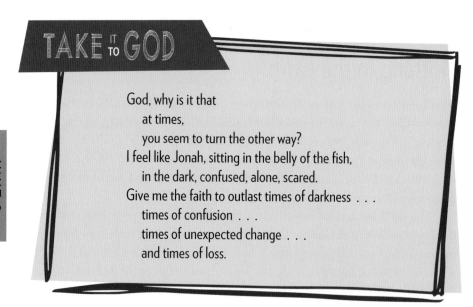

TAKE IT TO GOD

God, why is it that
at times,
you seem to turn the other way?
I feel like Jonah, sitting in the belly of the fish,
in the dark, confused, alone, scared.
Give me the faith to outlast times of darkness . . .
times of confusion . . .
times of unexpected change . . .
and times of loss.

The Burial of Jesus

Matthew 27:57–66, 28:11–15; Mark 15:42–47; Luke 23:50–56; John 19:38–42
All four Gospels name Joseph of Arimathea as the person who buried Jesus,
but their descriptions of him vary. John says that Joseph was secretly Jesus'
disciple (see 19:38). In Matthew, Joseph is described as a wealthy man (see
27:57) who laid Jesus in his own new tomb. Mark and Luke identify him as a
member of the council (the Sanhedrin). Regardless of these descriptions, we do
know that Joseph was able to approach Pilate to retrieve the body of someone
considered a criminal, so he probably was a man of respectable standing in the
community.

Matthew, Mark, and Luke's portrayals of Joseph of Arimathea make him
an unusual character to be found among Jesus' followers. As a member of the
wealthy class and of the Sanhedrin, he was associated with groups that Jesus
had criticized. Clearly, Joseph wasn't concerned about his wealth and status.
His courage in facing Pilate and his willingness to give up his own tomb points
to a deep faith in Jesus.

Most crucified bodies were just taken off their crosses and left for the wild animals to eat, but Jesus' body was removed quickly according to Jewish Law (see Deuteronomy 21:22–23). His body was then wrapped in a linen burial cloth and laid in Joseph's tomb. It was also the custom to anoint the body with spices and oils. However, Jesus was crucified on a Friday just before the beginning of the Sabbath (the Jewish Sabbath begins at sundown on Friday). This left no time to anoint his body before the Sabbath prohibition against unnecessary work took effect. So the women who had followed Jesus returned home and planned to return after the Sabbath was over to anoint his body (see Luke 23:55–56).

© Gino Santa Maria / Shutterstock.com

Just as God's plan of salvation was at work as Jesus' body lay in the dark tomb, God can also be at work during the dark times of our own lives. When have you felt God's presence during a difficult, dark time in your own life?

There is a detail about Jesus' burial that only the Gospel of Matthew includes. Matthew tells us that Pontius Pilate placed a guard at the tomb (see 27:62–66). In this account, the chief priests and Pharisees warn Pilate about Jesus' claim that he would rise three days after his execution (see 16:21). They are worried that the disciples will steal the body and claim that Jesus is raised, which will cause problems for them if the word spread to others. We learn that these guards are frightened when the Resurrection occurs (see 28:4). The guards are then paid by the chief priests and elders to lie and say that Christ's disciples stole the body while they were asleep (see 28:11–15)! By including this detailed story in his account, Matthew identifies non-Christians as witnesses of the empty tomb, establishing more credibility for Jesus' Resurrection.

CATHOLICS **MAKING** A **DIFFERENCE**

One of the most unique ways to observe the Corporal Work of Mercy of burying the dead is practiced by a group of high school students in Illinois. The St. Joseph of Arimathea Society is a group at Quincy Notre Dame High School (QND), who volunteer as pallbearers (those who carry the coffin at a funeral) for people in the community who have little or no family when they pass away. The group started informally with just a few seniors, and soon discovered from a local funeral home that there was a real need for it. For various reasons, some families cannot provide their own pallbearers. Jenna Zanger, a senior at QND, said, "The best part is seeing how we can make such a difference in their life doing such a small thing and taking a little bit of time out of our day" ("Quincy Notre Dame Students Serve as Pallbearers for Families in Time of Loss," *Herald-Whig*, February 24, 2018).

© AP Photo / Carlos Osorio

In the Belly

As we saw earlier, when Jesus was asked to perform a sign—some sort of miracle to prove himself—he said that the only sign he would give would be the sign of Jonah. Remember that the prophet Jonah was the one who was swallowed by a great fish and for three days and three nights remained in the whale's belly (see Jonah 2:1). After the great fish spit out Jonah, he went to the land of the Ninevites (who were Gentiles) and preached for them to repent, which they did (see 3:5). Similarly, after Jesus died, he remained three days in the belly of the Earth, so to speak, and was resurrected on the third day. Later, his Word was preached to the Gentiles and spread throughout the whole world.

Like Jonah, Jesus proclaims Good News to lost souls, but Jonah did his preaching after his three days in the fish, and Jesus did his during his three days in the tomb. The Apostles' Creed says that after his death and prior to his Resurrection, Jesus "descended into hell." This means that Jesus "experienced death and his soul joined the others in the realm of the dead. But he descended there as Savior, proclaiming the Good News to the spirits imprisoned there"[2] (*CCC*, number 632). Jesus descended into hell "to free the just who had gone before him"[3] (number 633). This answers the question of how all the just people who had died before Christ's Resurrection were brought into Heaven. Further, by descending into the realm of the dead, freeing the souls imprisoned there, and then returning to life in the Resurrection, Jesus truly conquered death and the Devil ("who has the power of death," [*CCC*, number 636]).

God's plan of salvation was already at work while Jesus' body was in the tomb, unseen by his disciples. So too God can be at work in the dark times of our lives, during the times when we might feel lost and confused. There is no trick to this; we must just stay faithful and trusting, doing what we know is right, persevering until the new path or the new light is revealed. This is one way the Paschal Mystery is true in our lives, even before our physical death and resurrection into glory. ✳

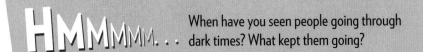

HMMMMM. . . When have you seen people going through dark times? What kept them going?

Article 25

What Is Resurrection?

During the season of autumn, flowers die, trees lose their leaves, some animals seek shelter and go into hibernation through the long winter months, the days grow shorter, and the nights grow longer. Life slows down. But, after several months of cold and darkness, the Earth wakes up: trees spring new leaves, flowers and plants break through the ground, animals come out of hibernation, the days grow longer, the nights grow shorter, and the sun shines and warms the Earth. Life abounds!

No one has experienced a resurrection like Jesus, but we can get a taste of what death and resurrection might be like through our observation of the Earth's cycle of seasons. Jesus truly died, but he conquered death and was resurrected. It was the same Jesus—his glorified body still had the wounds he suffered on the cross—but he was transformed.

What Jesus' Resurrection Is *Not*

Before addressing what it means to say that Jesus resurrected from the dead, it helps to understand what it does *not* mean.

- Resurrection is not **resuscitation**. Resuscitation is what occurs when someone's heart quits beating and then, perhaps due to some intervention like CPR, the person is revived. Jesus was not resuscitated; rather, he truly died.
- Resurrection is not **reincarnation**. Reincarnation is the belief that after death, one comes back to life in a completely new and different body. Jesus returned as the same person, not as anyone else.
- Resurrection is not becoming pure spirit. Becoming pure spirit would mean dying and leaving one's body behind. Jesus returned with a body.
- Resurrection is not **immortality**. Immortality is the state of never having to experience death. Jesus was truly divine, but he was also truly human; he experienced bodily death just as we will.

---

resuscitation ➤ When someone's heart quits beating and then, perhaps due to some intervention like CPR, the person is revived.

reincarnation ➤ The belief that our soul can be reborn into a new human body.

immortality ➤ The state of never having to experience death.

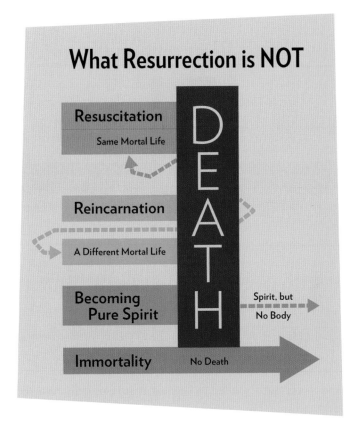

What Jesus' Resurrection *Is*

The **Resurrection** is the bodily rising of Jesus from the dead on the third day after his death on the cross. He is not simply resuscitated back to the same life he had before; rather, Jesus truly dies, passes through and conquers death, and returns to a new and different life. After the Resurrection, he is the same person, but he returns in a glorified body. Mortal bodies will get old, die, and decay, but a glorified body is eternal and incorruptible (see 1 Corinthians 15:42). This could explain why some of the disciples find Jesus unrecognizable after his Resurrection (see Luke 24:15–16; John 20:14, 21:4).

What Resurrection IS

Life

DEATH

Jesus dies and conquers death.

Jesus returns to a new and different life.

After the Resurrection, Jesus has a glorified body.

The Gospels certainly wanted to be clear that Jesus truly resurrected from the dead, body and soul. He was not simply a spirit who appeared to them. "Look at my hands and my feet, that it is I myself. Touch me and see, because a ghost does not have flesh and bones as you can see I have" (Luke 24:39). Thomas would not believe that Jesus had been raised until he touched him, which Jesus allowed him to do (see John 20:24–29). The Evangelists also noted that Jesus did something that a "ghost" would not do: he ate with them (see Luke 24:42–43, John 21:15). Saint Paul also points out that Jesus truly died and was buried (1 Corinthians 15:3–4).

Although Jesus truly had a body, there was something different about it. It was the same body that was crucified, because the wounds were still present for Thomas to witness. "Yet at the same time this authentic, real body possesses the new properties of a glorious body: not limited by space and time but able to be present how and when he wills"[4] (*CCC*, number 645). Jesus suddenly appeared in a locked room where the disciples were staying (see John 20:19). He appeared to the two people on the road to Emmaus, but abruptly "vanished from their sight" after breaking bread with them (Luke 24:31). In these experiences, his glorified body acts as a means to deepen the faith of his followers.

The Biblical Case for the Resurrection

Throughout the New Testament, the reality of Christ's Resurrection is defended and affirmed. One of the most important arguments the New Testament makes for the Resurrection is that many people witnessed the Risen Christ. The empty tomb witnessed by Jesus' disciples was an essential sign of his Resurrection, but that is not the only evidence. The New Testament writers offer many witnesses who testified to the Resurrection including the eleven remaining Apostles, Mary Magdalene and the other women, and the two disciples outside Jerusalem.

Saint Paul gives a passionate and detailed account of these witnesses in his First Letter to the Corinthians. Paul begins chapter 15 with a simple creedal statement: "that Christ died for our sins in accordance with the scriptures; that he was buried; that he was raised on the third day" (verses 3–4). He goes on to note that the Risen Jesus appeared to the Apostles and to more than five hundred people at one time (see verse 6). Many of these witnesses were probably known to the Corinthians. If the Corinthians doubted the reality of Christ's Resurrection they did not have to take Paul's word; they could verify it with other eyewitnesses.

Besides the numerous witnesses, there are a few other things that point to the Resurrection being an authentic historical event. If you were going to convince people that a lie was the truth, you would want to use the most convincing evidence to fool them, right? Jesus lived in a patriarchal society where women were considered subordinate to men. They thought so little of women's testimony that women were not allowed to be used as witnesses in court. Yet, in all four Gospels, the first witnesses of the empty tomb were Mary Magdalene and the other women. The Gospels also include them in numerous other appearances. If the disciples were going to lie about it, naming the women as witnesses would have been a terrible idea. The only logical reason the evangelists would do this is because *it really happened.*

UNIT 2

In a patriarchal society like that of first-century Palestine, women held no power. Yet all four Gospels make it a point to name women as the first witnesses of the empty tomb.

Another aspect to consider is the dangerous situation that Jesus' followers found themselves in immediately before and after his Crucifixion. Why would they continue to put their lives in danger for a lie? You have most likely heard this argument in previous texts. Paul makes this point very personally in his First Letter to the Corinthians. "Moreover, why are we endangering ourselves all the time? Every day I face death; I swear it by the pride in you [brothers] that I have in Christ Jesus our Lord" (15:30–31). Paul is almost sarcastic when he goes on to say, "If the dead are not raised: 'Let us eat and drink, / for tomorrow we die'" (verse 32). Paul isn't saying he regrets the dangers and the suffering he has endured to share in Christ's mission; he is saying that he certainly would not be doing this if he wasn't 100 percent certain that Christ had been raised!

The only reasonable explanation for all this evidence is that the early Christians experienced the true presence of the Risen Christ. This event forever changed their lives, and they dedicated themselves to spreading the Good News of Jesus' Resurrection. The Resurrection is the source of our faith. As Saint Paul says, "If Christ has not been raised, then empty [too] is our preaching" (1 Corinthians 15:14). ✳

Did you know that the Gospel of Mark has two different endings? Some scholars believe it originally concluded with: "They said nothing to anyone, for they were afraid" (Mark 16:8). If this is true, it may have seemed too bleak of an ending for the first Christians, for it seems a longer ending was soon added. Of the ancient manuscripts we have, most contain a longer ending that includes Jesus' appearances to his disciples and the Ascension (see 16:9–20). Four manuscripts also include a shorter ending in which Jesus sends the disciples to spread the Good News of his salvation (see the last two sentences of verse 20). In one manuscript, this shorter ending is the only ending. So which ending is correct? Both endings are included in the canon of Sacred Scripture! The entire development of the Bible was guided by the Holy Spirit and is truly inspired by God.

Which evidence of the Resurrection in this article makes the most sense to you and why?

Ascension ➤ The "going up" into Heaven of the Risen Christ forty days after his Resurrection.

UNIT 2

Article 26
Resurrection Appearances

After two weeks in hospice, Ginny felt the end was near. It was okay though. She was ninety years old and had lived a wonderful life. Her ten-year-old great-granddaughter, Sophie, visited, knowing that her great-grandma was near death. When she saw a tear in Sophie's eye, Ginny reassured her: "Now Sophie, it's okay to be sad. I know you will miss me, but you can still talk to me. I will be with Jesus, and I will hear everything you say. I'm not afraid of death, and I don't want you to be afraid either. Jesus showed us that death is not the end. One day, we will see each other again in Heaven. God loves you, and I love you too." After Ginny's death, Sophie was terribly sad, but she continued to talk to her great-grandma. Deep in her heart, Sophie knew that Ginny was listening.

Because Jesus was raised from the dead, we, like Ginny, can be confident that death is not the end of life. Jesus' Resurrection is the fulfillment of God's promise and a sign of his infinite and eternal love for us. Trusting God, we can be confident of our own welcome into his divine presence. We have already considered why it is reasonable to believe in the Resurrection accounts. Now let's consider what the Resurrection accounts teach us about our own personal response to Jesus' Resurrection, and the promise for our own **resurrection from the dead** on the last day.

We will rise again on the last day and can be confident that we will be with our loved ones again.

© Liukov / Shutterstock.com

---

resurrection of the dead ➤ The raising of the righteous on the last day, to live forever with the Risen Christ. The resurrection of the dead means that not only will our immortal souls live on after death but also our transformed bodies.

Thomas is the Apostle who is often noted for his lack of faith. Sure, like most of us, his faith had some room to grow, but one thing we can admire about Thomas was his self-awareness and honesty. There is never a need to exaggerate your faith or make it look any better than it is. In this sense, Thomas is a wonderful role model. Faith is not blindly accepting what others tell you to believe, but rather grasping the mysteries that God has revealed and living our lives accordingly. When you cannot find a reason to believe, and you have doubts and questions, do not ignore them. Be true to yourself and acknowledge the struggles. Find a competent and trusted spiritual mentor who can offer you some guidance. One thing you can count on: wherever you are on your faith journey, Jesus will come to meet you there.

UNIT 2

Burning Hearts (Luke 24:13–35)

Mark's Gospel briefly mentions Jesus' appearance to two disciples walking in the country away from Jerusalem (see Mark 16:12–13), but Luke goes into much greater detail on what seems to be the same event (see Luke 24:13–35). Luke notes that one of the disciples was named Cleopas and that the two men were on the road toward Emmaus. Like many others who saw Jesus after the Resurrection, they did not recognize him when he asked what they were talking about. Their downcast appearance and closeness to the events surrounding the empty tomb lead us to believe that they were disciples of Jesus. Through their conversation, Jesus shone some light on the teachings of the prophets and interpreted the scriptures, explaining why it was "necessary that the Messiah should suffer" (24:26).

Even though they still did not recognize him, the two were obviously captivated by Jesus. As they arrived at their destination, they urged him to stay. When Jesus sat at the table, "he took bread, said the blessing, broke it, and gave it to them" (Luke 24:30). It was then that their eyes were opened, but as soon as they recognized him, he vanished. Looking back, they realized that their hearts were "burning [within us]" the whole time they were with him (24:32).

If the words used to describe what Jesus did at the table look familiar, it is because you read them two chapters earlier in Luke. They were the same words used to describe the institution of the Eucharist (see 22:19). Like the two men who recognized Jesus in the breaking of the bread, we come to discover and know Christ through the sacraments, especially the Holy Eucharist.

What does it mean to have a "burning heart"? What does this account teach us about having a burning heart as a disciple today? We sometimes associate the word *heart* with our emotional life, but it refers more to our "center," the inner core of who we are. Though it certainly can be an emotional experience, listening to our hearts does not mean doing what makes us feel good emotionally. It means doing what God put us on this Earth to do. Fire is one of the symbols of the Holy Spirit, the one who guides us. A "burning" heart then is one that is filled with passion and excitement and guides us toward goodness.

Within each one of us, God has planted the ability to recognize him in all things. When our hearts burn, we are filled with passion and excitement for making God's love present in the world. It is like a compass that points our lives toward God and his mission for us. Walking with Jesus awakens that burning heart within us, giving us the drive and enthusiasm to be who we truly are.

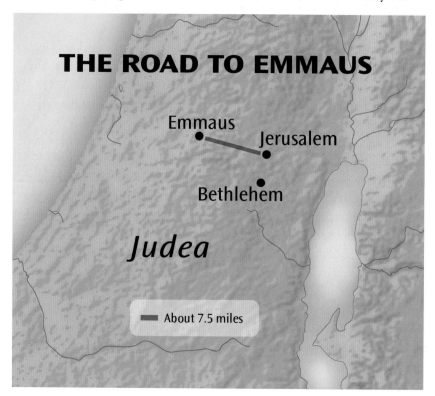

© Saint Mary's Press

THE ROAD TO EMMAUS

Emmaus

Jerusalem

Bethlehem

Judea

About 7.5 miles

Faith Responses to the Resurrection (John 20:1-8,11-16,20-29)

Another thing the Gospel accounts of the Resurrection teach us is how we might respond to the reality of Christ's Resurrection from the dead. John's Gospel offers us at least four different examples of the disciples' faith responses to the Resurrection:

- The first example to consider is the reaction of the disciple whom Jesus loved, or the "beloved disciple," who is believed to be the Apostle John. After Mary Magdalene reported the empty tomb, it says, "Then the other disciple also went in, the one who had arrived at the tomb first, and he saw and believed" (20:8). The beloved disciple believes before he sees Jesus. The *response of belief* is highlighted because it is the response of "the beloved disciple."

- The second response is the example of Mary of Magdala herself. She mistook Jesus for the gardener when he asked her why she was weeping. She saw the angels as well as Jesus himself but still did not understand. It was only when Jesus called her by name that she realized who he was (see 20:11–18). This is the *response of confusion*. Like Mary, we sometimes struggle to find God in our lives, even when he is right in front of our face. Confusion is not disbelief. We continue to trust that Jesus will call us and that we will awaken to find he was there all along.

- The Apostle Thomas offers us the third faith response. When he heard about Jesus' Resurrection, he said to the others, "Unless I see the mark of the nails in his hands and put my finger into the nailmarks and put my hand into his side, I will not believe" (20:25). Perhaps Thomas's response was harsh, but it was courageously honest. Thomas shows us the *response of doubt*. Note that doubt is not portrayed as a bad thing in this account. Only when someone can honestly state their doubts can they effectively address them. Thomas was honest about the gap between what he heard and what he was willing to believe. The account of Thomas is not so much about his lack of faith as it is about the length Jesus will go to bridge the gap between him and someone who longs to see him.

- The fourth faith response comes from all of Jesus' followers who never had the privilege of seeing Jesus' physical human presence on Earth—including us! This is the response of *faith without seeing*. There are many truths we believe in that we cannot directly see, nor can we prove their reality scientifically. Our belief in Christ's Resurrection is one of those truths.

UNIT 2

Faith in God and belief in the Paschal Mystery is a gift. Like any gift, all we have to do is open our hands to receive it . . . and wait. Like he did with Thomas, God will bridge the gap of our unbelief. Like he did with Mary, he will call us by our name so that we can recognize his presence in this life and see him face-to-face in Heaven.

The artist Carravaggio captures the moment when Jesus allows a doubtful Thomas to put his finger into his side, prompting Thomas to proclaim, "My Lord and my God!" (John 20:28).

© Schloss Sanssouci, Potsdam, Brandenburg, Germany / Bridgeman Images

Do You Love Me?

It must have been difficult for the disciples to face Jesus after they had abandoned him when he most needed them. Jesus had accurately predicted that Peter would deny knowing him three times (see John 18:15–18,25–27). After the Resurrection, Jesus offers Peter a chance to affirm his love for him. Just as Peter had denied him three times, Jesus asks Peter three times if he loves him (see 21:15–19). The Gospel offers a clue that ties these two events together. When Jesus questions Peter if he loves him, they are sitting near a charcoal fire (see 21:9). The only other time a charcoal fire is mentioned in John's Gospel is when Peter denies knowing Jesus (see 18:18). John appears to use this imagery to emphasize Jesus' forgiveness of Peter for his denial.

Each time Peter responds, Jesus commands him to take care of his sheep (disciples). In this we see Jesus' entrustment of the care of the Christian community to Peter, who is the first pope of the Church.

Jesus also changes Peter's job description. At the beginning of chapter 21, Peter is working at his trade as a fisherman (see verse 3), but Jesus gives him different work to do. Three times, Jesus asks Peter to tend or feed his sheep. No longer is Peter simply a fisher of men, but like Jesus, he is a shepherd for the flock.

This is what this Resurrection account teaches us: Just as Jesus met Peter on his level, Jesus also meets us where we are. If we are not prepared to freely give all to God, he still loves us and patiently waits until our hearts are filled with his love. If we have denied him in our lives, he will welcome us back. And if we are truly going to follow Jesus, he will lead us down the road of love where we will be called to freely give our lives to others.

This could sometimes put us in situations that are difficult and painful. For example, perhaps you will help refugees escaping poverty or oppression from their home country. Maybe you will listen to the stories of domestic violence victims and help them to find hope and health. Perhaps you will realize that the bully some of your classmates complain about is you. Acknowledging our own shortcomings will make us face our own insecurities that we were oblivious to. Despite the suffering we might endure, we slowly become aware of the power of God's love in our lives.

The Significance of Christ's Resurrection

It might seem obvious to call Jesus Christ's Resurrection from the dead a "significant" event. But focus on the first syllable of the word *significant: sign*. Jesus' Resurrection is significant because it is a "sign" pointing us toward a deeper understanding of salvation history and the Catholic faith.

First, the Resurrection confirms Jesus' divinity and the truth of his teachings. Because Jesus was resurrected from the dead, we can trust that he truly was the Son of God Incarnate. And because he is the Son of God, then we can rely on the truth of his teachings, even the ones that may be easy to understand but difficult to accept.

Second, the Resurrection is the fulfillment of the promises of the Old Testament and Jesus' earthly promises. He is the awaited Messiah. Jesus himself promised his Resurrection numerous times, sometimes using imagery of the Temple to represent his body (see John 2:19–21).

UNIT 2

Third, and most important, in Jesus Christ's Resurrection we find a promise for our own resurrection from the dead—the belief that we too will be raised on the last day, to live forever with the Risen Christ. The resurrection of the dead means that not only will our souls live on after death, but our transformed bodies will also.

Death does not own us, nor does it own the ones we love. Because of the Resurrection, we can be confident that we will see our loved ones again. After our earthly lives end, we will be welcomed into the warm embrace of God. ✳

Jesus' Resurrection assures us that death is not the end of life.

HMMMMM. . .
Why is Thomas's honest expression of doubt significant for our own faith life?

Article 27
The Ascension

When Pope Francis visited North America in 2015, he addressed the United States Congress and praised several well-known American Catholics. One of them was Thomas Merton, a Trappist monk of the Abbey of Gethsemani in Kentucky who died in 1968. Most famous for his autobiography *Seven Storey Mountain*, Merton also wrote poetry and essays on spirituality and social justice. In addition to being a writer, Merton taught the novices, or those aspiring to be monks. He once told them:

> God manifests himself everywhere, in everything, in people and in things and in nature and in events. It becomes very obvious that he is everywhere and in everything and we cannot be without him. You cannot be without God. It's impossible. It's simply impossible. (Monica Weis, *Thomas Merton's Gethsemani: Landscapes of Prayer,* page 117)

Merton's words assure us that even though Original Sin brought about a separation between God and humanity, it did not restrict God's presence. This is a paradox: sin brought about separation, but God is somehow no less available to us. We just do not always recognize his presence. The Incarnation allows humanity to overcome the separation caused by Adam's sin, but it also reminds us that the boundary between God and us is not so solid. The Ascension of Jesus into Heaven—with both his divine and human natures intact—is another reminder of God's "open border." We will focus more on this later in the article. First, let's explore what we know about the Ascension in Scripture.

The Acts of the Apostles describes Jesus ascending upward into Heaven, a reflection of Jewish understanding that God was in the heavens above the sky.

Jesus, Going Up

What does it mean to say that Jesus ascended into **Heaven**? The Gospels do not say a lot about it. The Gospel of John does not describe Jesus' Ascension into Heaven at all. Neither does the Gospel of Matthew. The Gospels of Mark and Luke briefly mention that Jesus was taken up to Heaven (see Mark 16:19, Luke 24:51), and the author of Luke delves deeper into it in the Acts of the Apostles.

The Acts of the Apostles focuses on the major events of the early Christian Church as the Apostles continued Jesus' mission after his Ascension. Acts begins with these two significant events:

- Jesus promised to send the Holy Spirit to guide them as they spread the Good News (see 1:8).
- When his disciples had gathered on Mount Olivet outside Jerusalem, Jesus "was lifted up, and a cloud took him from their sight" (1:9).

It is important to note that the direction "up" should be understood symbolically. We know that Heaven is a not a place but rather a state of eternal life and union with God. In this state, we experience complete happiness and the satisfaction of our deepest human longings. Since Heaven is not a place, why did Jesus have to go "up"? At that time, the Jewish People understood God to be in the heavens above the sky, so it was appropriate to describe Jesus as being lifted "up" as he returned to Heaven. This also creates a parallel with Jesus being "lifted up" on the cross at his death. This parallel emphasizes that Jesus' saving work, begun on the cross, is continued in his Ascension.

Another interesting thing to note is that when Jesus is "lifted up," a cloud takes him from the disciples' sight (Acts 1:9). Recall how often in the Old Testament God's presence is experienced as a cloud: God guided the Israelites out of Egypt in the form of a cloud (see Exodus 13:21); God called Moses from a cloud when he gave him the Ten Commandments on Mount Sinai (see Exodus 24:16); at the dedication of the Temple, God's holy presence was experienced in a cloud (see 1 Kings 8:10). Therefore, Jesus being taken from the disciples' sight by a cloud is yet another sign pointing to his divine nature.

Heaven and Earth

Knowing about the Jewish People's understanding of Heaven and Earth at that time can help deepen our appreciation of Jesus' Ascension. The Jewish understanding of Heaven and Earth was not quite so simple. They believed that the boundaries of Heaven and Earth sometimes crossed over each other. The

Old Testament records numerous appearances of angels on Earth (see Genesis 22:11, Exodus 14:19, Judges 13:3, for example). God was somehow present in the earthly Temple (see 2 Chronicles 5:14). The Psalms prayed that God's presence be known on Earth:

> Be exalted over the heavens, God;
>> may your glory appear above all the earth.
>>> (57:6)

Earth broke into Heaven with the sound of human voices as well:
> They would cry out to you,
>> and you would hear them from heaven.
>>> (Nehemiah 9:27)

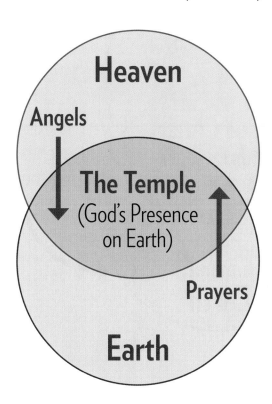

Heaven

Angels

The Temple
(God's Presence
on Earth)

Prayers

Earth

In the New Testament, God is most present in Jesus whose Ascension brings Earth to Heaven. Christ's mission is not only about leaving this world to enter into Heaven; it is also about making the Kingdom of Heaven present here on Earth. This is why Jesus begins his mission by proclaiming, "The kingdom of heaven is at hand" (Matthew 4:17).

Though some of the ancient people believed their body kept them from the spiritual world, Jesus' Ascension tells us the opposite: he ascended into Heaven *with a body*. This emphasizes the goodness of all God's creation and our physical bodies as well. We are not to deny or ignore our physical selves because we too will be transformed in our bodies, like Christ.

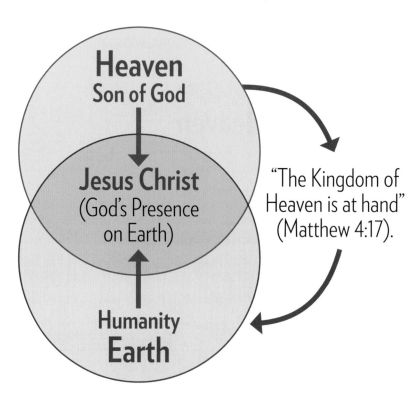

Chapter 6: Resurrection and Ascension 195

The Meaning of the Ascension

When Jesus says, "Follow me" (John 12:26), is he not saying that we should ultimately follow him to Heaven? Just as Jesus' conception and birth marked the Son of God's embrace of our human nature on Earth, the Ascension marked the entrance of Jesus' human nature into Heaven. His rising to Heaven in his body gives us reason to look forward to our own resurrection from the dead at the end of time.

We can also look to Mary's Assumption into Heaven for the same reason. The **Assumption** of Mary is the **dogma** that recognizes that the body of the Blessed Virgin Mary was taken directly to Heaven after her life on Earth had ended. Both Mary's Assumption and Jesus' Ascension give us hope that one day we will be reunited with all our loved ones in the unity of God's presence in Heaven.

© Saint Mary's Press

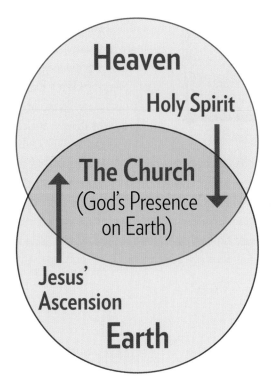

Assumption ➤ The dogma that recognizes that the body of the Blessed Virgin Mary was taken directly to Heaven after her life on Earth had ended.

dogma ➤ Teachings recognized as central to Church teaching, defined by the Magisterium and considered definitive and authoritative.

Recall that before Jesus ascended into Heaven, he promised to send the Holy Spirit. This is why the Ascension is closely tied to **Pentecost**, for it means that Christ's Ascension has cleared the way for the coming of the Holy Spirit. Remember that Pentecost commemorates the descent of the **Holy Spirit** on the Apostles, Mary, and the disciples. Pentecost occurs on the fiftieth day following Easter, just ten days after Jesus' Ascension. By sending the Holy Spirit, Jesus fulfills his promise to be with us forever (Matthew 28:20).

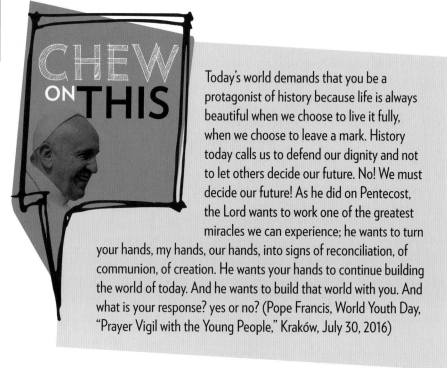

CHEW ON THIS

Today's world demands that you be a protagonist of history because life is always beautiful when we choose to live it fully, when we choose to leave a mark. History today calls us to defend our dignity and not to let others decide our future. No! We must decide our future! As he did on Pentecost, the Lord wants to work one of the greatest miracles we can experience; he wants to turn your hands, my hands, our hands, into signs of reconciliation, of communion, of creation. He wants your hands to continue building the world of today. And he wants to build that world with you. And what is your response? yes or no? (Pope Francis, World Youth Day, "Prayer Vigil with the Young People," Kraków, July 30, 2016)

Pentecost ➤ The fiftieth day following Easter, which commemorates the descent of the Holy Spirit on the Apostles and Mary.

Holy Spirit ➤ The Third Person of the Blessed Trinity, the perfect personal love between the Father and the Son, who inspires, guides, and sanctifies the life of believers.

The Ascension and the Church

Christ's Ascension also prepares the way for the Church to be revealed to the world. With the coming of the Holy Spirit after the Ascension, the Apostles are empowered to lead the early Christian community to continue Christ's mission. Just as Jesus was "filled with the holy Spirit" (Luke 4:1), the Church, the Body of Christ, is filled with the same Holy Spirit who inspires, guides, and sanctifies the life of believers. Through the Holy Spirit, we become the mingling of Heaven and Earth.

It is up to the Church, the Mystical **Body of Christ** to embody Christ's presence and continue his mission. The members of the Church are called to build up the Kingdom of Heaven that Jesus established on Earth. This requires that we not only go to church and worship God as a community but that we also live out this mission all our lives.

The Acts of the Apostles records that when Jesus ascended, the disciples continued to stare into the sky. Then two men in white garments who seem to be angels appeared to them and asked why they were just standing there looking up at the sky (see Acts 1:11). In other words, there is work to do here on Earth!

This passage also reminds us that Jesus is not to be found up in "the sky." Christ is found in the Eucharist when we celebrate Mass and when we gather in his name (see Matthew 18:20). You can see Christ in the people who make up the Church (see Colossians 1:24). Christ is also found in all those who are in need (see Matthew 25:37–40). The Ascension is a reminder that Heaven and Earth merge all around us, and that by following Jesus on Earth, we will also follow him into our heavenly home. ✳

UNIT 2

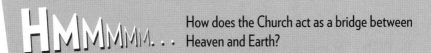

HMMMMMM. . .   How does the Church act as a bridge between Heaven and Earth?

Body of Christ ➤ A term that when capitalized designates Jesus' Body in the Eucharist, or the entire Church, which is also referred to as the Mystical Body of Christ.

1. Name the person who buried Jesus. Why would he be an oddity among Jesus' disciples?

2. Why were guards placed outside Jesus' tomb?

3. What does it mean to say that Jesus was resurrected?

4. How is Jesus different after the Resurrection?

5. Give three brief reasons that support the Resurrection as an actual historical event.

6. What did the two disciples on the road to Emmaus experience as they walked with Jesus? When did they finally recognize him?

7. After the Resurrection, Jesus asks Peter three times if Peter loves him, and Peter affirms his love for Jesus all three times. What pre-Resurrection event does this exchange address and heal?

8. With what event is Jesus' Ascension closely tied and why?

9. What was the Jewish understanding of Heaven and Earth, and how might that help our understanding of Jesus' Ascension?

ART STUDY

The Ascension of Christ was painted by surrealist painter Salvador Dali in 1958. It was inspired by a cosmic dream in which he saw the nucleus of an atom.

1. What initially strikes you about his painting?

2. Why do you think Dali painted Jesus from this perspective?

3. How does the painting show the unification of Heaven and Earth?

UNIT 2 HIGHLIGHTS

CHAPTER 4 The Life and Teachings of Jesus

The Infancy Narratives: Differences and Similarities

The infancy narratives of Matthew and Luke are primarily theological statements about the person and mission of Jesus Christ.

Matthew (Jewish audience)

Jesus is:

- a son of Abraham (Jewish)
- an important figure in their history
- the Son of David
- the Messiah
- Emmanuel: the Presence of God
- here for Gentiles too

Jesus is:

- conceived of a virgin
- the Son of God
- the Son of Mary

Luke (Gentile audience)

Jesus is:

- the Son of Man (Adam)
- here for all of humanity, both Jews and Gentiles
- concerned about the poor and outcasts
- appreciative of the contributions of women
- perceived as a threat to those in power

The Incarnation and the *Theotokos*

The Virgin Mary

Theotokos ("God-bearer")
The Mother of God

- The Incarnation refers to the mystery of Jesus Christ, the Divine Son of God, becoming human.
- Because of her "yes," Mary became the Mother of God.
- Mary is honored for her humility and faithfulness to God, and for bringing the Son of God into the world.

Dying and Rising

Jesus' teachings of self-denial and self-sacrifice point toward love of all people, hinting at his own sacrifice on the cross.

Poverty   Take Up Your Cross   Persecution   Crucifixion

Gospel accounts of Jesus raising someone from the dead offer hints toward his Resurrection from the dead.

Jairus's / Synagogue Official's Daughter   Raising of Lazarus   The Resurrection

CHAPTER 5   Jesus' Death: Four Perspectives

Motives of the Religious Leaders

Jesus is accused of blasphemy.	Jesus denounces religious leaders.
Jesus is accused of neglecting the Law.	Jesus refers to himself as Messiah / Son of God.
Jesus runs the money changers out of the Temple.	Jesus predicts destruction of the Temple.

Motives of the Political Leaders

Jesus said he came to bring about a new Kingdom.	Jesus was accused of inciting a revolt.
	To appease the Jewish religious leaders
Jesus was accused of opposing payment of taxes.	Fear of a Jewish messiah (military leader)

The Roman Practice of Crucifixion

Could last hours or days

Crime posted over the victim

Death penalty for non-Roman citizens

Victim usually died of asphyxiation

Public torture and humiliation

Aimed at frightening subjects into submission

Usually reserved for the lower classes

The Meaning of Jesus' Crucifixion

God's love

The New Covenant

Sacrifice

Freedom from sin

Selflessness

Victory over death

Following God's will

Service to others

CHAPTER 6 Resurrection and Ascension

Resurrection Is

- the bodily rising of Jesus from the dead on the third day after his death on the cross

- when Jesus passed through and conquered death, and returned to a new and different life

- Jesus' restoration to life as the same person but with a glorified body

Resurrection Is Not

- resuscitation—when someone's heart quits beating and then the person is revived

- reincarnation—coming back to life in a completely new and different body

- becoming pure spirit—dying and leaving one's body behind

- immortality—the state of never having to experience death

images. Shutterstock.com

Resurrection Appearances in the Gospels

The Gospel of Luke (24:13–35)

"Then the two recounted . . . how he was made known to them in the breaking of the bread" (verse 35).

The Gospel of John: The Four Responses (chapter 20)

The Response of Belief

"Then the other disciple also went in . . . and he saw and believed" (verse 8).

The Response of Confusion

"[Mary] turned and said to [Jesus], 'Rabbouni,'" (verse 16).

The Response of Doubt

"Unless I see the mark of the nails in his hands . . . and put my hand into his side, I will not believe" (verse 25).

The Response of Faith without Seeing

"Blessed are those who have not seen and have believed" (verse 29).

Shepherding the Flock (John, chapter 21)

Jesus commissions Peter for sacrificial leadership in the Church, not as a fisherman, but as a shepherd.

No Longer This

"'Simon, son of John, do you love me?' He said to him, 'Yes, Lord, you know that I love you.' He said to him, 'Tend my sheep'" (verse 16).

This!

UNIT 2

The Ascension:
Building on Old Testament Symbols

Old Testament Symbol	Ascension Connection

"Going Up"

Ancient Israelites believed God is in the heavens above the sky.

"Going Up"

In the Ascension, Jesus is the Son of God who returns to his Father in Heaven.

(See Mark 16:19, Luke 24:50–51, Acts 1:1–2.)

Clouds

An Old Testament symbol of God's holy presence:

- God guided the Israelites in the form of a cloud (see Exodus 13:21).
- God called "to Moses from the midst of the cloud" on Mount Sinai (Exodus 24:16).
- At the Temple dedication "the cloud [God's presence] filled the house of the LORD" (1 Kings 8:10).

Clouds

An Old Testament symbol of God's holy presence:

- God guided the Israelites in the form of a cloud (see Exodus 13:21).
- God called "to Moses from the midst of the cloud" on Mount Sinai (Exodus 24:16).
- At the Temple dedication "the cloud [God's presence] filled the house of the LORD" (1 Kings 8:10).

The Meaning of the Ascension

Jewish Understanding of Heaven and Earth

The boundaries of Heaven and Earth crossed over each other.

- Angels appear on Earth (see Genesis 22:11).
- God was present in the earthly Temple (see 2 Chronicles 5:14).
- The Psalms prayed for God's presence to be known on Earth: "Be exalted over the heavens, God; / may your glory appear above all the earth" (57:6).

Jesus' Ascension

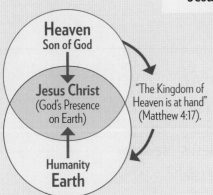

"The Kingdom of Heaven is at hand" (Matthew 4:17).

The Ascension brings Earth to Heaven.

- Christ's mission is not only about leaving this world to enter into Heaven; it is also about making the Kingdom of Heaven present on Earth.
- Jesus' Ascension in his body emphasizes the goodness of our physical bodies.
- The Ascension gives us hope that we too will enter Heaven.

The Church, the Mystical Body of Christ

The Ascension cleared the way for the coming of the Holy Spirit.

- The Holy Spirit inspires, guides, and sanctifies the Church.
- The Church gives us a foretaste of Heaven through true community and the sacraments.
- It is up to us to share in Christ's mission and build up the Kingdom of Heaven that he established on Earth.

UNIT 2
BRING IT HOME

HOW DID JESUS FULFILL GOD'S PLAN?

FOCUS QUESTIONS

CHAPTER 4 How does Jesus' life show he is the Messiah?

CHAPTER 5 Why did Jesus have to die to save us?

CHAPTER 6 Why is believing in Jesus' Resurrection so important?

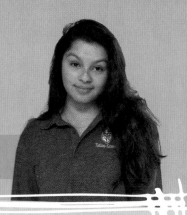

ROSA
Totino-Grace High School

Each Gospel writer had a specific audience they were writing to, which helped those people connect to Jesus. The Gospels have a lot of the same material, but each Gospel has unique parts that address a need or problem that was happening in those communities. Yet, all of the Gospels show us what God's plan really was— to send his only Son to guide the people and teach them how to live faithfully. I think many people get caught up in rules and what they can't do. But Jesus showed us it's more about what we can do. That is how Jesus fulfilled God's plan: by loving his enemies, challenging the status quo, and showing that it's possible to not give in to temptation.

REFLECT

Take some time to read and reflect on the unit and chapter focus questions listed on the facing page.

- What question or section did you identify most closely with?

- What did you find within the unit that was comforting or challenging?

UNIT 3
The Paschal Mystery:
Christ's Saving Work

WHY SHOULD WE BELIEVE IN LIFE AFTER DEATH?

LOOKING AHEAD

CHAPTER 7   Page 212

Redeemed by God

CHAPTER 8   Page 238

Our Salvation

I have always been taught to believe that there is a Heaven and Hell, and that God has a plan for all of us. But I never really had to think about it, because until last year, I had never experienced anyone close to me dying. When my aunt died, it shook my faith and made me doubtful about God's plan. I think a lot of people believe in life after death because it gives them something to hang onto. But I think there are other teenagers who might have doubts too, which makes me feel comforted, in a weird way.

OLIVIA
New Smyrna Beach High School

CHAPTER 7
Redeemed by God

HOW DOES JESUS' DEATH AND RESURRECTION AFFECT OUR LIVES?

SNAPSHOT

Article 28   Page 213
The Power of Love
- Pre-read: The Letter to Philemon

Article 29   Page 218
Paul's Theology of the Cross
- Pre-read: 1 Corinthians 1:18–25
- Pre-read: 1 Corinthians 4:10–16
- Pre-read: Romans, chapter 6
- Pre-read: Philippians 2:5–11

Article 30   Page 225
Resurrection of the Dead
- Pre-read: 1 Corinthians 15:1–58

Article 31   Page 230
Becoming One
- Pre-read: 1 Corinthians, chapter 12
- Pre-read: John 17:20–26

Article 28
The Power of Love

Salvatore grew up on the east side of downtown in a barrio that was notorious for its numerous gangs. He went to the local public high school, and despite how hard his parents tried to prevent it, he joined a gang when he was fourteen. "If you aren't down with a gang, nobody's got your back," he thought. Salvatore learned quickly that to survive in that world, you had to exert your power over others. For example, you had to be able to fight, you had to carry a weapon, and you had to look strong and make others look weak.

After several arrests, the violent death of a close friend, and a short prison sentence, Salvatore eventually began to see the harm of being in a gang. Over time he turned his life over to God. He realized that trying to wield power over others was not a strength, but a weakness rooted in fear. In reading the Gospels, he realized that Jesus never acted out of fear. Instead, he was true to himself even when doing so threatened his own life. Salvatore came to believe that Jesus' love was the greatest power in the world, and he vowed that he would do his best to love others in that same way.

UNIT 3

© Benjavisa Ruangvaree / Shutterstock.com

The Paschal Mystery reveals that true strength is found in the power of authentic love.

TAKE IT TO GOD

God,
Everyone seems so bossy—parents, teachers, coaches,
and even some of my friends!
I want to be free. I want to have the power to make my own decisions,
maybe even boss some other people around!
But then I remember that even the Son of God was obedient.
Jesus could have done anything, but he chose to be
a loving servant and friend.
He showed us that love is the only real superpower that matters.
Help me be obedient to you, Lord.
When I get selfish, remind me that I was made to love and serve.
Only then will I truly find happiness.
Amen.

Sources of Power

Jesus used the power of love, not force, to convert the hearts of those he touched while on this Earth and after his Ascension into Heaven. Before we dive deeper into the power of love, let's first understand some of the different sources and uses of power.

Source of Power	Use
Power from Authority	The power to direct and command others because of your office or position.
Power from Influence	The power to influence other people's attitudes and decisions because of the relationship you have built with them.
Power from Action	The power to take the initiative to make things happen or to inspire people with your actions.

Power, in and of itself, is neither good nor evil, but people can choose to use their power for good or for bad. Here are some examples:

Source of Power	Used for Good	Used for Evil
Power from Authority	A manager assigns her employees duties that are essential for a business to run smoothly.	A manager trains her employees to do something illegal.
Power from Influence	A person teaches someone how to perform CPR.	A person teaches someone how to steal a car.
Power from Action	A group devises and executes a plan to help aid the victims of a tragic event.	A group devises and executes a plan to rob a bank.

How Jesus Used Power

Power from Authority: Jesus had the authority that came with being the Son of God, the Second Person of the Holy Trinity. He also had the authority that came from his position as a rabbi, as a teacher and leader with disciples. Jesus used his divine power to control nature, to expel demons, and for physical healing. He used his position as a rabbi to direct the disciples' missionary actions. But he used his power from authority sparingly, and only used it to benefit others.

- He calmed the storm when he was with his disciples in a boat on the Sea of Galilee (see Matthew 8:23–27).
- He commanded an unclean spirit to come out of a possessed man (see Mark 1:21–28).
- He healed a paralyzed man (see Luke 5:17–26), and so many other people, too numerous to mention here!

Power From Influence: Jesus used this source of power to persuade people to accept his teachings and to follow him.

- He invited others to follow him and be his disciples; he did not force them to do so (see Mark 8:34).
- Jesus taught in a way that intrigued people and helped them accept his teachings on the New Covenant and the Law of Love.
- He avoided using his divine powers to impress and force others to follow him.

UNIT 3

Power From Action: Jesus didn't just preach; he practiced what he preached and confronted injustices and wrongdoing, even when it was a great risk to his own life. His actions changed people's lives and inspired his disciples to do the same.

- He denounced the hypocrisy of the scribes and Pharisees (Matthew 23:1–36).
- He drove the merchants and money changers from the Temple (John 2:13–16).
- He went out of his way to challenge cultural norms and hung out with people who were considered sinners (see Mark 2:13–17).

In short, Jesus used all three types of power but always used them to spread the Kingdom of God and for the good of others. He used his power lovingly, never using it to hurt people or to force them to do something against their will.

Jesus used his divine power to control nature when he calmed the storm on the Sea of Galilee (see Matthew 8:23–27).

The United States abolished slavery in 1865, but sadly it continues to this day in the form of human trafficking. Human trafficking is the sale of human beings, often for the purpose of forced labor or sexual exploitation. According to Polaris, an organization that fights modern slavery, over ten thousand victims were identified in the United States in 2017. You can help by educating yourself and your friends to make sure they do not become prey. Never reveal personal information that could identify you, your home, or school on the internet or to strangers. Be aware of your surroundings when you are alone in public. We must work to ensure that all human life is treated with the dignity that God intended.

UNIT 3

Authentic Love Is Power

Jesus' use of power is always focused on love. Some people would say that love is not powerful, that it makes a person vulnerable and weak. How often have you heard a villain in a book or movie say this to the hero? But the Paschal Mystery teaches us the opposite. It reveals that true strength is power used in and with love. Nowhere else is that more obvious than in Christ's choice to die on a cross (see Matthew 27:33–51, Mark 15:22–38, Luke 23:32–46, John 19:17–30). Through his sacrifice—which at first seemed like weakness to many—he makes God's saving love available to all people. Through Jesus' words and example, he taught us that love is the only true measure of our actions and that death is not a failure. The cross reminds us that our biggest failure comes when we fail to love one another.

One final thought: It is important to remember that power that comes from authority cannot be the primary basis for authentic love in relationships. Even though authoritative power can be used for good, it is not a relationship between equals. You cannot command someone to love you. Power that respects the freedom and equal dignity of the other is the basis for authentic love. This is one reason God took on our human nature, out of respect for our freedom and dignity and to approach us as an equal. ✳

How would you explain to a friend that true strength comes from using our power with love?

Article 29
Paul's Theology of the Cross

Have Jesus' teachings ever confused you? You aren't alone. In earlier chapters, we learned that many of Jesus' teachings were paradoxical. Much of what he taught often confused those who heard him two thousand years ago, including his disciples. At that time, people often believed that those who followed the Law were rewarded by God with prosperity and good health, while Jesus taught that the Kingdom of God belonged to the poor (see Luke 6:20). They expected the Messiah to be a powerful military ruler who would gain Israel's freedom. When the Apostles confessed their belief that he was the Messiah, Jesus said that he would suffer, be rejected, and die (see Luke 9:22).

Jesus turned people's perception of the world upside down. Often what they assumed to be good turned out to be bad, and vice versa. For example, he taught that spending time with sinners was a worthy thing to do in order to bring them to repentance, extending God's love and forgiveness toward them (see Luke 5:30–31); that blindness was not a punishment for sin, but rather the means by which God can show his glory (see John 9:1–3); that we are not supposed to hate our enemies, but rather love them (see Matthew 5:43–47). But the biggest paradox is Jesus' death on the cross. How can death bring new life? How can a shameful execution be Christ's hour of glory?

The New Testament author who wrote the most about the meaning of Christ's death on the cross is Saint Paul. On the road to Damascus, Saint Paul's life was turned upside down when he had a vision of Jesus. Paul saw the world in a new way, and he shared those insights in the letters he wrote.

Many of Jesus' teachings are paradoxical ("love your enemies" [Matthew 5:44]), but his death on a cross is probably the biggest paradox of all, because through his death, Jesus brings new life.

The Paradox of the Cross

Most of the religions at that time were **polytheistic**, and people would regularly offer sacrifices to a particular god in the hope that that god would grant the people what they wanted. The worshippers of a particular god believed that the strength of their god would enable them to defeat their enemies in battle. If they won, they assumed that it was because their god was stronger than their enemy's god. If they were defeated, they would sometimes start worshipping the god of the people who defeated them. It just made sense to try to gain the favor of the stronger god.

Considering this, you can probably imagine what it was like to try to convince people to accept the divinity of Jesus Christ. Christians preached that the Son of God was beaten, nailed to a cross, and died. This certainly did not match the common perception of a powerful god at that time. Saint Paul recognized these difficulties that potential converts had with Jesus' Crucifixion and death.

What is Paul's response to this stumbling block? He doesn't offer a logical or scientific proof. Rather, he appeals to what the Corinthians already know deep in their hearts. He speaks about the superiority of God's wisdom over human wisdom. What God has revealed will not make sense if we are only looking at it from the human perspective in which the power to control others is supreme. The Corinthians knew deep down—as we do—that controlling others isn't love; it isn't of God. True love shows itself in loving sacrifice, like the sacrifice of Jesus on the cross for the salvation of all who believe in him. This is true strength, only appearing as weakness, for "the weakness of God is stronger than human strength" (1 Corinthians 1:25).

What does this mean for us? Even today, following Jesus' Way of the Cross is not necessarily easy. We are still swayed by the ways of the world that says fame, power, and wealth are the things we should strive for. The path of loving self-sacrifice for others still seems like weakness to many people. Tripped up by this false belief, people are led away from loving others through humble words and actions—the wisdom of the cross.

UNIT 3

---

polytheistic ➤ Believing in many gods.

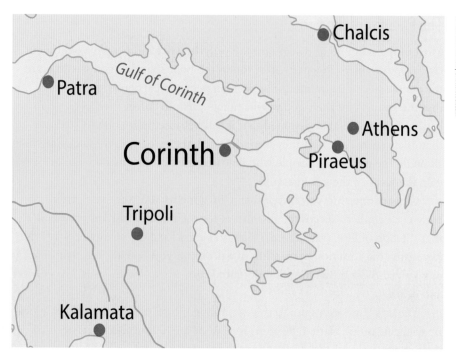

Saint Paul had originally helped set up the Christian church in Corinth. When the Corinthians ran into challenges, Paul wrote letters giving them much needed practical advice to respond to those challenges.

Our Role in Salvation

As Saint Paul prepared for his journey to Rome, he wanted to introduce himself to the Christian community there. Of course, he did this through a letter. In the letter, he addresses some common misunderstandings of Christ's saving work. One of those misunderstandings was the belief that because we are saved by God's grace, it does not matter how we act.

In his Letter to the Romans, Paul notes the absurdity of this idea. It's true that Jesus Christ "was handed over for our **transgressions** and was raised for our **justification**" (Romans 4:25). Justification is the removal of sin and the gift of God's sanctifying grace to renew holiness. This work of salvation was accomplished through Christ's Passion, death, and Resurrection, the Paschal Mystery. But there's more to it than that: we also have a role to play in our salvation.

---

transgression ➤ An act that goes against a law, rule, or code of conduct; sin.

justification ➤ God's act of bringing a sinful human being into right relationship with him. It involves removal of sin and the gift of God's sanctifying grace to renew holiness.

In chapter 6 of Romans, Saint Paul points out that we "were baptized into [Jesus'] death" (verse 3). What does that mean, exactly? It means we must think of ourselves "as [being] dead to sin and living for God in Christ Jesus" (verse 11). God's grace is offered freely to everyone, but we are not puppets that God simply manipulates. "Christians are called to lead henceforth a life 'worthy of the gospel of Christ'"[1] (*Catechism of the Catholic Church [CCC]*, number 1692). To put it another way, we have to accept this grace and participate in our salvation.

Praying for the coming of the Kingdom of God and working toward that goal is one way we can participate in our own salvation.

So, how do we participate in our salvation? One way is in practicing the **virtues**. A virtue is a habitual and firm disposition to do good. There are four **Cardinal Virtues** that are viewed as pivotal or essential for full Christian living: prudence, justice, fortitude, and temperance. The **Theological Virtues** are the God-given virtues of faith, hope, and love.

virtue ➤ A habitual and firm disposition to do good.

Cardinal Virtues ➤ Based on the Latin word *cardo*, meaning "pivot," four virtues that are viewed as pivotal or essential for full Christian living: prudence, justice, fortitude, and temperance.

Theological Virtues ➤ The name given for the God-given virtues of faith, hope, and love. These virtues enable us to know God as God and lead us to union with God in mind and heart.

UNIT 3

These virtues enable us to know God as God and lead us to union with him in mind and heart. "Christ's gift of salvation offers us the grace necessary to persevere in the pursuit of the virtues" (*CCC*, number 1811).

The Cardinal Virtues	
Prudence	The virtue that integrates knowledge with wisdom and understanding, so as to read the circumstances, discern what is good, and select the appropriate means for attaining that good, with patience and timing.
Justice	The virtue concerned with giving God and neighbor their due; the commitment to ensuring that all persons—particularly those who are poor and oppressed—receive what is due them.
Fortitude	Also called strength or courage, the virtue that enables one to maintain sound moral judgment and behavior in the face of difficulties, challenges, and pressure.
Temperance	The virtue by which one moderates his or her appetite for human pleasures and the use of created goods.

The Theological Virtues	
Faith	From the Latin *fides*, meaning "trust" or "belief," the gift of God by which one freely accepts God's full Revelation in Jesus Christ. It is a matter of both the head (acceptance of God's revealed truth) and the heart (love of God and neighbor as a response to God's first loving us).
Hope	The virtue by which we desire and expect from God both eternal life and the grace we need to attain it; having both a future dimension trusting in the promises of God and a present dimension cooperating with God's grace to make that future happen.
Love	Also called charity, the virtue by which we love God above all things and, out of that love of God, love our neighbors as ourselves.

UNIT 3

Paul reminds the Christians in Rome that before their Baptism, they were slaves to sin (see Romans 6:17), but because of their Baptism, they have been freed from sin (see 6:22). Slavery is an analogy that the Romans would have understood, as slavery was very common in Roman culture. Paul's point is that God's grace allows us to leave our old selves—trapped by sin—behind. It is as if the "old you" died and allowed the "new you" to be born. If it is a true transformation, the "new" person will not act like the "old" person. Christ's death on the cross and his Resurrection lead us toward the death of sin and our rising to new life in Christ Jesus (see 6:4). It does not happen by grace alone, but also by praying for the coming of the Kingdom of God and working toward that goal.

CATHOLICS MAKING A DIFFERENCE

Saint Simeon Salus (sixth century AD) took the idea of being a "fool for Christ" to the next level. After living the austere life of a monk in the desert for twenty-nine years, Simeon was called by God to serve his community. He walked into the town of Emessa, Syria, dragging a dead dog on a leash, and was immediately labeled a crazy old man. Simeon used unconventional tactics to knock down those who seemed too holy or wise for their own good. He went to the church and extinguished the candles, threw nuts at the women, and then flipped over the tables outside. He was ostracized and kept company with the poor and other outcasts. Meanwhile, Simeon secretly did acts of kindness, like feeding the hungry, healing the sick, and praying for everyone. It was not until after his death that his good works became widely known.

Emptying Yourself

Long before we physically die, we will most likely experience a number of losses during our lifetimes, such as the death of a family member or friend, the end of a friendship, moving to a different city, suffering a serious physical injury, and so on. These losses are almost like little deaths; they are always painful and often mean letting go of some important part of our lives.

Long before his Crucifixion and death, Jesus also experienced similar losses and painful experiences. It is instructive to see how he responded to them. When he was tempted by the Devil in the desert, Jesus accepted that his divinity would not be used to serve himself (see Matthew 4:1–11). When Jesus' closest friend denied knowing him, he forgave Peter anyway (see John 18:25–27, 21:15–17). Jesus also did not always get what he wanted (see Mark 14:35–36). In each of these situations, Jesus did not try to hang on to what was lost; rather, he emptied him*self*. He wasn't selfish; he was self-*less*.

This is the kind of self-emptying that Saint Paul refers to when he describes Jesus:

> He emptied himself,
> taking the form of a slave . . .
> he humbled himself,
>> becoming obedient to death,
>> even death on a cross.
>> (Philippians 2:7–8)

Jesus' cross is a symbol of death, yet it paradoxically leads the way to new life. The earliest Christians were considered foolish for believing that a crucified man was the Son of God. Saint Paul helped them understand that the cross is a symbol of Christ's selflessness that embodied his life's message and was his final earthly act of love. As followers of Christ, we are called to embody that same selflessness. ✳

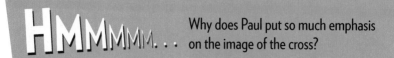

HMMMMM. . . Why does Paul put so much emphasis on the image of the cross?

Article 30
Resurrection of the Dead

When Therese and Alessandro walked into the hospital room, they asked the doctor to leave so they could be alone with their son, Dante, one last time. His body was underneath a white sheet, but the doctor folded down the upper half before he left so they could see him. They took turns holding his hand, caressing his face, stroking his hair, and hugging him. Of course, they knew he was dead and that his soul had left his body, but they still talked to him like he was in the room.

Even though Dante was gone, his body was still sacred. This was the body that had been in Therese's womb and that she had given birth to after nine months. These were the arms that Alessandro guided when he taught Dante how to swing a baseball bat. This was the forehead that they were both sure to kiss each night before he went to bed. In his short lifetime, Dante's ears helped him listen to his friend's problems. His hands helped clean a neighbor's flooded home. His right foot kicked the winning goal of his high school soccer team's state championship. These were not just "things" that he used—they were intimate parts of who he was. Without his body, it was impossible to even know Dante.

UNIT 3

We should always respect our body, even when it is dead! (No, we are not talking about the zombie apocalypse!) Because of our belief in the resurrection of the dead, our body "must be treated with respect and charity" (CCC, number 2300) when we die. Burying the dead, which is one of the Corporal Works of Mercy, is an example of treating the body with respect and charity. So why does the Church allow for autopsies, organ donations, and even scientific research to be performed on corpses? All of these are ways that seek to understand God's creation (e.g., research on diseases) and to help others (e.g., organ donation), and therefore are also signs of respect for the human body.

Every aspect of being human is sacred, including our bodies. Each human being is a union of body and **soul**—physical matter and spirit. The soul is what gives life to the body, but these "are not two natures united, but rather their union forms a single nature" (*CCC*, number 365). The body is not merely an enclosure for the soul, but rather both together make us who we are. Because of Jesus' Resurrection, we can be assured that at the end of time, we will be reunited with our bodies and will rise from the dead.

© Vatican Museums and Galleries, Vatican City / Artothek / Bridgeman Images (Resurrection of the Dead)

A section of Michelangelo's *Last Judgment* in the Sistine Chapel, Vatican City, depicts the bodily resurrection of the dead. Jesus' Resurrection assures us that we will be reunited with our bodies and will rise from the dead at the end of time.

soul ➤ Our spiritual principle; it is immortal, and it is what makes us most like God. Our soul is created by God at the moment of our conception. It is the seat of human consciousness and freedom.

Paul's Challenge

The early Christians accepted Jesus' Resurrection, but the thought of their own resurrection did not come so easily. In Saint Paul's First Letter to the Corinthians, it seems that many of the Christians in Corinth were having some difficulties understanding the resurrection of the dead. Paul was challenged with explaining this essential truth to them. Recall that the early Christian churches included both Jews and Gentiles. The church in Corinth was mainly Gentile, but it almost certainly included some Jewish converts to Christianity as well. Each of these groups had problems believing in a bodily resurrection from the dead but for different reasons.

Some of the Jewish Christians might have been troubled by the belief in the resurrection of the dead because the issue of an immortal soul was not yet resolved within Judaism. The belief in life after death was relatively new to the Jewish people and was not yet accepted by all Jews. So some Jews in Paul's time, like the Pharisees, embraced this belief. Others, like the Sadducees, did not believe in life after death (see Acts 23:7–8). The Sadducees thought that after death, one just disappeared into emptiness.

The Gentiles had a different understanding of life after death. Their beliefs were heavily influenced by Greek culture. Greek beliefs in life after death centered around the idea that there were two realms of existence: spiritual and material. The spiritual realm was understood as the eternal perfection of truth, beauty, wisdom, and goodness. On the other hand, the material world was imperfect and subject to decay.

The ancient Greeks believed that our souls were rooted in the spiritual realm. During our earthly lives, our material bodies were like cages trapping our souls, keeping us from spiritual perfection. Once we died, our souls would be freed from our bodies to spend eternity in the spiritual realm. Thus, the necessity of a bodily resurrection did not make sense to them.

So, in chapter 15 of First Corinthians, Paul addresses both of these issues. As you read the chapter, can you identify the arguments he is making?

UNIT 3

UNIT 3

One of Saint Paul's arguments supporting the Resurrection is that Jesus physically appeared to his disciples in a resurrected body.

Paul's Case for the Resurrection of the Dead

Saint Paul makes it clear how important Jesus' Resurrection is. He writes, "If Christ has not been raised, then . . . empty, too, your faith" (1 Corinthians 15:14). Jesus' Resurrection confirms "all Christ's works and teachings" and that he is "the fulfillment of the promises both of the Old Testament and of Jesus himself during his earthly life"[2] (*CCC*, numbers 651, 652). In the First Letter to the Corinthians, Paul lays out the following arguments to support this essential article of faith:

- **Jesus Christ truly resurrected from the dead.** (15:1–11)
  Paul cites Jesus' *physical appearance in a resurrected body* to Cephas (Peter), the Twelve, five hundred disciples, and James, as well as his own witness of the resurrected Jesus.

- **If Jesus' Resurrection occurred, then resurrection from the dead must be possible.** (15:12–19)
  Paul appeals to logic and says, "If there is no resurrection of the dead, then neither has Christ been raised" (verse 13).

- **Death has no power over God's salvation.** (15:20–28)
  If a man (Adam) can bring death into the world through sin, then all will be brought to life in Christ.
- **If there is no resurrection of the dead, then there is no reason to be good.** (15:29–34)
  Paul says that if we simply cease to exist at the end of our earthly lives, then all our works are pointless. He suggests that if there is not resurrection of the dead, we might as well just focus on selfish activities.
- **A resurrected body is different from a mortal body.** (15:35–58)
  Paul compares the two to a seed and a plant. Our earthly body is like the seed that must die (the way a seed is buried) before it can rise from the ground. Just as plants are different from seeds, our resurrected body will be different from our mortal body.
- **There is a direct connection between our pre-resurrection body and our resurrected body.** (15:42–49)
  "[Our body] is sown **corruptible**; it is raised incorruptible. It is sown dishonorable; it is raised glorious. It is sown weak; it is raised powerful" (verses 42–43). Paul is not saying that our pre-resurrection body is bad or evil, but rather corrupt*ible*. Corruptible refers to something that can be spoiled, contaminated, or made rotten.

These arguments address both the Jewish Christians' doubts and the Gentile Christians' misunderstanding about our bodily resurrection. Saint Paul reassures us that at our death, our soul will continue to live, and at the end of time, God will reunite us with our body. It is the same body, but it will have changed because it will be incorruptible. We will not suffer from illness, nor will we be tempted to sin. Our resurrected body will also not be constrained by the limitations of time and space. ✳

UNIT 3

HMMMMMM. . . How would you explain to someone what our own resurrection will be like?

---

corruptible ➤ Something that can be spoiled, contaminated, or made rotten.

Article 31

Becoming One

In the Last Supper Discourses in John's Gospel, Jesus offers a prayer to the Father in which he expresses a special desire for his disciples: "Holy Father, keep them in your name that you have given me, so that they may be one just as we are" (17:11). With this prayer, Jesus asks that we become one and offers the union of the Holy Trinity as our model. And he repeats his request several times (see 17:20–24). Maintaining our unity as his Church was very important to Jesus.

How do we "become one" like the Trinity? The union of the Father, Son, and Holy Spirit is a loving, communal relationship. It's also a mystery. In this article, we will acknowledge the challenges in "becoming one," the teachings of Saint Paul on this subject, and how we can bring unity to fruition in our own lives.

© wingedwolf / iStockphoto.com

The Church is called to be one unified Body of Christ that strengthens and loves one another. Think of a close-knit, loving community you belong to. What do you like most about it?

Community

If you've ever been part of a close-knit, loving community—friends, family, sports team, theatre group, school club—you know how wonderful it can be. Feeling wanted and included satisfies a basic human need. On the other hand, if you've ever been part of a community that is falling apart, you know how painful that can be. Cliques and peer pressure disrupt friendships. Before and after a divorce, a family can be torn apart by arguments and harsh words. Volleyball teams can have a star athlete who wants the spotlight all the time, leaving the others feeling left out. All sorts of groups can experience painful divisions.

The Church is called to be one, a unified Body of Christ. Although sin brought us separation from God and one another, our faith in Christ unifies us, and the sacraments heal us and strengthen us to better forgive and love one another. The Paschal Mystery is not simply a doctrine we must believe but something in which we are all called to participate. We look forward to the day when we will be perfectly united with God and one another in Heaven, but we are also called to help bring about the Kingdom of Heaven here on Earth. This is why Jesus prays that the Church "may all be one, as you, Father, are in me and I in you, that they also may be in us" (John 17:21).

The Church is not immune to disagreements and hurt feelings. Even though it is continually guided by the Holy Spirit, the Church includes human beings who are broken by sin. Even before his death, Resurrection, and Ascension, Jesus' disciples argued with one another (see Luke 9:46). What's important is that we disagree respectfully, always letting our love for Christ and one another unite us despite our differences.

UNIT 3

Many Parts, One Body

In his First Letter to the Corinthians, Saint Paul addressed a community that was in conflict. To begin with, they were already a diverse group of people—rich, poor, slaves, free, and so on. Second, some of the people split into rival groups who were attached to one church leader or another (see 1:11–12). Finally, some of the Corinthians also developed a sense of superiority because they claimed to have a special spiritual gift (see 13:1–2).

If the Christian community in Corinth was to survive and thrive, they needed to overcome these divisions. To help them realize this, Paul used the metaphor of a human body to express how their poor self-image served to further the divisions between them (see 1 Corinthians 12:14–20).

In this somewhat humorous metaphor, Paul portrays different body parts doubting their purpose in life. The feet and the ears appear to be suffering from a serious lack of self-esteem! Paul writes, "The eye cannot say to the hand, 'I do not need you,' nor again the head to the feet, 'I do not need you'" (1 Corinthians 12:21). Paul uses this absurd image to point out that while some gifts might not be given as much attention as others, everyone's gift is important and essential. No status or gift makes one body part more important than another. The same is true for people within a community.

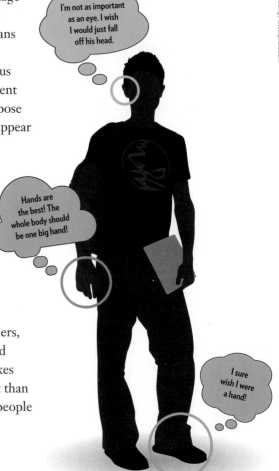

I'm not as important as an eye. I wish I would just fall off his head.

Hands are the best! The whole body should be one big hand!

I sure wish I were a hand!

© Vectorig / iStockphoto.com

Saint Paul used a humorous metaphor portraying the parts of the body doubting their purpose to point out that everyone's gift to the community, no matter how small, is important.

To remedy any arrogance the Corinthians might have, Paul takes it a step further and says that "the parts of the body that seem to be weaker are all the more necessary" (1 Corinthians 12:22). How are the weaker ones more necessary? Those who are weaker provide others an opportunity to practice compassion by loving those "unlovable" parts. By practicing compassion, we become closer to our true selves—the people God has called us to be—and closer to God. We also become closer to those we serve, discovering that we are not so different. Ironically, weakness has the power to unite people.

The Church: One Body

Paul's clever metaphor also points out that even though there are many parts to a body, there is still only one body. The parts are not separate from one another. If you get a serious wound on your leg, your hand does not say, "Whew! Thank God that wasn't me!" The body works together. Your hand reaches down to apply pressure and stop the blood flow; it does not know that it exists on its own. It is all you.

Similarly, the Church is one body. We are created to have the same concern for one another as we have for ourselves. Adam and Eve were created to be one body (see Genesis 2:24), but sin has created the illusion that we are separate from one another.

Though we might look like we are separate beings, Scripture repeatedly points to the intimate connections that tie us to one another. Paul reminds us that because we are one body, "If [one] part suffers, all the parts suffer with it; if one part is honored, all the parts share its joy" (1 Corinthians 12:26). We can get a sense of this unity by developing our ability to empathize with others. Empathy is the ability to recognize and share the emotions of another person. Consider your own experiences of empathizing with another: you might jump out of your seat and scream for joy when you see your best friend score the winning goal for the soccer team. Perhaps you feel your mom's pride and sense of accomplishment when she gets a promotion at work. You also might experience the sadness when a good friend's grandparent suddenly dies in a car accident.

UNIT 3

The Church is the ultimate community. We are intimately connected to one another and to Christ, who is truly present in a special way.

The Ultimate Community

Our connection to others takes on even more significance when we remember that Jesus said that whenever we gathered together in his name, he would be with us (see Matthew 18:20). Christ truly becomes present in a special way when we assemble as a Church community.

Saint Paul taught that people who are most vulnerable are even more necessary for the community. His teaching is rooted in the life of Christ who "identified himself with the least of his brethren"[3] (*CCC*, number 2448). Recall that Jesus stressed that his presence would be found in those who were in need (see Matthew 25:35–36).

The Church is not only an intimate connection to one another but also a union with Christ. It is the community where we come to know Jesus, hear his voice in the Word of God, and experience his real Presence in the Eucharist.

The Church is the ultimate community because it leads us toward union with God and one another in our heavenly home. Heaven is the state of eternal life and union with God, in which one experiences full happiness and the satisfaction of our deepest human longings. There we will fully experience the fulfillment of Jesus' promise and his desire for us to be one with God (see John 17:24). ✳

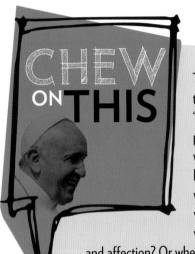

CHEW ON THIS

These words of Jesus answer the question that arises so often in our minds and hearts: "Where is God?" Where is God, if evil is present in our world, if there are men and women who are hungry and thirsty, homeless, exiles and refugees? Where is God, when innocent persons die as a result of violence, terrorism and war? Where is God, when cruel diseases break the bonds of life and affection? Or when children are exploited and demeaned, and they too suffer from grave illness? . . . These are questions that humanly speaking have no answer. We can only look to Jesus and ask him. And Jesus' answer is this: "God is in them." Jesus is in them; he suffers in them and deeply identifies with each of them. He is so closely united to them as to form with them, as it were, "one body." (Pope Francis, "Way of the Cross with the Young People," Poland, July 29, 2016)

HMMMMM. . .

Why does Paul call the Church the Body of Christ?

1. What are the sources of power, and how did Jesus use them?

2. What challenges did Paul face when he tried to convince people that Jesus was the Son of God?

3. Why did Paul chastise the Corinthians? Why did he suggest that they become "fools for Christ"?

4. Some of the early Christians believed that because we are saved by God's grace, it does not matter how we act. How did Paul respond to this false belief?

5. Why was the resurrection of the body difficult for Jewish Christians to believe? Why was it difficult for Gentile Christians?

6. In his First Letter to the Corinthians, what were the main points Paul made to support his case for the resurrection of the dead?

7. What metaphor does Paul use to explain the Church community to the Corinthians?

Yo Paul! Can u explain this dying for Jesus thing to me pls? 🤔

Sure! It's not about you. JC was always about doing the right thing – no matter what. 👍

But what about fighting evil? I don't want to die and let evil win.

Fight evil with goodness. Don't worry about the results. That's God's job.

I'll be honest - that sounds stupid! I don't like pain and I don't want to be a martyr.

Neither do I! Odds are, you won't be killed for doing good. But you will experience "little deaths" – sacrifices like shoveling snow for a neighbor in need instead of hanging out w/friends.

Doesn't sound like fun. 😨

Yeah, Jesus said something about that (Mark 8:34).

So why would I want to do that?

Doing good for others is...y'know – good! And the rewards are heavenly! Trust me! 😇

Okay – I get it. Thanks! Pray for me! 🙏

👍

AN IMAGINARY TEXT BETWEEN SAINT PAUL AND A TEEN TODAY

CHAPTER 8
Our Salvation

WHAT HAPPENS AFTER WE DIE?

SNAPSHOT

Article 32   Page 239
Saved *from* What?
• Pre-read: Ephesians 2:1–10

Article 33   Page 242
Saved *for* What?
• Pre-read: Romans 8:18–39

Article 34   Page 246
Judgment Day
• Pre-read: Matthew 25:31–46

Article 35   Page 250
Where Do We Go after Death?
• Pre-read: Revelation 21:1–4, 22:1–5

Article 32
Saved *from* What?

Imagine you are at the beach one summer day when you hear someone cry out: "Help! Save me!" You look up and see a young boy in the water a good distance away from the shore. He is waving his arms, trying to get the attention of anyone who might be able to help. Instinctively, you begin to consider the possibilities of why he needs to be saved. Maybe his float is deflating, and he cannot swim. Perhaps there's a strong undertow, and he is being pulled away from shore. Maybe a shark is lurking nearby, and the boy is starting to panic. Each of these situations requires adopting a different tactic that would aid in the boy's rescue. At this point, all you know is that he needs to be saved *from* something, but simply acknowledging this is only the first step to getting him back to shore safe and sound.

We often refer to Jesus Christ as our Savior. The title Savior implies that he saves us *from* something. And he does. But what exactly did we need to be saved from? Before going further, we need to take a step back and remember what happened to humanity long before Jesus walked the Earth and how his Paschal Mystery is intimately tied with our salvation.

UNIT 3

The Paschal Mystery—Jesus' Passion, death, Resurrection, and glorious Ascension—saves us from the consequences of both Original Sin and our own personal sins.

Saved from Sin and Its Consequences

Recall that sin entered the world when Adam and Eve disobeyed God's command and acted on their selfish desires (see Genesis, chapter 3). Their intimate union with God, with each other, and with all of creation was disrupted. Human nature was weakened, and as a result, we still suffer from the effects of their Original Sin. One of those effects is that we are more prone to making immoral choices, resulting in personal sin. Sin, both original and personal, damages our relationship with God, with one another, and with all of creation. Because we cannot repair that damage on our own, we need the help of a Savior.

The Paschal Mystery is God's gift that saves us from Original Sin as well as our own personal sins. It also saves us from the *consequences* of sin because it provides us the means to reconcile with God, both in this lifetime as well as after our death in our heavenly home.

Let's look at some of these consequences of sin:

- **Guilt and shame.** Sin causes us to feel guilt and shame. Consider how you might feel if your mother caught you stealing money from her purse. Hopefully you would feel guilty! Guilt can be a healthy response. But if that guilt leads to shame—doubting your own goodness—you might feel a desire to avoid your mom. She might be pretty mad at you too! Without any reconciliation between you and your mom, you might begin to feel depressed and unloved—and that's never a good feeling.

UNIT 3

TAKE IT TO GOD

Jesus, truly it is insanity to choose sin and experience its consequences:
  guilt, shame, loneliness, despair, and addiction.
Thank goodness you provide us with a path back!
Jesus, you are the fullness of joy.
Through your Paschal Mystery,
  you saved us from sin and death.
Lead me to the waters of forgiveness
  so that I may overflow with the joy of your salvation.
Help me to share this joy with everyone I meet.
Amen.

- **Loneliness, despair, and the feeling of being unloved.** It's natural to feel lonely at times, especially when we are separated from close friends and family members. But there is a deeper loneliness that we experience, caused by the shame that is the result of sin. Shame causes us to doubt our own goodness; we forget that we are made in the image of God. We fall into despair and start to believe that no one could love us. We end up isolated, separated from God and from the people who would love us. We can feel this kind of loneliness and despair even in a crowd of friendly people.

- **Addictions and unhealthy attachments.** When we feel guilty and ashamed, lonely and unloved, we look for ways to ease these negative and painful feelings. We might look for immediate gratification in unhealthy attachments to people, places, and things such as sex, drugs, alcohol, food, television, gaming, social media, and money. These attachments can easily lead to obsessive behaviors or active addictions. Our attempts to fill the emptiness caused by sin

One of the consequences of sin is a sense of deep, inner loneliness caused by shame, making us doubt our own goodness.

with all of these things are dead ends and don't deal with the real problem: our separation from God caused by Original Sin and our own personal sin.

- **Death.** When Adam and Eve disobeyed God and ate from the tree of the knowledge of good and evil, they lost their immortality (see Genesis 2:16–17). With their sin came death. Not just physical death but also the death of relationships, in both this lifetime and in the next. Original Sin and our personal sins break the bonds we have with others, and bring eternal separation from God.

Like the boy in the ocean who was in desperate need of saving, we need to be saved from sin and death. By the grace of God through the Paschal Mystery, our Savior has already arrived. ✳

UNIT 3

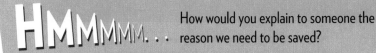

HMMMMM. . . How would you explain to someone the reason we need to be saved?

Article 33
Saved *for* What?

Imagine you are at the beach one summer day when you hear someone cry out, "Help! Save me!" You look up and see a young boy in the water a good distance away from the shore. You see that he appears to be caught in an undertow, is very tired, and cannot swim any longer. You take off on your jet ski and head out to the boy. You reach out your hand, pull him onto your jet ski, and check him for any serious injuries. As the boy catches his breath, you head back to shore to reunite him with his anxious but now grateful parents.

This might seem obvious, but it should be noted that to save someone, you have to both save them *from* something and save them *for* something. The boy becomes truly saved when he is safe and sound in the arms of his parents.

Jesus Christ saved us from sin, but he also saved us for something. Through his Passion, death, Resurrection, and Ascension, Jesus gave us the freedom of new life and reconciliation with God. The Paschal Mystery saves us for true happiness in this life and union with God in our heavenly home in the next life.

© Bruce Rolff / Shutterstock.com

Through his Paschal Mystery, Jesus saves us for new life,
true happiness, and full union with God in Heaven.

"For I do not do what I want, but I do what I hate" (Romans 7:15). Saint Paul is writing about the horrible guilt we feel after doing something we know is wrong. Then we ask, "Why did I do it?" Sometimes we make it worse by avoiding responsibility and blaming others. Alternatively, we can do something better: admit our sin and examine our weakness. Ask yourself: "Did I do it because I want others to like me? Because I did not want to look scared? Because I feel empty inside?" These questions can be painful because they make us face the dark places in ourselves. However, our weakness makes us reach out to God, and that is what makes us strong. Because he knew this, Paul could say, "for when I am weak, then I am strong" (2 Corinthians 12:10).

Saved for Eternal Life

By now, you are very familiar with what Jesus saved us *from* and why. So let's explore what it is that Jesus saved us *for*. In his Letter to the Romans, chapter 8, Saint Paul makes the case that the Paschal Mystery must have been *for* something. And it is! He writes, "I consider that the sufferings of this present time are as nothing compared with the glory to be revealed for us" (verse 18).

The things we are saved for are in many ways the opposite of what we are saved from. Christ "empties" us of sin, shame, loneliness, and unhealthy attachments so that he can "fill us" with his wonderful presence. Here are some examples:

- **Forgiveness and healing.** Our life with Christ is marked by the forgiveness of sins. In the Gospels, Jesus is constantly teaching about the importance of forgiveness. In fact, there are times when people come to him for physical healing, but he first focuses his attention on forgiving their sins. Christ's teaching and example is the reason why the forgiveness of sins is so central to the sacramental life of the Church. In Baptism, the mark of Original Sin is removed. The Sacrament of Penance and Reconciliation frees us from all personal sins. Hopefully you have known the joy and the freedom that come from being forgiven and from forgiving others.

- **Freedom.** Through Jesus' Paschal Mystery, we are freed from the oppression of sin, guilt, addictions, attachments, loneliness, and despair. Unburdened by sin, he saves us *for* the freedom to experience all the joy and love God wants us to have.

- **Joy.** With all of this talk about suffering for others, it is important not to overlook the joy that comes with following Christ. Saint Mother Teresa points out that "joy comes to those who in a sense forget themselves and become totally aware of the other." Through the Paschal Mystery, we are freed to experience all the joy God intends for us. Though we still feel the everyday sorrows and delights of life, beneath it all there is a profound joy that is never swayed. There is a deep sense of knowing that God can bring good out of any situation, no matter how troubling it might be.

- **Eternal life.** To be a Christian, we need to look beyond this earthly life to what comes next. Because of Jesus' Resurrection, we know that life does not end at death. Jesus saved us *for* eternal life in Heaven. There we will be in full communion with the Holy Trinity, and we will know God face-to-face.

Knowing that God can bring good out of any bad situation frees us to experience all the joy God intends for us.

Already but Not Yet

We know that Jesus Christ is the Son of God who established the Kingdom of God here on Earth, although it sometimes might not feel like it. It has been two thousand years since Jesus' Ascension, and sin still has a grip on humanity. War, poverty, racism, and other types of evil have not disappeared. We live in a sort of in-between state—the Kingdom of God is here already, but we are not yet in a state of perfect grace.

So, between our Baptism and our death, all of us are on a journey to become "perfect, just as [our] heavenly Father is perfect" (Matthew 5:48). Through Baptism, our sins were forgiven—both our personal sins and Original Sin. We died to sin and were raised to new life in Christ, yet we still suffer from the inclination to sin, concupiscence. Concupiscence keeps the door open for temptation. Each of the members of Christ's Church is in a state of "already but not yet" time.

The good news is that we are not alone in our work to do good and live our lives the way God intended. At our Baptism, we each received the **sanctifying grace** that heals our human nature wounded by sin. Likewise, it restores us to friendship with God by giving us a share in the divine life of the Trinity. With the guidance of the Holy Spirit, we are led to grow in goodness and are able to experience and share God's love with others. ✳

UNIT 3

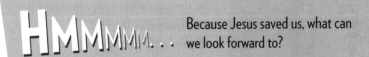

HMMMMM. . . Because Jesus saved us, what can we look forward to?

---

sanctifying grace ➤ The grace that heals our human nature wounded by sin and restores us to friendship with God by giving us a share in the divine life of the Trinity. It is a supernatural gift of God, infused into our souls by the Holy Spirit, that continues the work of making us holy.

Article 34

Judgment Day

As a student, you are used to being tested and judged. You have assessments and take tests in your classes. When you audition for the school play or try out for a team, you are judged by the director or coach to determine whether you qualify. What makes these judgments more bearable is knowing that the teacher, coach, or director really does like you and wants you to succeed.

We will all face a Final Judgment by Christ after we die. This might seem quite overwhelming and frightening. Let's remember, though, that Jesus loves us more than we can imagine—and he really wants us to succeed!

The Parable of the Prodigal Son gives us a glimpse of God's boundless love for us and how he will fully welcome us into Heaven when our mortal lives end.

Our Particular Judgment

In the Parable of the Lost Son (see Luke 15:11–32), Jesus gives us a glimpse of the infinite love God the Father has for us. He tells us that a father had two sons. The youngest son asked his father for his inheritance, which seems a bit presumptuous and bold. The father gives the money to his son, who takes it and squanders it (see 15:13). Soon, the son's life goes downhill, and he finds himself broke and hungry. After some serious reflection, he finally understands how poorly he treated his father and how he had wasted everything he was given.

I DIDN'T KNOW THAT!

Will all non-Christians go to Hell? The Church has always taught that the Sacrament of Baptism is necessary for salvation. But claiming that all non-Christians will spend eternity in Hell would contradict our belief in a loving and merciful God. The *Catechism of the Catholic Church* teaches: "'Since Christ died for all, and since all men are in fact called to one and the same destiny, which is divine, we must hold that the Holy Spirit offers to all the possibility of being made partakers, in a way known to God, of the Paschal mystery.' Every man who is ignorant of the Gospel of Christ and of his Church, but seeks the truth and does the will of God in accordance with his understanding of it, can be saved"[1] (number 1260).

UNIT 3

When the son returns home, the expectation is that the father would be angry at his son's foolishness and dishonorable life. The son was prepared to tell him that he was no longer worthy to be called his son (see Luke 15:19). But instead of banishing his son in anger, the father ran to greet his son, hugged and kissed him (see 15:20), and then he threw his son a party to welcome him home!

The father in this parable tells us something about the welcome that God will give us when our mortal lives end. Our **Particular Judgment** is the judgment that occurs immediately at the time of our death, when our immortal souls will be judged as worthy or unworthy of Heaven. Like the father in Jesus' parable, God wants to welcome us to our heavenly home and is infinitely glad to have us. But because we are inclined to the temptation of sin, we are sometimes like the lost son. It took the lost son quite some time before he was ready to admit his sin and return home. When our lives on Earth have ended and we face God, we too must come to grips with our own pride and sin.

It is important to know that God is not like the Santa Claus in the well-known song "Santa Claus Is Coming to Town." There is no list of your sins that God is checking twice to see if you've been naughty or nice. God does not

---

Particular Judgment ▶ The judgment that occurs immediately at the time of our death, when our immortal souls will be judged as worthy or unworthy of Heaven.

keep score. We do not believe in an angry God who, if disappointed, will close the gate to Heaven in our faces. At our Particular Judgment, whether we ultimately enter Heaven or Hell will depend on how we responded to God's grace and his invitation to put our faith in him. Pope Saint John Paul II said:

> God is the infinitely good and merciful Father. But man, called to respond to him freely, can unfortunately choose to reject his love and forgiveness once and for all, thus separating himself for ever from joyful communion with him. It is precisely this tragic situation that Christian doctrine explains when it speaks of eternal damnation or hell. It is not a punishment imposed externally by God but a development of premises already set by people in this life. ("General Audience," July 28, 1999)

This is not to say that we can do whatever we want in this lifetime and still reach Heaven. Accepting God's love and mercy is not so simple. It is like a momentum we set in motion in this lifetime that will extend into the afterlife. We create this momentum by daily admitting our need for God, by putting our faith in Jesus Christ, and by acknowledging our sins and asking for forgiveness.

In addition to these things, we should also consider Jesus' description of the Last Judgment in Matthew 25:31–46. In this parable about sheep and goats, Jesus tells us that the Kingdom of Heaven is prepared for those who feed the hungry, give drink to the thirsty, welcome the stranger, clothe the naked, care for the sick, and visit those in prison. This parable emphasizes that the good that you do in this lifetime—especially for those most in need—will prepare you to accept the infinite goodness of God in the afterlife.

This modern fresco of the Last Judgment, by Fredericao Spoltoze, reminds us that all of humanity will face such a judgment besides our own personal one.

© Renata Sedmakova / Shutterstock.com

The Last Judgment

In addition to our Particular Judgment, we will also face the Last Judgment. Also called the Final Judgment, the **Last Judgment** is the judgment of humanity by Jesus Christ at the **Parousia**. The Parousia is the second coming of Christ as judge of all the living and the dead, at the end of time, when the Kingdom of God will be fulfilled.

In terms of our eternal destination, the Final Judgment will not override or change our Particular Judgment. It is more like coming to a deeper understanding of what we did and did not do in our lives. The *Catechism of the Catholic Church* describes it like this: "In the presence of Christ, who is Truth itself, the truth of each man's relationship with God will be laid bare. The Last Judgment will reveal even to its furthest consequences the good each person has done or failed to do during his earthly life" (number 1039). Those destined for eternal union with God will be united with their glorified, resurrected bodies.

When will Christ return? Saint Paul urged his fellow Christians to be constantly vigilant and prepared for that day because we don't know when the second coming will occur (see 1 Thessalonians 5:2). Even Jesus said that he did not know! (see Mark 13:32–33).

The second coming is not something that we should fear, because we can count on the infinite love and mercy of God. But we must choose our eternal destination now. You cannot shoot an arrow and complain when it lands in the direction where you aimed. We must keep our eyes on the Lord, and at the end of our lives we can say, like Paul, "I have competed well; I have finished the race; I have kept the faith. From now on the crown of righteousness awaits me, which the Lord, the just judge, will award to me on that day, and not only to me, but to all who have longed for his appearance" (2 Timothy 4:7–8). ✳

HMMMMM. . . What role do we play in deciding how we spend eternity?

Last Judgment ➤ The judgment of the human race by Jesus Christ at his second coming. It is also called the Final Judgment.

Parousia ➤ The second coming of Christ as judge of all the living and the dead, at the end of time, when the Kingdom of God will be fulfilled.

Article 35
Where Do We Go after Death?

What do you think happens to us after we die?

Where do we go after we die? That's a big question. Many people would probably rather not think too much about their own death. Most young people can
get all the way through high school and attend only a handful of funerals. Yet
occasionally, because of an accident, a serious illness, or the death of someone
close to us, we have to face the possibility of our own death.

It may surprise you to know that the Old Testament rarely refers to an
afterlife. Nevertheless, we do find evidence that a concept of life after death
did emerge among the Jewish People. We know this because two of the
last Old Testament books to be written—a couple of centuries before the
birth of Jesus—contain references to life after death (see 2 Maccabees 7:23,
Daniel 12:1–3).

As Christians, however, we know what happens to us when we die, because the person who supplied us with the answers actually died and rose from
the dead. After death, our souls will be judged, and those who have remained
faithful to God will be united with him in Heaven. Those who separated themselves from God in this life will be separated from him for all eternity in Hell.
Let's look further at the concepts of Heaven and Hell.

What Is Heaven?

When asked for an image of Heaven, people often think of it as a place up in the sky. There are numerous artistic representations of God the Father as an old man in the clouds. Even some of the language in the Bible encourages this perception:

> "No one has gone up to heaven except the one who has come down from heaven, the Son of Man." (John 3:13)

Heaven is not a particular place. It is a state of eternal life and union with God, where our deepest human longings are met.

Despite how often it is described as being "up" or "in the clouds," let's be clear that Heaven is not a place in this universe. It is probably better to think of it as a state of being. Heaven is the state of eternal life and union with God, in which one experiences full happiness and the satisfaction of our deepest human longings. In Heaven, our relationship with God—injured by Original Sin—is restored, and we enter into full communion with the Holy Trinity.

Hell

If Heaven is complete and eternal union with God, **Hell** is the opposite. Hell is the state of permanent separation from God, reserved for those who die in a state of mortal sin, that is, those who freely and consciously choose to reject God to the very end of their lives. "God predestines no one to go to hell; for this, a willful turning away from God (a mortal sin) is necessary, and persistence in it until the end" (*CCC*, number 1037). The Church has formally canonized numerous saints as sharing eternal life with God but has never declared any deceased human being to be in Hell.

If the image of Heaven is up in the sky, its opposite, Hell, would naturally be below ground in the worldview of the ancient Israelites. Hell is often portrayed as a fiery pit ruled by demons who torture the dead. Some scholars think this image was inspired by the garbage pit outside of Jerusalem. The images of fire and demons with pitchforks are metaphors that attempt to express the pain of Hell. The real torture of Hell is not a physical pain but the spiritual anguish of being separated from God.

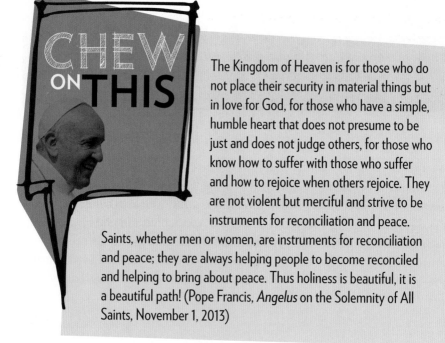

CHEW ON THIS

The Kingdom of Heaven is for those who do not place their security in material things but in love for God, for those who have a simple, humble heart that does not presume to be just and does not judge others, for those who know how to suffer with those who suffer and how to rejoice when others rejoice. They are not violent but merciful and strive to be instruments for reconciliation and peace. Saints, whether men or women, are instruments for reconciliation and peace; they are always helping people to become reconciled and helping to bring about peace. Thus holiness is beautiful, it is a beautiful path! (Pope Francis, *Angelus* on the Solemnity of All Saints, November 1, 2013)

Hell ➤ Refers to the state of definitive separation from God and the saints, and so is a state of eternal punishment.

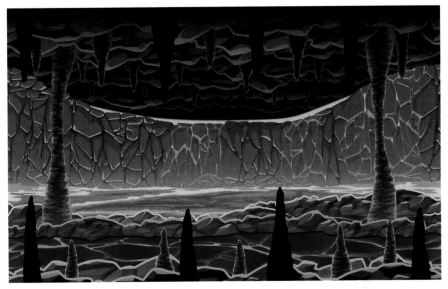

© November_Seventeen / Shutterstock.com

Some scholars believe that the image of Hell as a fiery place with demons was inspired by the garbage pit just outside of Jerusalem.

UNIT 3

Purgatory

When we die, most of us are probably not in a perfectly holy state ready to enter Heaven. Very few are perfect saints or perfect sinners. This is why those who die in God's grace and friendship, but who are not perfectly purified to enter Heaven, undergo a stage prior to their entry called **Purgatory**. Purgatory is a state of final purification or cleansing, which one may need to enter following death and before entering Heaven.

The belief that souls in Purgatory are assured of entering Heaven once their purification is complete is part of the truth God has revealed in Tradition and Sacred Scripture. In Scripture, we encounter references to the idea of purification after death in both the Old Testament and the New Testament. In Second Maccabees, we read of making atonement for the dead to free them from sin (see 12:39–46). In the New Testament, Saint Paul speaks of a person being saved through a purifying fire (see 1 Corinthians 3:15). ✳

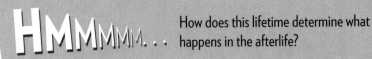

HMMMMM. . . How does this lifetime determine what happens in the afterlife?

Purgatory ➤ A state of final purification or cleansing, which one may need to enter following death and before entering Heaven.

1. Why do we call Jesus a Savior?

2. What does Jesus save us *from?*

3. What does Jesus save us *for?*

4. What does it mean to say that the Kingdom of God is "already but not yet"?

5. What is our Particular Judgment, and when will it happen?

6. When is the Last Judgment, and when will it happen?

7. What is Heaven?

8. What is Hell?

9. Can someone go to Hell after Purgatory? Explain.

THE LAST JUDGMENT

1. *The Last Judgment* by Michelangelo covers the entire wall behind the altar in the Sistine Chapel. What are you immediately drawn to when you look at this painting? How does it make you feel?

2. Cover the right side of the painting so you only see the left side. What is depicted on the left side?

3. Cover the left side of the painting so you only see the right side. What is depicted on the right side?

UNIT 3 HIGHLIGHTS

CHAPTER 7 Redeemed by God

Sources and Uses of Power

Power from Authority
Direct and command others because of your office or position.

Power from Influence
Influence other people's attitudes/decisions because of the relationship you have built with them.

Power from Action
Take the initiative to make things happen or to inspire people with your actions.

Used for Good	Used for Bad	Used for Good	Used for Bad	Used for Good	Used for Bad
A manager assigns her employees duties that are essential for a business to run smoothly.	A manager trains her employees to do something illegal.	A person teaches someone how to perform CPR.	A person teaches someone how to steal a car.	A group devises and executes a plan to help aid the victims of a tragic event.	A group devises and executes a plan to rob a bank.

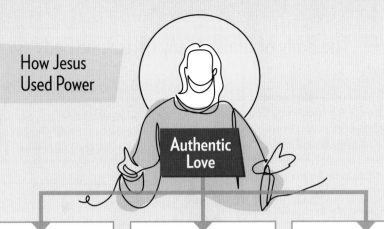

How Jesus Used Power

Authentic Love

Power from Authority

- had authority that came with being the Son of God
- healed people, expelled demons, controlled nature
- used it sparingly and only to benefit others

Power from Influence

- invited people to accept his teachings and to follow him

Power from Action

- practiced what he preached
- confronted injustices and wrongdoing

UNIT 3

The Paradox of the Cross

- "Jesus' death brings new life"
- True love shows itself in loving self-sacrifice

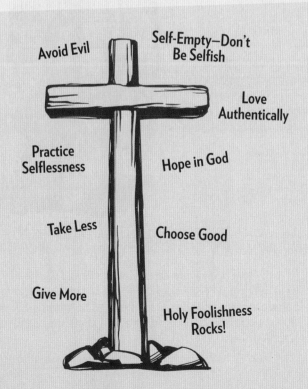

Avoid Evil

Self-Empty—Don't Be Selfish

Love Authentically

Practice Selflessness

Hope in God

Take Less

Choose Good

Give More

Holy Foolishness Rocks!

The Body of Christ: Many Parts, One Body

The Church includes human beings who are broken by sin. Sin brings separation from God and from one another. Jesus' Passion, death, and Resurrection redeem us from sin.

"May all be one, as you, Father, are in me and I in you, that they also may be in us" (John 17:21).

The Church is one Body. We are created to have the same concern for one another as we have for ourselves.

We are called to participate in the Paschal Mystery to bring about the Kingdom of Heaven here on Earth.

"If the whole body were an eye, where would the hearing be? If the whole body were hearing, where would the sense of smell be? But as it is, God placed the parts, each one of them, in the body as he intended. If they were all one part, where would the body be? But as it is, there are many parts, yet one body." (1 Corinthians 12:17–20)

CHAPTER 8 Our Salvation

Death

"The last enemy to be destroyed is death, for 'he subjected everything under his feet.'" (1 Corinthians 15:26–27)

Guilt and Shame

"No one who believes in him will be put to shame." (Romans 10:11)

SAVED FROM

Addictions and Attachments

"Now those who belong to Christ [Jesus] have crucified their flesh with its passions and desires." (Galatians 5:24)

Loneliness and Despair

"We are afflicted in every way, but not constrained; perplexed, but not driven to despair; persecuted, but not abandoned; struck down, but not destroyed." (2 Corinthians 4:8–9)

UNIT 3

Freedom

"For freedom Christ set us free; so stand firm and do not submit again to the yoke of slavery." (Galatians 5:1)

Joy

"I have told you this so that my joy may be in you and your joy may be complete." (John 15:11)

SAVED FOR

Eternal Life

"The gift of God is eternal life in Christ Jesus our Lord." (Romans 6:23)

Forgiveness and Healing

"He delivered us from the power of darkness and transferred us to the kingdom of his beloved Son, in whom we have redemption, the forgiveness of sins." (Colossians 1:13–14)

What Happens after We Die?

We Face Two Types of Judgment after We Die

Particular Judgment

What: Our immortal souls will be judged as worthy or unworthy of Heaven.

Why: God wants to welcome us to our heavenly home and is infinitely glad to have us. But because we are inclined to the temptation of sin, we must come to grips with our own pride and sin.

When: Immediately at the time of our death.

Last Judgment

What: The judgment of the living and the dead by Jesus Christ. Also called the Final Judgment.

Why: Those destined for eternal union with God will be united with their glorified, resurrected bodies.

When: At the second coming of Christ (the Parousia) at the end of time, when the Kingdom of God will be fulfilled.

The Final Judgment will not override or change our Particular Judgment. It is more like coming to a deeper understanding of what we did and did not do in our lives.

Where Do We Go after Death? Three Options:

Heaven

- The state of eternal life and union with God, in which one experiences full happiness and the satisfaction of the deepest human longings.
- In Heaven, the relationship broken by humanity through Original Sin is restored, and we join in full communion with the Holy Trinity.

Purgatory

- A state of final purification or cleansing, which one may need to enter following death and before entering Heaven.
- Most of us are probably not in a perfectly holy state ready to enter Heaven when we die. Purgatory is that step toward Heaven.

Hell

- The state of permanent separation from God, reserved for those who die in a state of mortal sin, that is, who freely and consciously choose to reject God to the very end of their lives.

UNIT 3

UNIT 3
BRING IT HOME

WHY SHOULD WE BELIEVE IN LIFE AFTER DEATH?

FOCUS QUESTIONS

CHAPTER 7   How does Jesus' death and Resurrection affect our lives?

CHAPTER 8   What happens after we die?

OLIVIA
New Smyrna Beach High School

After reading this unit, I realize that maybe Heaven and Hell are not necessarily what I was taught when I was in elementary and middle school. Instead of Hell being a burning pit of fire and Heaven being a place of clouds and angels, I read that Heaven and Hell really depend on your relationship with God. This idea is much more interesting to me than what I learned before. So, instead of taking the bad things that happen in life personally, and feeling like God is punishing me, the material I read actually made me curious to learn about Catholicism and other religions and all of their ideas about the afterlife. I think trying to understand the afterlife as a spiritual state of being is something I want to know more about.

REFLECT

Take some time to read and reflect on the unit and chapter focus questions listed on the facing page.

- What question or section did you identify most closely with?

- What did you find within the unit that was comforting or challenging?

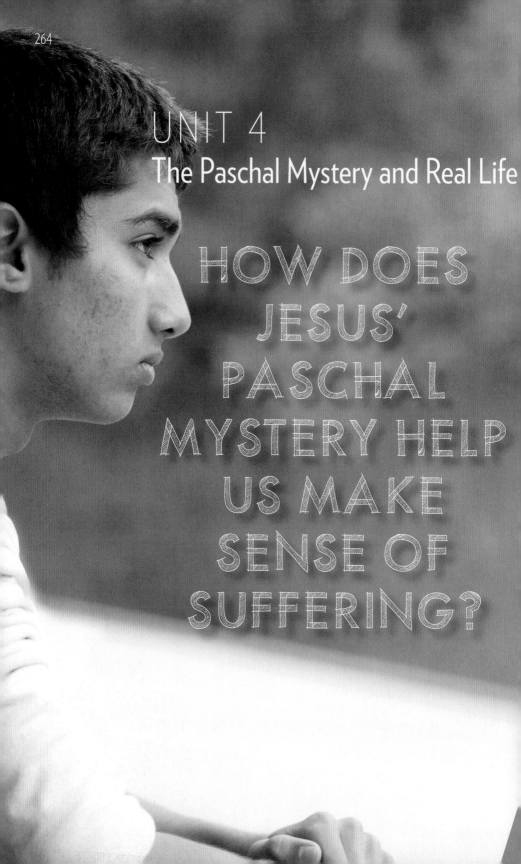

UNIT 4
The Paschal Mystery and Real Life

HOW DOES JESUS' PASCHAL MYSTERY HELP US MAKE SENSE OF SUFFERING?

LOOKING AHEAD

CHAPTER 9   Page 266
Personal Suffering and the Paschal Mystery

CHAPTER 10   Page 288
Communal Suffering

UNIT 4

Personal sin, communal sin, all sin brings pain and suffering to ourselves and others. Everyone experiences suffering in some way. But then we have to think about Jesus' sacrifice. He was willing to suffer and die because he loves us. This is the kind of pure love that means he loves us for who we are. He suffered during his time on Earth, so he has experienced what we experience. So, we suffer because of sin, but Jesus' love offers us hope that there is happiness beyond the suffering.

DUC
Totino-Grace High School

Personal Suffering and the Paschal Mystery

WHAT GOOD CAN COME FROM SUFFERING?

SNAPSHOT

Article 36   Page 267
Making Sense of Suffering
- Pre-read: Job 1:1–2:13

Article 37   Page 273
Is Accepting Suffering a Sign of Weakness?
- Pre-read: 1 Peter 4:12–19

Article 38   Page 277
Finding Strength in Times of Weakness
- Pre-read: 2 Corinthians 12:1–10

Article 39   Page 281
How Do I Cope with Suffering?
- Pre-read: Colossians 1:24–29

Article 36
Making Sense of Suffering

Betty was a young mother when she had her third son, Joseph. He arrived two months early, and while Betty was giving birth, the umbilical cord got wrapped around Joseph's neck, depriving him of oxygen long enough to cause brain damage. He had cerebral palsy, and in his first few years of life, doctors discovered that the parts of his brain that controlled both his legs and his right arm were severely impaired. The damage also compromised his ability to read, write, and grasp difficult concepts. Joseph would be confined to a wheelchair for his entire life.

Betty struggled with this painful situation. Her two older sons were able to run, swim, play baseball, climb trees, and do all the things that kids normally do. It made no sense to her that God would allow this to happen to Joseph. Some friends explained that it was all part of God's plan, but Betty could not believe that God would "plan" for her son to have brain damage. She believed that God is loving and wants only good for people. She wholeheartedly did not believe that God did this on purpose, but she still had no reasonable explanation for why this occurred.

Painful experiences like this can bring people face-to-face with the most profound questions about life, such as "Why does God allow bad things to happen?" and "Why do we suffer?" To help us understand suffering, we can look to the Paschal Mystery. The Paschal Mystery reveals that suffering can play a role in our salvation. Jesus Christ's Passion and death led to his Resurrection and Ascension, so we know that God can bring good out of suffering. Still, the Paschal Mystery is exactly what it says it is: a mystery, a truth we can never fully understand. Though we may never completely grasp why bad things happen to innocent human beings, this mystery does invite us into a deeper relationship with God.

UNIT 4

Why Do We Suffer?

In much of the Old Testament, there is a simple explanation for suffering: when someone does something wrong or bad, God punishes that person. You may recall this concept of **divine retributive justice** discussed in an earlier course. This explanation for human suffering might appeal to our sense of fairness and justice, but it is not correct. For example, when people do not study for tests, they tend to fail. When people are mean, they are often avoided by others and feel lonely. What happens to people in such circumstances is a natural consequence of their behavior. It is not a punishment from God.

© Hilary Morgan / Bridgeman Images

Is suffering a punishment for our sins? The Jewish People addressed this question in the Book of Job. Job experiences great suffering despite his being a good and upright man, so sin can't be a punishment.

Another reason we can know that suffering isn't God's punishment for our sins is because good people experience suffering too. The Jewish People realized this and addressed this problem in the Book of Job. Job is described as a good and righteous man (see 1:1), yet he was hit with one disaster after another. His friends were convinced that this was a punishment from God, that Job must have done something wrong. Job, however, maintained his innocence.

Eventually, Job demanded that God explain why this was happening to him. After much debate with his friends, he finally received a response from the Lord, who bombarded Job with questions that no human being could answer. God admonished Job until he finally comprehended that there are things only God can understand.

---

divine retributive justice ➤ The belief that God punishes people for their sins during this lifetime.

In the end Job accepted that like so many other things in this world, suffering is a mystery we cannot comprehend because we do not see the world from God's perspective. God is unbound by space and time and knows all things past, present, and future. Grasping why good people suffer is not within our capability, so it remains a mystery to us. Job, however, did eliminate one aspect of the mystery—suffering is not God's punishment for our sin.

Jesus further reinforces this insight with his teaching. For example, in the Gospel of John, a blind man is brought to Jesus. The disciples ask Jesus if the man is blind because of his sins or the sins of his parents. Jesus says neither the man nor his parents. In the Gospel of Luke, Jesus is asked about some Jewish people who were killed by the Romans and about another group of people who were killed by a falling tower (see 13:1–4). In both cases, Jesus affirms that these people were no greater sinners than anyone else, clearly implying that these tragedies were not punishments from God.

Ultimately, the best evidence we have that suffering is not a punishment for sin is that Jesus suffered. Jesus, who was without sin, was falsely accused of a crime, tortured, and put to death by crucifixion. With all this biblical evidence, we can be confident that the pain and misery we experience in life is not a punishment from God.

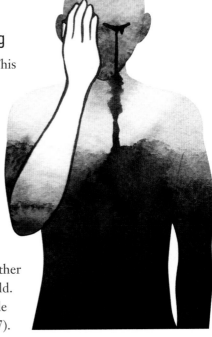

A Better Understanding of Suffering

We want life to be fair, to make sense. This is why we sometimes struggle with the reality of suffering. One important step to better understand suffering is to realize that it is not caused by God. The Creation accounts teach us that suffering was never part of God's plan. What we do know is that since the Fall and the introduction of Original Sin, suffering has been part of the human condition. To save us from meaningless suffering and death, the Father sent his only begotten Son into the world. By assuming a human nature, Jesus made our suffering his own (see Matthew 8:17).

UNIT 4

Suffering has been part of the human condition since the Fall and the arrival of Original Sin, as told in Genesis, chapter 3.

We can't avoid physical and emotional suffering; it is part of human life. But we can control how we deal with it. If we choose to find the good in our suffering, it can be a path toward growth and maturity. For example, our suffering can help us become less self-centered and more sympathetic to others' pain. True, it's difficult to think about the good that can come from our suffering while we're in the midst of it. It may take a little time—or a lot of time—and that's okay. If we're open to this possibility, God can and will transform our suffering and sacrifice into healing and new life.

The ultimate example of good coming from suffering is in Jesus' Paschal Mystery. His suffering and self-sacrifice lead us on a path toward **redemption** and salvation. Through Christ's painful but perfect sacrifice, death was destroyed and the doors to Heaven were opened, restoring the possibility of our full communion with God for all eternity. Following Christ's example, we are called to make our own sacrifices for others and to participate in Christ's saving mission through our suffering. Uniting our personal sufferings and sacrifices with Christ's is part of being a disciple. Saint Paul teaches us that the sufferings we endure can mean that "in my flesh I am filling up what is lacking in the afflictions of Christ on behalf of his body, which is the Church" (Colossians 1:24). In essence, our sufferings, when offered up to God, continue the work of Christ's sacrifice. Our participation in Christ's suffering objectively helps accomplish the mission of the Church, which is the redemption of human beings! We do this not only because of our hope and faith in our eternal reward in Heaven but also to make **reparation** for the hurt and harm caused by our own personal sins.

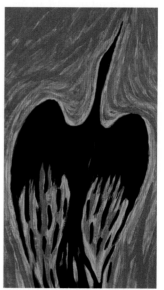

© robodread / Shutterstock.com

The phoenix is a fabled bird that would burn itself to ashes every 540 years and rise again to begin a new life. Early Christians used the phoenix as a symbol of resurrection and eternal salvation. You can find images of the phoenix among other symbolic art on the walls of Christian catacombs.

---

redemption ➤ From the Latin *redemptio*, meaning "a buying back," referring, in the Old Testament, to Yahweh's deliverance of Israel and, in the New Testament, to Christ's deliverance of all Christians from the forces of sin. As the agent of redemption, Jesus is called the Redeemer.

reparation ➤ The act of making amends for something one did wrong that caused physical, emotional, or material harm to another person.

CATHOLICS **MAKING** A DIFFERENCE

© Bibliotheque Nationale, Paris, France / Bridgeman Images

Thérèse became very sensitive and spoiled after her mother died when she was only four. At the age of fifteen, she entered a Carmelite convent, where her delicate temperament was tested. She learned to accept criticism in silence and practice small acts of kindness. She learned to follow Christ by "making some small sacrifice, here by a smiling look, there by a kindly word; always doing the smallest right and doing it all for love." Saint Thérèse of Lisieux was canonized in 1925, but not because she was martyred or performed some great heroic deed. Rather, she provided a simple example of holiness through her "little way" of following Christ.

UNIT 4

Practical Examples of Everyday Sacrifice

At this point, you might be saying, "I don't get when and where I would possibly accept suffering as part of my life as a disciple!" Sacrifice does not have to be a grand, life-threatening endeavor. Consider the following practical, everyday examples of small sacrifices you can make:

- spending time with a sick classmate or family member instead of going out to have fun with friends
- sacrificing your popularity by not giving into pressure to participate in immoral activities
- donating your time and money to those in need instead of spending it on yourself
- taking care of the environment by giving up a Saturday to clean up the beach or a local park
- making your faith known to others, despite the rude comments you might receive
- sacrificing any short-term pleasures by remaining a virgin until you are married

Giving your time and energy to volunteer in an environmental cleanup instead of hanging out with friends is an example of sacrifice.

UNIT 4

Christians all over the world make sacrifices like these daily and accept the suffering that comes with them. Not only have they discovered that the Holy Spirit provides the strength they need, but they've also discovered that they have received much more than they have ever lost. ✳

OVERVIEW of the Book of Job

- **Author:** Unknown, written during the sixth or fifth centuries BC.
- **Theme:** Why do good people suffer? God's power, presence, and wisdom are beyond human understanding.
- **Of note:** Job is a story within a story. Chapters 1–2 and 42:7–17 constitute a folktale. Set within that tale, 3:1–42:6 is a poetic debate about the cause of suffering.

HMMMMM. . .

In what way is God calling you to embrace the suffering that comes with sacrifice?

Article 37

Is Accepting Suffering a Sign of Weakness?

Some people avoid suffering at all costs, avoiding any situations that might bring pain or discomfort in their lives. Others accumulate power over others, trying to make themselves invulnerable to painful situations. These people often see suffering as a sign of weakness. Are they right? Simply put: no. Accepting suffering is not a sign of weakness. The Paschal Mystery of Jesus clearly shows that the willingness to accept suffering takes a great deal of courage and strength.

Jesus Suffered

Recall that Jesus was not only fully divine, he was also fully human. "He has truly been made one of us, like us in all things except sin" (*Pastoral Constitution on the Church in the Modern World* [*Gaudium et Spes*, 1965], number 22). When

he cut his hand, it hurt. When those close to him died, he grieved their loss. When his friends betrayed him, he felt abandoned. He was not immune to any of the pain and suffering we feel. When faced with the future of a painful death, he did not want to do it. Yet he was ready to do whatever his Father asked him (see Luke 22:42).

Jesus' suffering was not limited to his Passion and death. He endured pain and insult throughout his ministry. Sometimes Jesus did not have a place to sleep (see Matthew 8:20). In Nazareth, where he grew up, people ran him out of town after he preached in the synagogue (see Luke 4:29). The religious authorities regularly confronted and harassed him (see Luke 11:53–54). Sometimes Jesus' disciples rejected his teachings and quit following him (see John 6:66). Being the Son of God did not make his life easy!

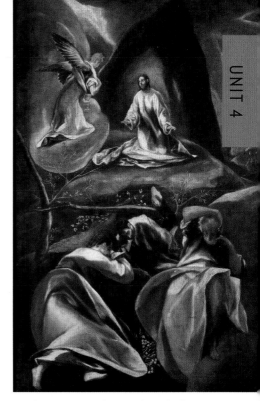

© Musee des Beaux-Arts, Lille, France / Bridgeman Images

UNIT 4

Jesus was scared yet ready and willing to suffer a painful death to bring about God's plan of salvation.

TAKE IT TO GOD

Jesus,

Do I really have to?

Do I really have to give up my Saturday to volunteer at the homeless shelter?

Do I really have to donate my "me" money to the collection for world hunger?

Do I really have to take care of the environment by recycling?

Do I really have to go to a family member's birthday party instead of hanging out with friends?

If I really have to make some sacrifices in life to be your disciple, send your Holy Spirit to provide the strength and courage I need to make it happen.

Amen.

Similarly, knowing that sacrifice and suffering have an important role in God's plan of salvation doesn't automatically make it easy for us to accept and endure suffering in our own lives. History is full of people who do the right thing, but they are still persecuted or even face death for their good works. Because sin exists in the world, doing good can be an uphill battle. Still, faithful Christians have always accepted this as the necessary consequence of building up the Kingdom of God.

Jesus himself made it clear that following him was not always going to be easy (see Mark 8:34). The good news is that we don't have to do it alone. Such sacrifice is possible only through our loving and compassionate God who desires to help us on this journey.

Public domain

Following Jesus' Example

The life of Saint Damien of Molokai (1840–1889) is an extraordinary example demonstrating that suffering for the sake of Christ is not a sign of weakness. Born in Belgium, Damien de Veuster became a missionary priest in the Hawaiian Islands. During that time, leprosy was spreading through the islands. Leprosy, or Hansen's disease, is an infectious disease resulting in numbness, paralysis, physical deformities, and ultimately death. The people's fear of contracting the deadly disease led to their forming an isolated colony on the island of Molokai. Those who were infected with the disease were often rounded up and dropped off on the island. Sometimes they were forced off the boat and made to swim to shore.

Saint Damien of Molokai (1840–1889) was a missionary priest who cared for the lepers of Hawaii. His willingness to minister to those with leprosy despite the likelihood of his contracting the disease showed his commitment to live as Jesus did.

UNIT 4

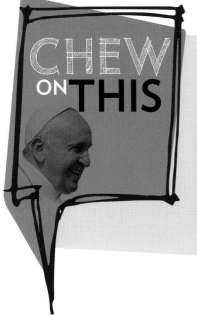

CHEW ON THIS

If God could weep, then I too can weep, in the knowledge that he understands me. The tears of Jesus serve as an antidote to my indifference before the suffering of my brothers and sisters. His tears teach me to make my own the pain of others, to share in the discouragement and sufferings of those experiencing painful situations. (Pope Francis, "Prayer Vigil to 'Dry the Tears,'" May 5, 2016)

Despite knowing that he would be exposed to a contagious deadly disease, Father Damien volunteered to minister to this neglected community at Kalaupapa on Molokai. When he arrived, he found their living conditions in terrible shape. Father Damien built homes and churches, celebrated Mass and heard confessions, counseled those who were suffering from the disease, and buried the dead.

After twelve years at Kalaupapa, Father Damien contracted leprosy. At first, he wondered why God allowed this to happen, but soon his concern turned toward the people he served. He was worried about who would carry on his mission after he died. He reached out, and help arrived when four new missionaries came. Despite his illness, he continued his hard work, constructing new buildings and organizing the community for the last few years of his life. Father Damien died in 1889.

Public domain

Father Damien is a beloved hero to the people of Hawaii. His suffering was a sign of his love for them and his commitment to live as Christ did. He was canonized as a saint by Pope Benedict XVI on October 11, 2009. Saint Damien is the patron saint of lepers and people with HIV and AIDS. ✳

UNIT 4

After twelve years of serving the leper community in Molokai, Father Damien contracted leprosy. This photo was taken shortly before his death. Despite his suffering, he remained committed to live as Christ did by loving and serving the leper community.

HMMMMMMM. . .
If someone told you that suffering is a sign of weakness, how would you respond?

Article 38
Finding Strength in Times of Weakness

Frankie fell in love with weightlifting when he was a teenager, and becoming an Olympic athlete was his dream. He worked hard, and because he was very successful in his high school competitions, he received athletic scholarship offers from numerous universities. In college, Frankie went to his first major competition and did not even make the finals. He was devastated and walked away from the event visibly shaken.

One of his coaches could see how the loss deeply troubled Frankie, so he called him into his office. When he sat down, his coach honestly told him, "Frankie, you didn't make the finals because you haven't yet fully addressed your weaknesses." Frankie was speechless. No one had ever told him this. He just stared blankly at his coach. The coach continued: "You've got the upper body strength of a gorilla, but that's not enough. Your legs still need work." Then he moved from his desk and sat down next to Frankie. "Son, you've got what it takes to be great in this sport, but to be successful, you have to work on your weaknesses. If you ask any great athlete, I would bet that their list of weaknesses would be much longer than their list of strengths. Frankie, make friends with your weaknesses, because they are just signposts leading to your growth, that's all." Frankie would recall the words of his old coach from that moment on and use them as guidance and comfort throughout his life whenever he faced any adversity.

Like Frankie, we all have personal strengths as well as limitations and weaknesses. Sometimes our weaknesses cause us to suffer in some way. The good news is that knowing our personal strengths and weaknesses raises our self-awareness and can help us make good life decisions.

UNIT 4

© Africa Studio / Shutterstock.com

When faced with a daunting task, how often have you said, "I can't!"? The next time you feel that way, turn to God for help. When we learn to embrace our weaknesses, we can begin to see them as strengths and opportunities for growth.

Your Weakness Is Your Strength

Saint Paul struggled with weaknesses too, but rather than avoid or deny them, he chose to embrace them with a very unique attitude. While offering some advice to the church in Corinth, Saint Paul presented a paradoxical description of himself as being strong in his weakness (see 2 Corinthians 12:10). That makes no sense at all . . . or does it?

What is Paul talking about? It's important to understand that Saint Paul was dealing with people who criticized him for his inadequacy as an Apostle (see 2 Corinthians 10:10). They bragged about their own abilities as being far superior to his. Yet, Paul chose to boast about his weaknesses. Why?

The point that Paul is trying to make is that it is our weaknesses that help us turn to God for help. Because of this, our weaknesses can paradoxically be counted as our strengths and opportunities for growth. This is why Paul was proud of his weaknesses.

Finding Strength through God and Others

God did not intend for us to be alone (see Genesis 2:18). We were made to be in communion with him and with others. This becomes all the more apparent when we face our weaknesses and sufferings. There is a vast difference between the experience of facing these things alone and facing them with someone.

MAKE IT SO

Helping someone else when you yourself are in need of help has an amazing effect on your outlook and perspective (this, of course, depends on whether your situation allows it). When we suffer, we often feel vulnerable and powerless, and it is easy to become narrowly focused on our own loss. By actively supporting others in need, we naturally lose the feeling of being powerless. When you serve someone, you become intimately aware that you are not alone in your pain.

The following are some ideas for reaching out to God and to others, which can help us to find strength in times of weakness:

One way we can find strength in times of weakness is by reaching out to family and friends to talk about our struggles.

- Reach out to family and friends to talk about your struggles.
- Read the accounts of Jesus' Passion. Here we are reminded that we are not alone, that God is not aloof, and that he has suffered as a human being too.
- Pray the Psalms. The Psalms can be a source of reassurance and confidence that, even in the most trying circumstances, God is there with us. Psalm 23, for example, is well known for its message of God's presence in times of trouble.
- Set aside some time for daily prayer, even if it's only a couple of minutes. (See chapter 12 for more about prayer.)
- Participate in the Sacrament of Penance and Reconciliation.
- Attend the youth ministry events at your parish.
- Get some spiritual advice from a trusted adult or priest. The Church is not just a community that worships together; it also provides practical care and help for people going through difficult times.
- Journal or do other creative writing activities to address your weaknesses.
- Join a Bible study group.
- Spend some quiet time in nature.
- Read a biography of a saint or another figure who inspires you.

Remember, God is **omnipotent** and can appear to us in the form of a stranger (see Genesis 18:1–3) or in the silence of nature (see 1 Kings 19:11–13). Cultivating a desire for God and a readiness to find him anywhere at any time is what's most important, regardless of how you choose to do it.

UNIT 4

---

omnipotent ➤ From the Latin *omnia*, meaning "all," and *potens*, meaning "powerful"; refers to the divine attribute that God is almighty and so has unlimited authority and power.

Taking our weaknesses to God and others can help us envision our situation differently. Rather than seeing it as a burden we must endure, we might be able to start looking at it as a time to grow, a time to strengthen ourselves and our relationships with God and with loved ones. There is something to learn in every situation no matter how painful. Each moment we live is important, each of us matters, and we don't have to face our challenges alone (see Matthew 10:30).

© oneinchpunch / Shutterstock.com

Spending quiet time in nature is another way we can find strength within during times of weakness.

Remember the End of the Story

Another key to finding hope and strength in difficult times is remembering that suffering is not the end of the story. The Paschal Mystery begins with Christ's Passion and death but ends with his Resurrection and Ascension. Almost all of the suffering we experience in this lifetime will be temporary. We can be confident that better days are ahead. Ultimately, our story does not end in this lifetime. We can find hope in looking forward to the joy and peace we will share with God in our heavenly home. ✳

HMMMMMM. . . How can our suffering and weaknesses bring us closer to God?

Article 39

How Do I Cope with Suffering?

The pain and suffering that people experience can be overwhelming at times, and it is natural to want to relieve someone's pain. In coping with our own and others' suffering, we can do practical things to prevent future pain and anguish when it is possible to do so. For example, if a friend is struggling with a school subject in which you excel, you could offer to help him or her. But sometimes there is little we can do to alleviate a person's suffering.

When someone we know experiences a great loss, like a death, or is dealing with immense physical or mental suffering, there is often a desire to help them make sense of what has happened or is happening. However, we should avoid trying to come up with easy explanations. Well-intentioned Christians sometimes state, "It's part of God's plan." On the one hand, it is true that we are called to trust in the **providence** of God, his loving care in our lives, bringing what is needed in every situation and even bringing good out of evil. On the other hand, it can be understandably difficult for someone to hear that God had planned for their pain. God never intends our unhappiness.

UNIT 4

© Antonio Guillem / Shutterstock.com

One of the most important things we can do to help someone who is suffering is to just be there, say nothing, and listen.

providence ➤ God's divine care and protection.

Just Be There

One of the most important things you can do for anyone who is suffering is to just be there and listen. Let them talk about their pain without trying to fix their problems. If they do not want to talk, offer to do something with them. Sometimes just normal, everyday activities can be comforting. Something as simple as playing basketball with a friend in the driveway can help them see that despite the pain, not everything has been lost. And if they want to be alone, do not take it personally. Be patient.

Another important thing to remember is to avoid saying something that may make the person feel worse, no matter how well intended it might be. If you feel the need to say something, here are some examples of what *not* to say and what *to* say (from "The 10 Best and 10 Worst Things to Say to Someone in Grief" at *https://grief.com*):

What Not to Say	What to Say or Do
1. I know how you feel.	1. I wish I had the right words—just know that I care.
2. She was such a good person that God wanted her to be with him.	2. I don't know how you feel, but I am here to help in any way I can.
3. He's in a better place.	3. My favorite memory of your loved one is . . .
4. There's a reason for everything.	4. I'm so sorry (for your loss).
5. Be strong.	5. I'm always just a text away.
6. She brought this on herself.	6. We all need help at times like this; I am here for you.
7. Aren't you over him yet?	7. Give a hug (instead of saying something).

A Different Way to Question

Suffering is often accompanied by an investigation into the meaning of life. It is natural to question why bad things happen. Some questions have no answer, though—at least not one that we can grasp in this lifetime. If someone is not comfortable with the mystery of suffering, these questions can sometimes lead to a deep sense of frustration or even despair.

So, what if we were to take another perspective? What if we made slight adjustments to these questions, so they lead us toward a life of hope and meaning? Consider the question: "Why did this happen to me?" There is nothing wrong with this question and it is natural to struggle with it. The problem is that the answer may be unknowable. A similar question that can be helpful is "Where is God leading me?" This question is rooted in the trust that God can bring good out of any situation.

Instead of "What does it mean?" it might be better to ask, "How can I make this meaningful?" Many service organizations, like Alcoholics Anonymous (AA), and Mothers Against Drunk Driving (MADD), were started from tragic situations. Their founders took a tragedy and made something good come from it. Since its founding in 1980, MADD, for example, has reduced drunk-driving deaths by 50 percent, saved more than 370,000 lives, and helped over 840,000 victims.

The grappling with questions such as "Why did God allow this to happen?" must be given special care. There are no easy answers to questions that seek to understand the spiritual significance of suffering. However, the struggle to understand can lead us to a closer relationship with God and with one another. We can find hope in firmly believing "that God is master of the world and of its history. But the ways of his providence are often unknown to us. Only at the end, when our partial knowledge ceases, when we see God 'face to face,'[1] will we fully know the ways by which—even through the dramas of evil and sin—God has guided his creation to that definitive sabbath rest[2] for which he created heaven and earth" (*Catechism of the Catholic Church* [*CCC*], number 314).

UNIT 4

Can something good come from suffering? The organization MADD (Mothers Against Drunk Driving), founded by women who lost children to a drunk drivers, has reduced drunk-driving deaths by 50 percent since its founding in 1980.

Life as It Is

For reasons only God knows, we sometimes find ourselves in painful circumstances over which we have no control. But we do have a choice in how we respond to these circumstances: we can accept them and move forward, or we can agonize over them and try to force them to be different. Complaining about the life that we have can keep us from seeing the beauty in life as it is. In these difficult situations, we can find peace by placing ourselves in God's presence and trusting that he will guide us. This notion is summed up nicely in the well-known Serenity Prayer: "God, grant me the serenity to accept the things I cannot change, courage to change the things I can, and wisdom to know the difference."

If you have ever complained about having to do some tedious chore around the house, you may have heard your parents say something like, "Offer it up to God." Before delving into that expression, it will help to look at a similar phrase first: "Suck it up." This is not necessarily bad to say. It simply means to do the job and quit complaining. There are certainly times when that attitude is appropriate, but it does suggest that you ignore your burdens.

"Offer it up to God" is a suggestion for you to look at your struggles differently, to use your pain, discomfort, or worries as a prayer. Much of our suffering is, in some way, rooted in sin—our own or that of others. Ironically,

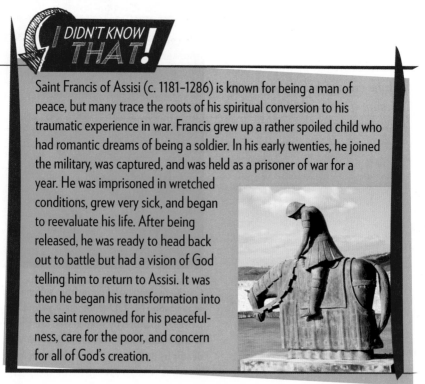

I DIDN'T KNOW THAT!

Saint Francis of Assisi (c. 1181–1286) is known for being a man of peace, but many trace the roots of his spiritual conversion to his traumatic experience in war. Francis grew up a rather spoiled child who had romantic dreams of being a soldier. In his early twenties, he joined the military, was captured, and was held as a prisoner of war for a year. He was imprisoned in wretched conditions, grew very sick, and began to reevaluate his life. After being released, he was ready to head back out to battle but had a vision of God telling him to return to Assisi. It was then he began his transformation into the saint renowned for his peacefulness, care for the poor, and concern for all of God's creation.

© Mia Garrett / Shutterstock.com

it was Jesus' suffering that saved us from sin. Offering our burdens up to God can act as a sort of training in selflessness and a way of participating in Christ's work of salvation. This practice does not yield quick results, though. After a while, we do become more comfortable with the mysterious nature of Christ's and our own suffering. Because Jesus "has in some way united himself to every man, 'the possibility of being made partners, in a way known to God, in the paschal mystery' is offered to all men"[3] (*CCC*, number 618). Moreover, as disciples, we can serve as a means by which Christ pours out more grace for the salvation of souls, truly accomplishing something concrete in Christ's mission. Though participating in Christ's suffering is a mystery, we can certainly grasp that offering up our suffering is an active way to help others and carry forth the mission of Jesus Christ.

Saint John Henry Newman (1801–1890) encouraged us to turn to God, who has the ability to use all parts of our lives, even our suffering, for his purposes.

Saint John Henry Newman (1801–1890) was an English priest, cardinal, theologian, and poet, who was canonized by Pope Francis in 2019. Newman once wrote a reflection on our mission as Christians, as well as God's ability to use all parts of our lives—even our suffering—for his purpose. ✳

UNIT 4

> God, you have created me to do some specific service.
> You have committed some work to me which you have not committed to another.
> I have my mission.
> I am a link in a chain, a bond of connection between persons.
> You haven not created me for naught.
> I shall do good; I shall do your work.
> . . . If I am in sickness, my sickness may serve Him,
> in perplexity, my perplexity may serve Him.
> If I am in sorrow, my sorrow may serve Him.
> He does nothing in vain.
> He knows what He is about.
> He may take away my friends. He may throw me among strangers.
> He may make me feel desolate, make my spirits sink, hide my future from me.
> Still, He knows what He is about.

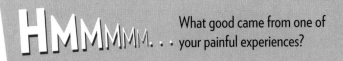

HMMMMMM. . . What good came from one of your painful experiences?

1. What belief does the Book of Job question?

2. Does God want us to suffer?

3. What is the best evidence that suffering is not God's punishment for sin?

4. How was Saint Damien's suffering a sign of his love for the people of Kalaupapa and his commitment to Christ?

5. What did Saint Paul mean when he said, "For when I am weak, then I am strong" (2 Corinthians 12:10)?

6. How does recalling the Paschal Mystery help us when we are suffering?

7. What is one of the most important things we can do for someone who is suffering?

8. What does it mean to offer up our suffering to God?

Hey. How ya doin?

My forecast is partly miserable with a chance of despair. 😩

I get it. I'm sorry. I know it's been tough 4 U.

Why does God just sit there and let bad stuff happen? 🙄

IDK. 😶

If God REALLY loves us then why does he make us suffer?????

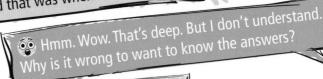

Fr. Phil told a story at Mass bout a guy in the Vietnam War. He got tired of asking God y all those bad things happnd, b/c he never got an answer. Then he started asking God, "Where are those bad experiences leading me?" The soldier said that was when he started finding peace.

😲 Hmm. Wow. That's deep. But I don't understand. Why is it wrong to want to know the answers?

Not wrong – it just ain't gonna happen.

What's the point of it all?????????????????

I think Fr. Phil's point was that God can bring good from bad. He said the soldier went back to Vietnam to help start an orphanage for kids whose parents were killed in the war.

OMG! I guess I've been asking the wrong question.

THNX! 🔺🔺

It's never too late to ask the right one. Hang in there!

UNIT 4

WHERE IS GOD WHEN WE SUFFER?

CHAPTER 10
Communal Suffering

WHY DO WE HAVE TO SUFFER FOR THE SINS OF OTHERS?

SNAPSHOT

Article 40   Page 289
Sinful Violence
- Pre-read: Genesis 4:1–16
- Pre-read: Romans 12:9–21

Article 41   Page 295
Human Failings
- Pre-read: Leviticus 4:13–21
- Pre-read: Luke 16:19–31

Article 42   Page 302
God's Creation Suffers
- Pre-read: Genesis, chapter 1
- Pre-read: Romans 8:18–27

Article 40
Sinful Violence

In 2012, a young man suffering from mental illness shot and killed his mother. He then drove to Sandy Hook Elementary School in Newtown, Connecticut, which he had attended as a child. There he killed twenty children, between six and seven years old, and six adult staff members. Then he took his own life. The news reports horrified the world. The youth and innocence of the children just compounded the senseless nature of what occurred that day. Soon after the incident, there were numerous public discussions about gun control, care for the mentally ill, and how we can work to prevent events like this from occurring. The numerous mass shootings since then emphasize the fact that we still have more work to do.

Sin comes in many forms, and some of the most disturbing are the violent acts that human beings commit against one another. In the case of mass shootings such as the one at Sandy Hook, violence not only affects the victims but also leaves an unforgettable impression on all those involved: witnesses, relatives of the victims, and first responders. It can even create a fear that touches those who simply hear about it. The evil of these violent acts ripples through the entire human community.

So it probably shouldn't surprise us that God's saving work of the Paschal Mystery includes a terribly violent sin: the Crucifixion and death of Jesus Christ. But we can find comfort in the fact that God was able to bring good out of such an evil. Jesus' response to the violence inflicted upon him is not only admirable but also a standard for which we should strive. Before proceeding further with this concept, let's quickly review the evolution of the biblical understanding of violence.

© Gina Jacobs / Shutterstock.com

UNIT 4

Sinful, violent acts committed by human beings against other human beings, like the shooting at Sandy Hook Elementary in Connecticut in 2012, affect the entire human community.

Violence in the Bible

As you know from previous courses, some of the Bible's content can be strikingly violent, especially in the Old Testament. The Book of Genesis alone contains several sinful acts of violence: Cain murders his brother Abel (see 4:1–8); Jacob's sons seek vengeance for the rape of their sister Dinah and massacre all the men in a nearby village (see 34:13–29); Jacob's sons plot to kill their youngest brother, Joseph, and leave him in the bottom of a well to die (see 37:18–24).

Some parts of the Old Testament even depict God as the instigator of violence. God sends the Flood that wipes out nearly the entire human population (see Genesis 6:7). The First Book of Samuel portrays God demanding the deaths of Israel's enemies, even their infant children (see 15:1–3). Despite these accounts, the lesson is not that God advocates violence; rather, God is teaching that those who commit grave evils will be brought to justice, if not in this life, then in the next. You may recall that early in their history, the Israelites equated God with divine retributive justice. They understood that God's just nature required justice for the terrible sins people committed. Yet throughout their history, God also revealed to them his merciful and loving nature (see Wisdom 11:23–24).

© Thoom / Shutterstock.com

Can we really find God's loving forgiveness in the Paschal Mystery, even for perpetrators who kill innocent people?

UNIT 4

TAKE IT TO GOD

God, help me be an instrument of your peace.

Help me to reflect on how my behavior and the choices I make affect others;

to be welcoming and hang out with people who are different from me;

to put myself in someone else's shoes before I make a decision that could affect their well-being and happiness;

to admit my errors and ask for forgiveness;

to forgive and not hold grudges;

to be kind and loving to others, knowing that I could stop a future violent act from ever happening.

Amen.

They Know Not What They Do

In the New Testament, Jesus fully and truly reveals God because he *is* God. If we look to Jesus' words and actions, it's clear that God's nature is not primarily rooted in divine retributive justice. Or, as some have put it, God's justice is rooted in mercy: "I say to you, offer no resistance to one who is evil. When someone strikes you on [your] right cheek, turn the other one to him as well" (Matthew 5:39). "I say to you, love your enemies, and pray for those who persecute you" (5:44).

If those teachings weren't clear enough, consider Jesus' actions when confronted with violence. Jesus and his followers are the primary victims of violence in the New Testament. We can look to them and their response to violence as models for our own lives. Saint Paul recalls both the Old Testament and the teachings of Jesus in his advice to the Romans:

> Do not repay anyone evil for evil; be concerned for what is noble in the sight of all. . . . "If your enemy is hungry, feed him; if he is thirsty, give him something to drink; for by so doing you will heap burning coals upon his head." Do not be conquered by evil but conquer evil with good. (12:17,20–21)

UNIT 4

CATHOLICS MAKING A DIFFERENCE

In 1965, about six hundred nonviolent civil rights marchers crossed the Edmund Pettus Bridge in Selma, Alabama, and were brutally beaten by state troopers. Sr. Antona Ebo, FSM, an African American nun in St. Louis, saw the televised images of the "Bloody Sunday" attack. She was no stranger to racism. As one of the first black members of her religious community, she had already addressed prejudice within her own order. Within two days, she was chosen as a delegate and sent to the next march in Selma.

She left home knowing she was risking her life. She later said: "I didn't want to be a martyr. But it was either put up or shut up." For the rest of her life, Sister Ebo continued to serve as an activist against the violence of racism. Sr. Antona Ebo died in 2017.

© David Carson / St. Louis Post-Dispatch / Polaris

Saint Paul points out that vengeance is not for us to decide. Dealing with the consequences of sin is the work of God alone. He also says that by being kind to your enemy, you will "heap burning coals upon his head." In other words, your kindness will make them ashamed of the evil they do. This expression of love has the possibility of bringing about a conversion of their hearts.

Jesus didn't just "talk the talk" about loving one's enemies; he truly "walked the walk." From the cross, he asked the Father to forgive those who were crucifying him (see Luke 23:34). The Roman soldiers knew they were putting someone to death. However, it is unlikely they knew they were crucifying an innocent man, and they certainly didn't know they were killing the Son of God.

This is often the case with horrific mass violence perpetrated by people in our world today. In some cases, there is a psychological illness that prevents them from completely understanding the consequences of their actions. In the case of terrorism by religious extremists, they are often under the influence of misguided leaders. Racist violence is often the result of ignorance and unchallenged prejudice. This does not necessarily relieve them of their guilt, but rather it points to how sin affects our ability to see goodness and act accordingly.

Because of its obviously disturbing nature, sinful violence can feel unforgivable. How could God ever welcome the brutal murderer of small children into his heavenly home? Yet, in the events of the Paschal Mystery, we find God's loving forgiveness for even those who killed the most innocent of all. The love that God has for his people calls us not only to forgive but also to prevent these violent acts from occurring.

Stop Violence before It Happens

Why are we talking about violence and its effects in a book on the Paschal Mystery? Through the Paschal Mystery, Christ brings his healing to the world, saving us from sin and the effects of sin. And violence is one of the most visible effects of sin. Because we are called to participate in Christ's saving work, we are also called to combat violence and heal ourselves and others from its impact on our lives.

Violence does not happen without a reason. It is most often rooted in one form of sin or another: jealousy, greed, fear, falsehood, or injustices like poverty or oppression. To end violence, we must address its root causes in our own hearts. Here are small steps you can take to address the things that can lead to violence in your own life:

- **Reflect.** Consider how your behavior and the choices you make affect others. What prejudices do you have and how can you avoid acting on them?
- **Be truthful.** Make sure the information you pass on is factual and worthy of being circulated.
- **Be welcoming.** Get to know and hang out with people who are different from you.
- **Practice empathy.** Put yourself in someone else's shoes before you make decisions that could affect their well-being and happiness.
- **Confess.** Be willing to admit your errors and ask for forgiveness.
- **Forgive.** Do not hold grudges. When others have wronged you, forgive them—even if they do not acknowledge or ask for it.
- **Take responsibility.** Write to your representatives in government and hold them accountable for their inaction or actions they've made on your behalf.
- **Be peaceful.** Your kindness and love for others could stop a future violent act from ever happening.

All of these can help us to be faithful to the teachings of Jesus Christ, who was willing to die rather than betray his divine mission. ✳

UNIT 4

A small step you can take to address the things that can lead to violence in your own life is to engage in nonviolent protest. Pictured here, teenagers stage a lie-in at the White House to protest gun laws in Washington, DC.

HMMMMM. . .

What is one practical way you can help stop violence?

Article 41
Human Failings

When a fight broke out in the yard two houses down from him, Harris went out to help break it up. One man was seriously wounded and unconscious, and another fled away on foot. A crowd of people quickly gathered outside, and Harris was mistakenly identified as the person who started the fight. When the police did their background check, they learned that Harris was an ex-convict. He had a record for a minor offense he had committed years ago when he was still a teenager. He was arrested and taken to jail.

Harris had a steady job but could not afford to post bail, which would have allowed him to go home while he awaited his day in court. As he sat in jail, he lost his job. Because he could not afford to pay his rent, the landlord got rid of all of his belongings. His court-appointed attorney was overwhelmed with work. He tried to convince Harris to plead guilty to a lesser crime so he could get out of jail earlier. Harris maintained his innocence, the plea deal was refused, and the prosecutor postponed the court date. A year after he was arrested, he finally got his day in court. The victim had recovered and showed up to testify that another man had injured him, not Harris. The prosecutor then dropped the case. The court declared that justice was served, but Harris left the courtroom a homeless man without a penny in his pocket or a job to earn a living.

Perhaps this story made you angry because you recognize the injustice done to Harris. But, consider this: the people involved were doing their job to the best of their ability. The police arrested a man who was identified as the suspect and had a criminal record. The court-appointed attorney and prosecutor often do their best, but the criminal court system is overburdened. Because it's impossible to go to trial in every case, they try to swiftly end them through plea bargains. In the end, justice is not served and innocent people, like Harris, suffer.

Racism is an example of communal, or social, sin. Pictured here is the March Against Racism national demonstration in London protesting the dramatic rise in race-related attacks.

UNIT 4

I DIDN'T KNOW THAT!

The ones who brought out the wrath of Jesus more than anyone else were the religious leaders of his day! More specifically, they were hypocritical religious leaders. Regarding the scribes and Pharisees, Jesus complained that they didn't practice what they preached (see Matthew 23:3). Their positions allowed them to easily exploit people's trust. What made it so despicable was that evil was being done in the name of God. They did this to secure their positions of power and wealth, and this infuriated Jesus (see Matthew, chapter 23).

Communal Sin

The injustice and suffering that Harris experienced is an example of **communal (or social) sin.** Communal sin is "the negative influence exerted on people by communal situations and social structures that are the fruit of men's sins"[1] (*CCC*, number 408). In Harris's situation, the criminal justice system in his city was so dysfunctional that it prevented timely justice and victimized an innocent man.

Jesus was also a victim of communal sin. The Romans ruled the citizens of Palestine with a tyrannical hand that kept its people in line. Most Jewish People did not enjoy the same rights as Roman citizens. Religious freedom, fair trials, and economic opportunities were not open to all. Jesus was victimized by the Roman governors as well as the Jewish leaders who felt threatened by his works and teachings. Jesus' Crucifixion was not the result of a single person's actions, but rather the culmination of the condemnation of many.

Communal sins are often the results of ignorance, neglect, or a lack of compassion. Even though there is no single person to blame, a communal sin is no less sinful. A community's failure to acknowledge problems like a broken penal system, drug abuse, poverty, and poor health care can be devastating.

---

communal sin ▸ The negative influence exerted on people by communal situations and social structures that are the fruit of man's sins; also refers to the collective effect of many people's sins over time, which corrupts society and its institutions by creating "structures of sin."

Despite their leaders' treatment of Jesus, the Israelites had a very good understanding of communal sin and its detrimental effect on them as a community. The Mosaic Law included rules and regulations on how they, the Chosen People, were to behave as a community. They even had rituals seeking God's forgiveness for their communal sins (see Leviticus 4:13–14). Note that in this passage, they are asking for forgiveness of sins committed inadvertently.

Quite often, we are unaware of the unjust situations and systems that deny people the freedom and justice to live fully. Although it is impossible to be aware of every situation, Christians are called to inform themselves about the world around them and to act when necessary. Put another way, we need to read the Bible and watch the news. Saint Paul warned, "Watch carefully then how you live, not as foolish persons but as wise, making the most of the opportunity, because the days are evil" (Ephesians 5:15–16).

Like the Israelites and early Christian communities, we seek God's forgiveness of our sins as a community too. At the beginning of Mass, we participate in the **Penitential Act** when the priest asks the faithful to reflect on their sins and then ask for God's mercy: "Lord, have mercy . . . Christ, have mercy . . . Lord, have mercy." We also ask that God pardon "us" when we offer the Lord's Prayer: "forgive us our trespasses." When you pray these prayers, consider the ways in which your community allows sinful situations to occur, seek God's forgiveness, and vow to make a difference in whatever way you are able.

Corruption

Unfortunately, there are people in governments, businesses, and even churches who use their power from authority for their own gain and to the detriment of others. They've become **corrupt**. Corruption is the dishonest conduct by those in power by which they take advantage of those they lead or serve.

Because of the power that politicians exercise in the life of the community, the temptation to misuse that power is always present. This can include corrupt activities like taking bribes or accepting favors for supporting certain legislation. Corruption also includes making politically motivated decisions that do not benefit the community they serve. Because politicians often rely on the donations of wealthy people and corporations to get elected, they feel the need to please them for their continued support. In doing so, they often end up serving the needs of the elite few instead of the entire community.

UNIT 4

Penitential Act ➤ The invitation by the priest at Mass, after the opening greeting, to have the congregation acknowledge their sins and place their trust in God's mercy.

corrupt ➤ Having or showing a willingness to act dishonestly in return for money or personal gain.

Business people, politicians, and other people in positions of power—even Church leaders—are tempted to misuse their power for their own good and to the detriment of others. This leads to corrupt activities, such as bribery or the acceptance of favors.

The same is true for business leaders. When their main concern is how much money the business can make, the impact of their business practices on their employees, their customers, and the environment can take second place or even be ignored.

What happens behind closed doors in our city councils, state and national capitals, business offices, and boardrooms has real consequences in people's lives, for good or for bad. Politicians and business leaders make decisions that directly affect issues like abortion, health care, poverty, employment, immigration, and numerous other social justice issues. As citizens and Christians, we are called to make sure that our representatives and business leaders are held accountable. We also must work to free them from influences that keep them from serving their community.

Within Jesus' closest group of followers, it was Judas who served as treasurer (see John 12:6). Though there may have been other reasons that Judas betrayed Jesus, the Gospels make it clear that his desire for money was a primary motive. "Then one of the Twelve, who was called Judas Iscariot, went to the chief priests and said, 'What are you willing to give me if I hand him over to you?' They paid him thirty pieces of silver, and from that time on he looked for an opportunity to hand him over" (Matthew 26:14–16). Corruption was one of the many reasons that led to Jesus' death.

The Root of All Evils

Jesus consistently warned his disciples of the sin of greed, and he didn't shy away from expressing his anger about it! He toppled the tables of the money changers in the Temple (see John 2:14–16). He condemned "the Pharisees, who loved money" (Luke 16:14). He insisted that you cannot serve God and wealth at the same time (see Matthew 6:24). He told the rich man that to enter Heaven, he had to sell everything he owned and give it to the poor (see Luke 18:18–23).

What is it about money that is such a problem? Money in and of itself is not the problem. We know that the faithful disciple who buried Jesus in his own tomb, Joseph of Arimathea, was a wealthy man (see Matthew 27:57). We also know that the early Church often gathered for the Eucharist in the homes of wealthy Christians. Still, there must be something about wealth that would cause Saint Paul to declare that "the love of money is the root of all evils" (1 Timothy 6:10).

The key word that Paul uses is *love*. It is our *love* of money that can lead us toward sin, not the money itself. With wealth comes responsibility to use it wisely and justly. But the temptation to use it only for one's selfish desires can be very strong and therein lies the problem. Greed can lead to a lack of concern for the suffering of other human beings. Sometimes people make money at the expense of their workers or consumers. While some are so focused on buying the extra luxuries of life, there are others who cannot afford the necessities (food, shelter, health care, and so on).

The sin of greed is a failure to acknowledge the pain and suffering of someone in our human family. It is a choice to love something over someone. In the Parable of the Rich Man and Lazarus, Jesus warned those who ignore the needs of the poor while tending to their own extravagant desires. The temptation of wealth is seductive and convincing enough to draw people away from Christ.

Young people do not have much control over their family's wealth. No one chooses to be born into a wealthy or poor family. However, you do have control over your buying habits as well as what you ask your parents to purchase for you. The most important first step is to inform yourself. Research how your food and clothing are produced. The Human Thread is an organization based on Catholic social justice principles that raises awareness and promotes ethical standards for workers in clothing and shoe factories. And what about

UNIT 4

your favorite candy bar? The Food Empowerment Project puts out a list of companies that sell chocolate that does not involve the exploitation of child or slave labor. Was your snack worth supporting child slavery? It only takes a minute to find out.

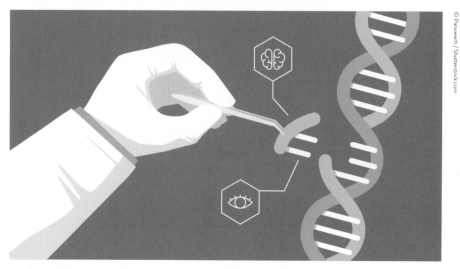

We have the technology to manipulate the genetic material of humans, but should we? How would such decisions affect us individually and as a society?

We Can but Should We?

When the first car was built in the late 1800s, the people almost certainly did not imagine that this invention would contribute to an environmental crisis. Over a hundred years later, we know that emissions from machines using carbon-based fuel play a role in climate change. We live in a world that is changing fast. Technological advancements are allowing us to do things that were not even imagined a hundred, fifty, fifteen, or even five years ago. But just because we have the technical ability to do something, does that mean we should do it? Opening the door to certain possibilities can potentially lead to disaster. You might have seen this theme reflected in movies about bringing back dinosaurs by using the DNA retrieved from their fossils. How did that go over? Not well!

Today, we have the means to manipulate the genetic material of both plants and animals—including humans. Scientists have the means to identify and alter the genetic code of human embryos. This could mean the end of medical issues like heart defects, cystic fibrosis, or congenital blindness. But it could also lead to such practices as genetically made-to-order designer babies. It is very possible that in the future someone could decide their child's gender, eye and hair color, athletic ability, intelligence, and other genetically determined characteristics. However, we cannot look into the future to see the consequences of how these decisions will affect us individually and as a society.

It is good to be reminded that the desire to play the role of God led to humanity's first sin (see Genesis 3:5–6). Pope Saint John Paul II emphasized that outside of improving the health of the child, humans should not tamper with the dignity of human procreation: "No social or scientific usefulness and no ideological motivation could ever justify intervention on the human genome which is not therapeutic in character" ("The Charter for Health Care Workers," number 3.1).

Because we are already able to identify certain medical issues in children in the womb, and because abortion is currently legal, parents can choose to end the life of a child who has a genetic disorder. Weeding out the sick and disabled through abortion is morally wrong and contradictory to the Gospel of Christ. This is not to say that it is easy to accept raising a disabled child. Raising a child with severe disabilities is a daunting task that requires the support of the entire community. Refusing to offer that support makes the community liable if the child is aborted.

God is not confined by space and time. Unlike God, we humans are limited in our ability to see the unintended consequences of our actions. We must be extremely careful that we do not create the conditions for sin. It is important to identify and repair the evil situations we, as a human family, have created. It is also equally important to acknowledge that God knew what he was doing when he created everything. Humans should not be messing with the natural order that God set in place. Pope Francis said this about his namesake: "Saint Francis of Assisi bears witness to the need to *respect all that God has created and as he created it, without manipulating and destroying creation*; rather to help it grow, to become more beautiful and more like what God created it to be" (Homily, "Pastoral Visit to Assisi, " October 4, 2013). ✳

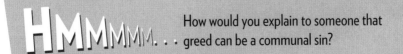
HMMMMMM. . . How would you explain to someone that greed can be a communal sin?

Article 42
God's Creation Suffers

The oceans are filling up with our garbage. When sea turtles are young, they sometimes get ensnared in the plastic six-pack rings that hold our canned beverages together. Unfortunately, they are often unable to free themselves from it. As they continue to grow, their bodies become compressed in the area where the ring is lodged. Their lungs and other internal organs do not grow properly. In order to avoid injuring more sea turtles, a Florida company started using biodegradable six-pack rings that the sea turtles can actually eat! Innovations like these show respect for God's creation. We can participate by making sure the products we purchase do not harm any of God's creatures.

Human activities have taken their toll on creation in other ways. The machines that burn carbon-based fuel (cars, airplanes, etc.) account for much of the greenhouse gases that heat up our atmosphere. Did you know that animals like cows, buffalo, and sheep release large amounts of methane into the atmosphere? Raising livestock actually contributes around 15 percent of the total gas emissions in the world each year, according to *The New York Times*. Convincing people to give up their hamburgers is not easy! Scientists are devising new ways to provide plant-based meat substitutes that look and taste like the real thing. But even if the idea does succeed, it does not completely solve the problem. We still have a long way to go to solve the issues causing climate change. It will take numerous innovations of this kind to bring humanity back into a healthy balance with the Earth.

When it comes to sin, suffering, and God's salvation, all of creation has something at stake. As we become free from the slavery of sin, creation itself will also enjoy the fruits of our salvation.

Courtesy the Missouri Department of Conservation

What do you do with the plastics you use?

UNIT 4

A Mission from God

When God created humans, he told us to have dominion over the Earth and all creation (see Genesis 1:28). *Dominion* is a word that was used in relation to kings having authority over the people. It was not unlimited power to use as they saw fit. Kings were expected to care for their people. This is God's commandment to protect and nurture creation, and it is a mandate that needs more of our attention.

Much of our environmental crisis can be blamed on waste. Just a few decades ago, empty bottles of milk would be picked up, cleaned, and used again. Today, milk is often purchased in plastic bottles that take about four hundred years to decompose naturally. Recent studies report that around the world, humans buy a million products served in plastic bottles *per minute*. Though most of these bottles could be recycled, studies have shown that only about 9 percent of all plastic makes it to the recycling bin.

Most of our plastic trash ends up in landfills or the ocean. The Pacific Ocean now holds what has been dubbed "The Great Pacific Garbage Patch." It is more than twice the size of Texas and consists mostly of plastic items that even the salt water of the ocean cannot break down. Unfortunately, it is not the only one, as there are other floating patches of trash polluting our oceans. In 2018, marine officials discovered a sick whale and took care of it for five days before it died. The autopsy found over seventeen pounds of plastic inside the whale, including over eighty bags. These garbage patches endanger sea life worldwide, and because our fate is tied to the health of the oceans, human life is at stake too.

In his encyclical "On Care for Our Common Home" *("Laudato Si'")* Pope Francis speaks of Mary, the Mother of God, and her care and concern for all life: "Just as her pierced heart mourned the death of Jesus, so now she grieves for the sufferings of the crucified poor and for the creatures of this world laid waste by human power" (number 241). Through the Paschal Mystery, we, with Mary, know that death is not the end. Likewise, through our concern and care for the Earth, we can find new life ahead for all of God's creation.

UNIT 4

Garbage patches, like this one, are large areas of the ocean where litter, fishing gear, and other debris left by humans collects.

As climate change causes the oceans to warm, storms become larger and more intense. In September 2017, Hurricane Harvey battered Texas. In the wake of the destruction, neighbors came out to help one another by sharing chain saws, generators, ice coolers, and so on. We often strive to be strong and independent, and in some ways that is good. But if you were totally self-sufficient, why would you need anyone? Why would you need God? When we suffer, we reach out for help, and that allows others to live out their Christian mission. When we see others suffer, it becomes our opportunity to love those in need, just as Christ did. Suffering encourages us to reach out to one another and to God too, and that is what makes us whole.

Peace, Poverty, and the Environment

There is a connection between the environmental health of a country and the wealth and peace they enjoy. In developing countries, poverty can impel governments to resort to ways of supporting their people that they would not normally pursue. For example, some countries have resorted to the logging industry for income, but this only provides short-term relief. After the trees are sold, the land is useless for farming because forests typically have nutrient-depleted soil. On top of that, when large sections of forests are removed, the tree roots that provided stability to the soil are gone. This can lead to erosion and flooding problems. Because trees naturally remove carbon dioxide from the air and release oxygen into the atmosphere, the loss of these forests also adds to the climate's change. In the end, the people are left with an ecological disaster, their poverty has not been solved, and climate change is intensified.

Ecological disaster and poverty make a situation ripe for social turmoil, government instability, and war. Countries that are suffering from economic and environmental crises become vulnerable to terrorist organizations as well. The environment, poverty, and peace are so interconnected that Pope Benedict XVI insisted, "If you want to cultivate peace, protect creation" ("Message for the Celebration of the World Day of Peace," number 1, January 1, 2010).

When We Lose Rainforests, We Lose

Losing rainforests would create a dire situation for our planet:

- Many isolated indigenous people would likely die due to their lack of resistance to sickness and disease.
- Fifty percent of the Earth's species would be without a home.
- Millions of plants and animals would become extinct.
- Thousands of plants and animals would never even be discovered.
- Twenty percent of the world's oxygen production would be lost.
- Resources for scientific research would vanish.
- Medical cures for illnesses such as AIDS, cancer, and other terminal diseases would not as easily be discovered, if at all.

Our beautiful planet Earth is a gift from God that requires our care and attention. What do you do to care for the Earth?

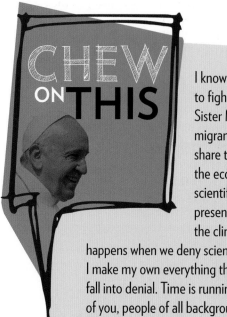

I know that you have committed yourselves to fight for social justice, to defend our Sister Mother Earth and to stand alongside migrants. I want to reaffirm your choice and share two reflections in this regard. First, the ecological crisis is real. "A very solid scientific consensus indicates that we are presently witnessing a disturbing warming of the climatic system." . . . [We] know what happens when we deny science and disregard the voice of Nature. I make my own everything that concerns us as Catholics. Let us not fall into denial. Time is running out. Let us act. I ask you again—all of you, people of all backgrounds including native people, pastors, political leaders—to defend Creation. (Pope Francis, "Message on the Occasion of the World Meetings of Popular Movements," February 10, 2017)

UNIT 4

What We Pass On

One of the biggest environmental problems we face is rooted in a false understanding that the Earth is simply a lifeless thing that is here for us to exploit. Some see it merely as a resource with infinite capabilities to provide us with the natural goods we need to live. The Earth is neither lifeless nor is it an endless supply source. Instead, it is an interconnected dynamic entity that requires our care and attention. It is a gift from God that continues to provide for us, but only as long as we ensure its safety.

We are called to be stewards of God's creation. **Stewardship** is the careful and responsible management of someone or something that has been entrusted to a person's care. This includes responsibly using and caring for God's gift of creation. A steward is not someone who is the final recipient of a gift, but rather one who manages and cares for something so that it can be passed on to another.

The Earth has been passed on by faithful stewards for hundreds of thousands of years. Most have taken good care of it, though there have been difficult burdens from which the Earth has had to rebound. These moments have brought a variety of sufferings upon us. In the past fifty to one hundred years, humanity has painfully pushed Earth to its limitations. Its future, and the future of humanity, is at stake now. In what condition will the Earth be when you pass it on to your children? ✳

HMMMMM. . .

Why is our concern for the environment a faith issue?

UNIT 4

---

stewardship ➤ The careful and responsible management of someone or something that has been entrusted to a person's care. This includes responsibly using and caring for the gifts of creation that God has given us.

1. How do we explain the violent portrayals of God in the Bible?

2. How did Jesus respond to violence?

3. What are some ways we as individuals can stop violence before it happens?

4. What is communal sin, and who is to blame for it?

5. Why is money a cause for so much sin?

6. Why should we carefully consider the sinful possibilities of technological advancements?

7. How is taking care of the environment a commandment from God?

8. What did Pope Benedict XVI mean when he said, "If you want to cultivate peace, protect creation"?

9. Why is it important that we consider ourselves stewards of God's creation?

UNIT 4

Courtesy National Gallery of Art, Washington

UNIT 4

1. What imagery in this painting by Albert Bierstadt entitled *Mount Corcoran* (circa 1876-1877) strikes you the most and why?

2. How do greed, corruption, and violence threaten our landscape?

3. How could this painting help remind you to be a good steward of our Earth?

UNIT 4 HIGHLIGHTS

CHAPTER 9 Personal Suffering and the Paschal Mystery

We Cannot Fully Understand Why We Suffer

"I have spoken but did not understand; things too marvelous for me, which I did not know."
(Job 42:2–3)

Suffering for Others Is a Strength

"Whoever wishes to come after me must deny himself, take up his cross, and follow me."
(Mark 8:34)

UNDERSTANDING MY PERSONAL SUFFERING

Weakness Helps Us Rely on God

"[The Lord] said to me, 'My grace is sufficient for you, for power is made perfect in weakness.'"
(2 Corinthians 12:9)

We Are Not Left to Suffer Alone

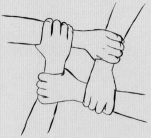

"If [one] part suffers, all the parts suffer with it."
(1 Corinthians 12:26)

CHAPTER 10   Communal Suffering

Ways in Which Communities Suffer

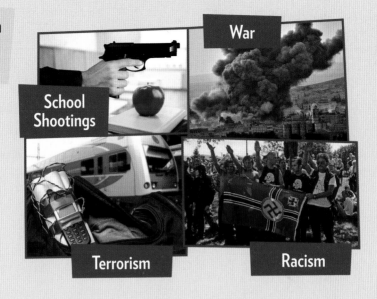

War

School Shootings

Terrorism

Racism

Ways in Which Communities Cause Suffering

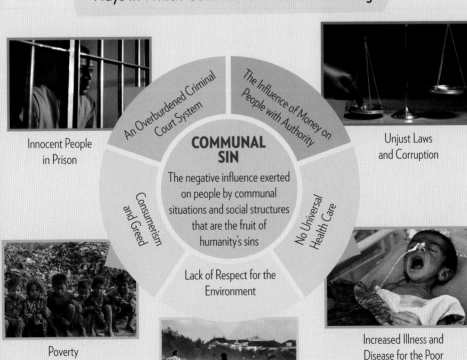

Innocent People in Prison

An Overburdened Criminal Court System

The Influence of Money on People with Authority

COMMUNAL SIN

The negative influence exerted on people by communal situations and social structures that are the fruit of humanity's sins

Consumerism and Greed

No Universal Health Care

Lack of Respect for the Environment

Unjust Laws and Corruption

Increased Illness and Disease for the Poor

Poverty

Environmental Crisis

UNIT 4
BRING IT HOME

HOW DOES JESUS' PASCHAL MYSTERY HELP US MAKE SENSE OF SUFFERING?

FOCUS QUESTIONS

CHAPTER 9 What good can come from suffering?

CHAPTER 10 Why do we have to suffer for the sins of others?

DUC
Totino-Grace High School

So, suffering exists and we all experience it, but what is the connection to the Paschal Mystery? I think it's the idea that Jesus was willing to sacrifice himself for us that gives us a clue as to how we can help to relieve the suffering of others. Each of us is called to become less self-centered and immerse ourselves in the suffering of others. Just as Jesus was willing to suffer and die to save us from our sins, we too are called to sacrifice ourselves for others. If we follow Jesus' example, the world will be filled with compassion.

UNIT 4

REFLECT

Take some time to read and reflect on the unit and chapter focus questions listed on the facing page.

- What question or section did you identify most closely with?

- What did you find within the unit that was comforting or challenging?

UNIT 5
Prayer and Holiness

HOW DOES PRAYER BRING US CLOSER TO GOD AND ONE ANOTHER?

LOOKING AHEAD

CHAPTER 11 Page 316
Holiness and Union with God

CHAPTER 12 Page 338
Communing with God

CHAPTER 13 Page 360
Praying with the Triduum

UNIT 5

To me, prayer has always been kind of unimportant because it has always been boring. As I grow older, I do realize the importance of prayer, but I still struggle to pray daily. When I do pray, I get a feeling that I don't get when I'm anywhere else or when I'm doing anything else. So, praying helps bring me closer to God, because I feel at peace and have a sense of relief when I pray. I think that is how it should feel when you are close to God.

RICHARD
Mater Dei High School

CHAPTER 11
Holiness and Union with God

WHAT DOES IT MEAN TO BE HOLY?

SNAPSHOT

Article 43   Pazge 317
Being Holy
• Pre-read: Colossians 3:5–17

Article 44   Page 323
Discipleship: The Path to Holiness
• Pre-read: Matthew 5:17–7:29

Article 45   Page 327
Mysticism: Seeking Union with God
• Pre-read: John 17:17–23

Article 46   Page 333
The Church's Sacramental Life Unites Us
• Pre-read: John 6:51–58

Article 43
Being Holy

In her high school theology class, Becca was asked to describe a "holy person" that she knew personally. She had never really thought about it but figured that it must be someone who goes to church a lot. So she mentioned her grandmother, who attended Mass every morning. The more she thought about it, she concluded that her grandmother really *was* a holy person, but not for the reason she had given. Becca realized that her grandmother attended daily Mass because of her great devotion to God, not because she felt obligated to do so.

When Becca asked her grandmother about it, she responded: "I love God with all my heart. Going to Mass allows me to pray in a special way and to glorify God, but it also reminds me to love all people. It reminds me of something *my* grandmother told me: being holy means being aware of the needs of others, responding to those needs the best way we can, and treating everybody as a holy person—which everyone is."

All of us are called to be holy. This is a lifelong commitment and challenge, but it is not an impossible goal. Because each one of us is made in God's own image and likeness, all human life is sacred and potentially holy. However, our personal holiness is not a given; all of us must cooperate with God's grace to become the holy people God intends us to be. Put another way, holiness not only describes who we are but also includes what we do and how we act.

We are holy from the moment of our conception because we are made in the image and likeness of God.

UNIT 5

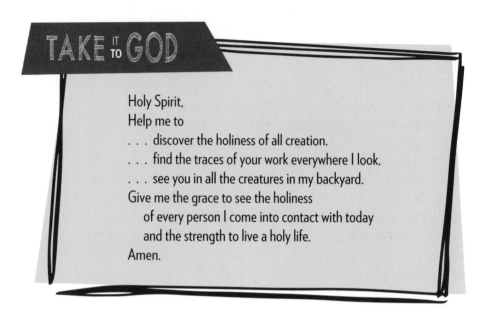

TAKE IT TO GOD

Holy Spirit,
Help me to
. . . discover the holiness of all creation.
. . . find the traces of your work everywhere I look.
. . . see you in all the creatures in my backyard.
Give me the grace to see the holiness
     of every person I come into contact with today
     and the strength to live a holy life.
Amen.

What Is Holiness?

Holiness is difficult to describe because it has many dimensions and meanings. Let's consider a couple of these dimensions to help us understand our own call to be holy.

First, something is holy because it somehow reveals God and shares in God's own life. Therefore, in a general sense, all creation is holy. But in a particular sense, every human being is holy in a special way. Each of us is made in God's own image and likeness. Each of us reveals God and is in communion with God in a way no other part of creation is. Simply put, we are holy because we are made in the image of God (see Genesis 1:26). Still, there is more to being holy than this.

UNIT 5

---

holiness ➤ The state of being holy. This means to be set apart for God's service, to be devoted to God and united with him and his Church, to live a morally good life, to be a person of prayer, and to reveal God's love to the world through acts of loving service.

When it comes to interacting with people, our actions can be more or less holy. Simply following God's Laws can help lead us to holiness, but it is only a beginning. Jesus criticized those whose strict interpretations of the Law seemed to be a way to avoid fulfilling the goodness of God's commandments. He condemned this attitude (see Mark 7:6).

Jesus called his disciples to a conversion of the heart that leads to the perfection of love and a more complete union with him. He said, "A good person out of the store of goodness in his heart produces good, but an evil person out of a store of evil produces evil; for from the fullness of the heart the mouth speaks" (Luke 6:45). The good that we do comes from an inner goodness that all of us possess but which needs to be nurtured. God calls every person to be holy, and each of us must choose whether to respond to that call. Christ's teachings on loving God and one another (see Mark 12:28–34) challenge us to respond to that call. Once our hearts are truly converted, we realize that all human beings are holy and naturally act accordingly.

MAKE IT SO

Daily Schedule for a Holy Teenager

6:30   Rise and say morning prayers.
6:40   Shower, dress, and eat breakfast.
8:00   Go to school.
3:00   Participate in extracurricular activities.
6:00   Eat dinner.
7:00   Do homework and chat online.
10:30 Say night prayers and go to bed.

Being a holy person is not so much about *what* you do but rather *how* you do it. Strengthening your relationship with God is essential, which is why prayer is essential. This does not mean you have to sit alone to pray for hours. Short prayers before, during, and after meals and other activities work well for a young person's daily life. Besides prayer, living a holy life means many things: helping your friend study for a test; being honest in school and in your relationships; giving thanks to God; feeding your body, mind, and soul with good things; and treating everyone as children of God. As Saint Teresa of Kolkata (Calcutta) (1920-1997) said, "You have to be holy where you are—wherever God has put you."

UNIT 5

Second, something is holy when it has been **consecrated** to God; that is, it has been solemnly designated or set aside for service to God. For example, the vessels that are used in Mass (like the **chalice** and **ciborium**) are holy because they have been set aside for a sacred task. It would be inappropriate to use them for regular meals. We are holy in a similar way, because through our Baptism, we have been consecrated for service to God. We live to spread the Gospel of Jesus Christ and bring about the Kingdom of God on Earth.

So what does it mean to be holy? We could summarize it like this: We are holy from the moment of our conception because we are made in the image and likeness of God. Although our original holiness is corrupted due to Original Sin, Baptism restores our original holiness and consecrates us to God's service. As baptized people, we perfect our holiness by growing in our relationship with God, avoiding sin, and dedicating our lives to the service of others, following the example of Jesus.

© Impact Photography / Shutterstock.com

One way we can perfect our holiness is by living lives in service of others. What's one of your favorite ways to serve other people?

consecrate ➤ To declare or set apart as sacred or solemnly dedicated to God's service; to make holy.

chalice ➤ The cup used during the Mass that holds the wine before the Consecration and the Blood of Christ after the Consecration. It represents the cup used at the Last Supper and is a symbol of Jesus' sacrifice and eternal life.

ciborium ➤ From a Latin word for *cup*, a cup-shaped vessel for holding the consecrated hosts, the Body of Christ, at the Mass.

Aids to Holiness

"Be holy; for I, the LORD, your God, am holy" (Leviticus 20:7). How is it possible to be holy like God? Being holy like the Lord sounds like a tall order, but God provides us with a number of tools and plenty of assistance to lead holy lives. There are many gifts that can help us grow in holiness. You've heard of these gifts in previous courses, but it helps to be reminded of them.

- **Intellect and free will.** First and foremost are the gifts of our intellect and free will. Our intellect helps us to see and understand the natural order God has created. It helps us weigh decisions and evaluate outcomes, and in so doing, we can make good moral choices. Our free will allows us to act on those good choices that lead us to love God and one another.

- **Grace.** Grace is God's gift that empowers us to respond to his love. Through grace, we receive a holiness that is a greater blessing than original holiness. Through grace, we participate in the life of the Holy Trinity with God as our Father, Jesus as our brother, and the Holy Spirit as the one who lives within us and gives us strength and guidance. Various kinds of grace assist us on our way to perfection.

Type of Grace	Description
Sanctifying grace	• heals our human nature wounded by sin
	• restores us to friendship with God by giving us a share in the divine life of the Trinity
	• a supernatural gift of God, infused into our souls by the Holy Spirit, that continues the work of making us holy
	• received in Baptism, when we were freed from Original Sin and initiated into the Church
Actual grace	• refers to God's interventions and support for us in the everyday moments of our lives; for example, if you have ever been depressed or lonely, and someone stepped into your life at just the right moment to cheer you up
	• refers to the Holy Spirit acting within and through other people in our lives, enabling us to become closer to God and know true happiness

UNIT 5

- **Self-Reflection.** God has also given us the ability to reflect on our own thoughts and actions. This is sometimes called **interiority**, which is the practice of developing a life of self-reflection and self-examination to attend to our spiritual life and call to holiness. To do this, you need to take a break from the normal distractions of daily life. It could be a few moments of quiet in your bedroom as you begin or end your day. You could take a walk through a park to consider how you handled a particular troubling event. Retreats are excellent times to practice this skill, which is necessary for a healthy spiritual life. All of these are ways to help strengthen and listen to our conscience, that small inner voice, making it easier for us to live holy lives.

- **The Church.** It is well known that human beings are influenced by the people who surround them. So it should be no surprise that God's gift of the Church is an important aid to holiness. The Church provides us with opportunities for education, for prayer, for community, and for service to the world. As the Body of Christ, the members of the Church give strength, hope, and support to one another in our common goal of becoming holy people. ✳

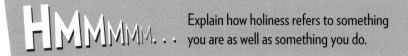

HMMMMM. . . Explain how holiness refers to something you are as well as something you do.

---

interiority ➤ The practice of developing a life of self-reflection and self-examination to attend to our spiritual life and call to holiness.

Article 44

Discipleship: The Path to Holiness

Have you ever heard the phrase "talk is cheap"? Generally, this phrase is used as a challenge to a friend to actually do the things they have been talking about doing for a long time. Or perhaps you heard it when your mom was criticizing a politician for not fulfilling his campaign promises. Maybe it was when your teacher got tired of your promises to turn in your homework assignments on time. Regardless of the situation, when people say "talk is cheap," they are pointing out that it is easy to say that you are going to do something, but much harder to actually do it.

Without ever using the phrase, Jesus pointed out that talk is cheap. He told his disciples, "Not everyone who says to me, 'Lord, Lord,' will enter the kingdom of heaven, but only the one who does the will of my Father in heaven" (Matthew 7:21). In other words, it's easy to *say* that Jesus Christ is your Lord. But living as a disciple of Jesus requires that we follow his teachings and live as he did.

CATHOLICS **MAKING** A DIFFERENCE

Would your love be so strong that you'd be willing to risk your own life so that others may live? Irena Sendler, a Polish Catholic (1910–2008), did just that. Sendler was twenty-nine years old when the Germans invaded her native Poland in 1939. Without concern for her own life, Sendler and

other activists worked to save thousands of Jews from the Nazis' concentration camps. They provided food, money, and forged documents to aid those in the Warsaw ghettos. Sendler also smuggled children out to live in the homes of other Catholics. In 1943, Sendler was captured, tortured, and sentenced to die, but through a bribe to a guard, she was able to avoid death. Irena Sendler was named "Righteous Among the Nations," an honor bestowed by Israel to those who aided Jews during the Holocaust.

UNIT 5

Doing What Jesus Taught

Jesus' teachings require that we not only accept them as true but also put them into practice. Below are just some of Jesus' key teachings that should act as guideposts on our path toward holiness.

Be Humble	Don't overestimate your own worth, importance, or goodness. Always examine your motives; acknowledge that your gifts for service come from God and are to be used for the good of others.
Do Not Judge	Condemning others does not bring anyone closer to being holy. Be concerned about your own faults, not the faults of others.
Forgive Others	When we forgive, not only is the sinner released from the burden, but we are as well. When someone harms you, do not retaliate, which would create a continuing loop of hatred and vengeance. Only forgiveness and refusal to retaliate can interrupt this cycle.
Love Everyone, Especially Enemies	We are called to love everyone—even our enemies. No one is outside the reach of God's love. Ultimately, love frees us from harboring ill will toward those who have wronged us, and brings us closer to becoming holy.
Do Not Let Money Lead You Astray	There is nothing wrong with earning money honestly and fairly. But when wealth rises to the level of a false god, it can prevent us from using our wealth as God wants us to. Our abundance, then, could potentially come at the cost of those who are in need and could lead us from the path to holiness.
Care for Those in Need	Jesus says that our eternal welfare is dependent on our care for those in need, especially the poor and marginalized. All of us have been given certain gifts, talents, and resources. Our journey to holiness requires that we use our gifts in service to those in our community.
Service and Sacrifice	Jesus washed the disciples' feet as a model of service to others and emphasized that their service would require sacrifice. He warned that to be holy, we will need to set aside our own needs and desires to do God's will.
Dedicate Yourself to God	Dedication to God requires that we stay in touch with God through prayer. Jesus suggested that we set aside some time to be alone with God and that prayer should lead us to know and do God's will. Our desire to be holy should make us persistent in prayer, and ultimately God will provide for all our needs.

Love Never Fails

When asked about the Greatest Commandment, Jesus responded that it was to love God and love your neighbor (see Matthew 22:34–40). Love is the teaching on which the Apostles also focus. In his First Letter to the Corinthians, Paul points out that "love never fails" (13:8). This is important to remember, because sometimes it *feels* like love fails. When you are kind to people who are mean to you, and they still treat you poorly, it might *feel* like love failed. If you served lunch for homeless people at a soup kitchen, and they complained about the meal, it might *feel* like love failed there too. Sometimes love can challenge people and make them uncomfortable. People do not always respond to love immediately.

Nonetheless, your job is to love, not to control or even judge the outcome. Acts of love are good. Period. But if it helps, look at the love you offer as a seed you have planted. There is no telling when it will sprout and grow. Like Jesus' disciples after the Crucifixion, we will certainly face times when our dedication to spreading God's love is challenged. We can rest assured knowing that the Resurrection is a sure sign that love never fails.

Doing What Jesus Did

Jesus "is 'the perfect man,' who invites us to become his disciples and follow him"[1] (*Catechism of the Catholic Church [CCC]*, number 520). His ultimate teaching is expressed in the Paschal Mystery. His sacrifice on the cross offered us an example of how we are supposed to take up our own cross and follow in his footsteps. His suffering for our salvation teaches that the pain and discomfort we might experience when we serve others can be redemptive. We learn through his Resurrection that when we leave this world, we can rely on God's promise of eternal life with him in Heaven.

Before he ascended into Heaven, Jesus told his disciples to "make disciples of all nations, baptizing them in the name of the Father, and of the Son, and of the holy Spirit, teaching them to observe all that I have commanded you" (Matthew 28:19–20). This is also our call to engage in the mission of evangelization. Fortified by the Holy Spirit, we are called to continue Jesus' mission to build up the Kingdom of God here on Earth. ✳

UNIT 5

© Quality Stock Arts / Shutterstock.com

Jesus taught us to love God and love our neighbor regardless of whether it is accepted or challenged by someone.

HMMMMM. . . Explain how love is at the heart of Jesus' teachings such as "Do not judge" and "Be humble."

Article 45
Mysticism: Seeking Union with God

Thomas Merton, a priest and a Trappist monk, wrote an autobiography called *Seven Storey Mountain*, detailing his journey to becoming Catholic.

In 1941, Thomas Merton entered the Abbey of Gethsemani, a Trappist monastery in Kentucky, and dedicated the rest of his life to prayer and work. He became a world-renowned author through his autobiography, *Seven Storey Mountain*, which detailed his journey from a painful childhood to becoming Catholic and eventually becoming a priest and monk. The Trappist monks were, in some ways, very isolated from the world, as they only left the monastery grounds on rare occasions. One day on a visit to see a doctor in the city, Merton had a deeply moving experience that he later described:

> In Louisville, at the corner of Fourth and Walnut, in the center of the shopping district, I was suddenly overwhelmed with the realization that I loved all those people, that they were mine and I theirs, that we could not be alien to one another even though we were total strangers. It was like waking from a dream of separateness. . . . The whole illusion of a separate holy existence is a dream. . . . They are not "they" but my own self. There are no strangers! (*Conjectures of a Guilty Bystander,* pages 156 and 158)

What happened to Thomas Merton on that street corner in Louisville could be described as a **mystical** experience. A mystical experience is typically a spiritual event that is neither apparent to the senses nor obvious to the intellect. Because of this, it is difficult to describe, even by the person who has experienced it. Still, this doesn't make a mystical experience any less real. In recalling the event, Merton lamented, "But it cannot be explained. There is no way of telling people that they are all walking around shining like the sun" (page 157).

UNIT 5

---

mystical ➤ Having a spiritual meaning or reality that is neither apparent to the senses nor obvious to the intelligence; the visible sign of the hidden reality of salvation.

THOMAS MERTON (1915~68)

Trappist monk, poet, social critic, and spiritual writer. Born in Prades, France. After education at Cambridge, and Columbia Univ., he entered Abbey of Gethsemani, Trappist, Ky., 1941; ordained as priest, 1949. His autobiography The Seven Storey Mountain (1948), earned international acclaim. He is buried in abbey cemetery.

Presented by Thomas Merton Center Foundation

On his way to see his doctor, Thomas Merton had a mystical experience while standing on a street corner in Louisville, Kentucky.

What Is Mysticism?

Mysticism refers to intense experiences of the presence and power of God, resulting in a deeper sense of union with God. Those who regularly experience such union are called mystics. Notice that the word *mysticism* is related to the word *mystery*. Even though these experiences are mysterious and ultimately unexplainable, they are no less powerful.

You may have seen a comedic movie or a TV show that portrays someone having an experience with God. Often sunlight breaks through the clouds and shines a beam of light directly on that person, then a choir of angels sings from the heavens. The person comes to a new realization about his life and he feels at one with God and the universe. The new insight brings comfort and understanding to the troubling situation he is experiencing, and a peaceful smile slowly appears on his face.

UNIT 5

mysticism ➤ An intense experience of the presence and power of God, resulting in a deeper sense of union with God; those who regularly experience such union are called mystics.

When it comes to depicting mystical experiences, this type of imagery can be misleading. It is difficult to visually portray mystical experiences because there is nothing to see. It is purely a spiritual event known only to the person experiencing it. How people encounter God is as different as the people themselves. These experiences can be overwhelming and glorious, but they can also be kind of scary and disturbing. For one person, the experience can offer immediate insights and understanding. For another, it might seemingly lead to a dark and empty path. In the end, these experiences will bring one to a closer union with God, humanity, and all of creation.

These personal encounters with God not only assist a person on their spiritual journey; they can also offer hope and guidance to others. We can look to many Catholic mystics from all times, places, and various life circumstances for inspiration. Some of these people were priests, monks, nuns, or theologians, and some were not. For a better understanding of the mystical experience, let's explore a few Catholic mystics and their unique experience of the presence of God.

Did you know that there is a saint who spent over thirty years of his life on top of a pillar? Saint Symeon the Stylite (c. 390–459) was an ascetic who lived in modern-day Syria. After trying other forms of self-denial, Symeon imposed this life on himself in part to get away from the numerous people who sought him out in the desert. His first pillar was only about 10 feet off the ground, but over the years his pillars grew to over 50 feet high. Symeon mainly devoted himself to prayer, but he did regularly meet with those who sought him for advice and spiritual direction. Bishops and emperors revered him and sought him out for his wisdom and piety. Symeon also inspired a number of other ascetics to become "pillar-hermits" like him.

UNIT 5

Saint Teresa of Ávila

Saint Teresa of Ávila (1515–1582) was born in Spain. She was an extroverted teenager, more interested in falling in love with boys and less interested in faith. Her mother died when she was fifteen, and she was sent to a convent where her love of God was restored. At age twenty, she entered a monastery of the Carmelite sisters, a religious order founded in the twelfth century.

The heart of the Carmelite **charism** is prayer. But because Teresa suffered from repeated, painful, physical illnesses, she often struggled with prayer. Then, in her forties, Teresa began to have numerous mystical experiences. She had visions of Christ in which she felt blessed by his physical presence. She also experienced a fiery angel who pierced her heart with a spear.

While her illnesses caused her terrible physical pain, they also brought her a spiritual bliss she had never experienced before. She once described the union of the soul with God "as if a tiny streamlet enters the sea, from which it will find no way of separating itself, or as if in a room there were two large windows through which the light streamed in: it enters in different places but it all becomes one" (*Interior Castle*, page 153).

© Classic Image / Alamy Stock Photo

Saint Teresa of Ávila (1515–1582) and Saint John of the Cross
(c. 1541–1591) were both Carmelites, good friends, and mystics.

Teresa is recognized as a Doctor of the Church (someone whose writings have had a major impact on the Church) for the spiritual path she outlined in her writings.

---

charism ➤ A special grace of the Holy Spirit given to an individual Christian or community, for the benefit and building up of the entire Church.

Brother Lawrence

Nicolas Herman (1614–1691) was born in eastern France to a poor peasant family. At the age of eighteen, he had a simple but powerful experience that stayed with him for the rest of his life. It was wintertime, and he saw a bare tree. As he considered that soon new leaves, flowers, and fruit would appear again, he became overwhelmed by the power and wisdom of God. Later, he joined a monastery where he was given the name Brother Lawrence of the Resurrection. He never attained any notable status within his religious order, as he often worked in the monastery kitchen or fixed shoes. However, he became known for his humility and wisdom, and many people reached out to him for advice.

After his death, the brothers found a collection of short sayings and spiritual advice he had written and published them along with some of his letters and a record of conversations in a book called *The Practice of the Presence of God*. In this book, Brother Lawrence teaches us that God can be found in the normal activities of daily life. Simply reminding yourself that you are in the presence of God, again and again, can have a profound effect on your life. He wrote: "God is present before you as you carry out your duties, and you know that He is at the depth and center of your soul, [so] why not stop from time to time, whatever you are doing . . . to offer your heart to Him, and to thank Him?" (page 126).

Saint John of the Cross

The mystical experiences of Saint John of the Cross (1542–1591) were gained through a grueling punishment he had received. Saint John was attempting to reform his religious order, the Carmelites, which he believed had strayed from its original routine and regimen. This led to a dramatic, sometimes even violent disagreement between different factions within the Carmelites order. As a result, John was charged with disobedience and imprisoned. He spent nearly nine months alone in a dark, dank prison cell and was subjected to regular beatings. During this time, he came to intimately know the sufferings of Christ. He began to understand the mystical connection between suffering and loss and the search for God.

UNIT 5

Later, in his poem "Dark Night of the Soul," Saint John uses the metaphor of a wife searching for her husband to represent the human soul in search of union with Christ. The darkness of night represents the unknowable dimension of God. Ironically, the night is better suited than the dawn to lead the wife to her beloved. The poem highlights the painful but necessary part of the spiritual journey when we let go of our limited ideas of who God is. In his book *The Ascent to Mount Carmel*, Saint John describes how the ascetical life can lead to a mystical union with God. **Asceticism** is the spiritual discipline in which a person leads a strict life of simplicity and self-denial.

Numerous other Catholic mystics have been privileged with the gift of mystical experience. Their encounters with God have inspired many of the faithful. Some of the more well-known mystics include Saint John Cassian, Saint Catherine of Siena, Meister Eckhart, Julian of Norwich, Saint Padre Pio, and Saint Faustina Kowalska.

You Can Be a Mystic!

You do not have to be a priest, monk, or nun to be a mystic. You also do not have to sit for weeks in deep contemplation on the top of a mountain. Mystical experiences with God are not reserved for any particular groups of people. The *Catechism of the Catholic Church* assures us that "God calls us all to this intimate union with him" (number 2014).

On your journey toward union with God, it is important to remember that mystical experiences cannot be programmed or produced by you. They are first and foremost gifts from God. Just as an open hand is far more likely to receive a gift than a clenched fist, you too have to be open to receiving God. One way to do this is through a dedicated life of prayer. Prayer is an essential exercise in preparing to receive God. "The wonder of prayer is revealed beside the well where we come seeking water: there, Christ comes to meet every human being" (*CCC*, number 2560). ✳

HMMMMM. . . Does the idea of having a mystical experience appeal to you? Why or why not?

asceticism ➤ The spiritual discipline in which a person leads a strict life of simplicity and self-denial.

Article 46
The Church's Sacramental Life Unites Us

The Church is certainly God's greatest gift to help us live a holy life. One of the most important ways it does this is through the **sacraments**. A sacrament is an outward, visible expression of God's invisible grace that plays an essential role in connecting us with God. You will learn more about the sacraments in another course, but for now, let's discover ways in which the sacraments lead us toward union with God and with one another.

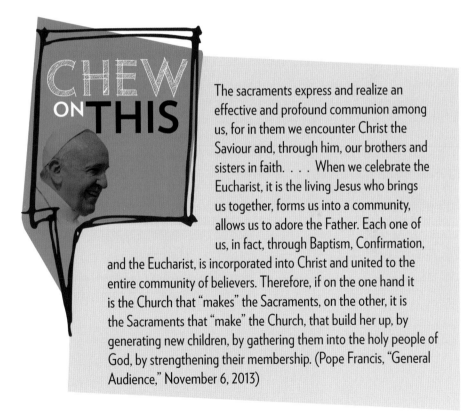

The sacraments express and realize an effective and profound communion among us, for in them we encounter Christ the Saviour and, through him, our brothers and sisters in faith. . . . When we celebrate the Eucharist, it is the living Jesus who brings us together, forms us into a community, allows us to adore the Father. Each one of us, in fact, through Baptism, Confirmation, and the Eucharist, is incorporated into Christ and united to the entire community of believers. Therefore, if on the one hand it is the Church that "makes" the Sacraments, on the other, it is the Sacraments that "make" the Church, that build her up, by generating new children, by gathering them into the holy people of God, by strengthening their membership. (Pope Francis, "General Audience," November 6, 2013)

---

sacrament ➤ An efficacious and visible sign of God's grace, instituted by Christ and entrusted to the Church, by which divine life is dispensed to us. The Seven Sacraments are Baptism, the Eucharist, Confirmation, Penance and Reconciliation, Anointing of the Sick, Matrimony, and Holy Orders.

The Seven Sacraments

Though all Seven Sacraments are avenues for God's grace, each has its own particular gifts to bestow. Consider this chart:

Sacrament	Type	Gift Bestowed
Baptism	Initiation	One becomes a member of the Church and a new creature in Christ.
Confirmation	Initiation	Through an outpouring of special Gifts of the Holy Spirit, Confirmation completes the grace of Baptism by confirming or "sealing" the baptized person's union with Christ and by equipping that person for active participation in the life of the Church.
Eucharist	Initiation	Based on a word for *thanksgiving*, it is the central Christian liturgical celebration, established by Jesus at the Last Supper. In the Eucharist, the sacrificial death and Resurrection of Jesus are both remembered and renewed.
Penance and Reconciliation	Healing	The liturgical celebration of God's forgiveness of sin, through which the sinner is reconciled with both God and the Church.
Anointing of the Sick	Healing	A gravely ill, aging, or dying person is anointed by the priest and prayed over by him and attending believers. One need not be dying to receive the Sacrament.
Matrimony	Service of Communion	A lifelong covenant, modeled on that between Christ and the Church, in which a baptized man and a baptized woman make an exclusive and permanent commitment to faithfully love each other and to cooperate in the procreation and education of children.
Holy Orders	Service of Communion	The sacrament by which baptized men are ordained for permanent ministry in the Church as bishops, priests, or deacons.

UNIT 5

In general, the Seven Sacraments offer us a path to holiness and union with God. They touch all the stages of our lives, from birth to death. Because they touch both our body and soul, they are the means by which our invisible God becomes both tangible and present. ✳

HMMMMM. . .   How do the sacraments restore and strengthen our relationship with God?

1. Why are human beings called to holiness?

2. What are some of God's gifts that can help us grow in holiness?

3. List some of Jesus' key teachings.

4. Why are mystical experiences difficult to explain?

5. What is mysticism?

6. What is a sacrament?

7. How do the Sacraments of Initiation bring about union among humanity and between humanity and God?

UNIT 5

Being Holy

1. How do each of the things depicted in this diagram help us become holy?

2. What can you do to move forward on your journey toward holiness?

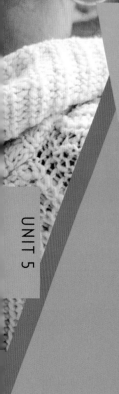

CHAPTER 12
Communing with God

HOW DOES PRAYER BRING US CLOSER TO GOD?

SNAPSHOT

Article 47 Page 339
What Is Prayer?
• Pre-read: James 5:13–18

Article 48 Page 343
Forms of Prayer
• Pre-read: Luke 11:9–13
• Pre-read: 2 Timothy 3:14–17

Article 49 Page 350
Expressions of Prayer

Article 50 Page 355
Scripture: A Source and Guide
• Pre-read: Matthew 6:5–15
• Pre-read: Luke 11:1–4

Article 47

What Is Prayer?

Think about one of your best friends. That friendship probably did not happen instantly. Friendships develop in stages over time. First you meet someone. Is that person now automatically your best friend? Rarely does this happen. You have to get to know the person over time. You find out if they like the same music as you. You learn whether or not they have a short temper. You might discover that you have the same hobbies. Or you might even be opposites, yet there is still some kind of connection between the two of you that you might not be able to explain.

If you made a list of ways to develop good friendships, what would it include? Here are some things many people would include on such a list:

- Make time for your friend.
- Talk about things that are important, such as hopes and dreams.
- Do things together or just hang out.
- Listen to your friend.
- Seek reconciliation and forgiveness when there has been a break in the relationship.

These and other facets of making and keeping strong friendships also apply to another important relationship: the personal relationship we develop with God through prayer.

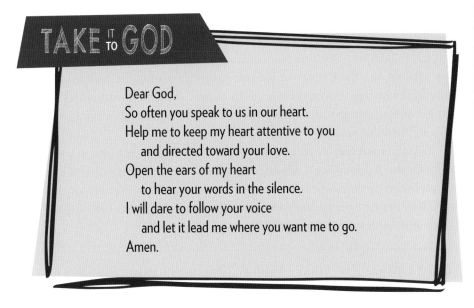

TAKE IT TO GOD

Dear God,
So often you speak to us in our heart.
Help me to keep my heart attentive to you
    and directed toward your love.
Open the ears of my heart
    to hear your words in the silence.
I will dare to follow your voice
    and let it lead me where you want me to go.
Amen.

UNIT 5

Prayer is lifting up one's mind and heart to God or requesting good things from him. It is communication with God in a relationship of love. Saint Teresa of Ávila (1515–1582) described prayer as a "sharing between friends; it means taking time frequently to be alone with [God] who we know loves us" (Peter Tyler, *Teresa of Ávila: Doctor of the Soul*). For Christians, prayer is an essential part of our lives that allows us to enter into a deeper relationship with Jesus Christ.

Listening to God is just as important in prayer as talking to God.

How to Pray

Let's acknowledge two things that are really important. First, Jesus is now physically present not in the ordinary manner, but rather in a sacramental manner, in the Eucharist. So, talking with God, whose presence is in these forms, is indeed very different from talking with a friend. Second, God is more than a friend; he's the Creator of the universe, worthy of our complete adoration and worship. Prayer, then, requires ways of communicating with God that are different from the ways we would use with a friend. (See article 48 on different forms of prayer.)

Talking is certainly an important part of conversation, but listening is just as significant, if not more so. If one person is asking and talking all of the time, it is no longer an authentic relationship. This is also true in our relationship with God. Prayer does not only consist of asking God for help; listening to God is how we learn what his will is for our lives.

prayer ▶ Lifting up of one's mind and heart to God or the requesting of good things from him. The six basic forms of prayer are blessing, adoration, praise, petition, thanksgiving, and intercession. In prayer, we communicate with God in a relationship of love.

UNIT 5

But how does one listen to God? People often say that God speaks to them in silence. When they say "silence," they don't always mean that there is no sound. Quiet places can help, but external physical silence is not necessary. It just means that *you* have to be silent inside. This can be very difficult to do—we might be able to close our mouths, but our minds ramble on long after our voices stop. Practice and persistence is the key here. Saint Mother Teresa of Kolkata (Calcutta) (1910–1997) said, "It is in the silence of the heart that God speaks. God is the friend of silence—we need to listen to God because it's not what we say, but what he says . . . that matters" (*Mother Teresa: A Simple Path*, page 7). In the following articles, you will discover some ways to listen to God's voice.

Overcoming Obstacles to Prayer

It might seem like prayer ought to be an easy thing to do, but developing a consistent and regular prayer life is often challenging. There are many obstacles that can get in the way of prayer. Here are a few:

- **Distractions.** We live in a noisy, fast-paced world; outside distractions are many. But sometimes, it's the inner distractions that can really make it challenging to enter into prayer. The mind is never quiet; it races with ideas, concerns, worries, etc. You become distracted and find yourself focusing on things other than prayer: "Oh no! I forgot to text Brianna!" "I wonder what I should wear to the dance?" "I have so much homework to finish!" As a result, you might feel frustrated and think you are the least holy person in the world. Do not scold yourself for this; it happens to even the most prayerful people. Even as he retreated to the desert, Jesus faced temptations (see Luke 4:1–13). As distractions come, respond just as you would to interruptions in conversation: notice them, let them go, and then turn your focus back to the Lord. Eventually, you will find it easier to hear God's voice in the midst of so many others.

- **Spiritual dryness.** This is similar to those times in even the best friendship when the spark seems to have faded. You seem to be growing apart; you no longer have as much fun when you are together. Remaining faithful to your friend and exploring new activities together are important if you do not want the friendship to die. In prayer, dryness is experienced as feeling separated from God. When this happens, the strength, joy, and peace of prayer run dry, and nothing seems to change the situation. If this is the case, keeping faith will see you through.

© Cookie Studio / Shutterstock.com

Many obstacles can get in the way of prayer, such as outside distractions. What gets in the way of your prayer life?

- **Expertise needed?** That you need to be some kind of prayer expert is a misconception about prayer. Anyone can pray, and you probably already do. For example, do you ever sit in your room listening to music, caught up in the rhythm and how the verses express your own thoughts and feelings about your relationship with God? When you are caught in a difficult situation, do you turn to God and ask for help? Have you ever looked at a beautiful sunset or a tiny infant and thought, "Way to go, God!" If you do any of these, you are already praying. Most people pray at some level, even if it is only occasional and unplanned.

It is important not to judge your prayer life based on obstacles you experience. Like any good habit, prayer can be difficult to get going, but once you develop the habit, it is easier to maintain. Prayer brings God's peace and joy into our lives, and once we have had a taste, we will want to keep coming back for more. ✳

HMMMMM. . . How is prayer like a conversation with a friend? How is it different?

UNIT 5

Article 48
Forms of Prayer

Friendships are based on many things, and you'd probably agree that different friends bring out different aspects of your personality. Although each friendship brings out a part of you, you probably aren't comfortable sharing everything about yourself with everyone.

The really wonderful thing about prayer is that it is the one relationship in which you can share all of yourself and know you are loved. God wants to be in relationship with you in every aspect of your life, in all your concerns, gifts, faults, and feelings. Different forms of prayer—blessing and adoration, petition, intercession, thanksgiving, and praise—are appropriate in different times and situations in your life, strengthening your relationship with God. In this article, we learn more about each of these prayer forms.

Prayers of Blessing and Adoration

"Bless you!" How often do you say or hear this when someone sneezes? When we say it, we are asking God to offer some sort of special care for a person who might be ill. This is one form of **blessing** prayer—asking God to care for a particular person, place, or activity. We ask God to bless people when they are sick or in danger. When people move into a new home, they sometimes ask a priest or deacon to come to the house to bless it. In a prayer before an athletic event, a team will request that God bless them and their activity. When we ask for God's blessing, it is because we are confident that God, in some way, will come through for us.

Another form of blessing is a two-step movement. First, God gives us a gift. Second, we respond with joy and gratitude. An example of a grateful response is the prayer "Blessed is he who comes in the name of the Lord. / Hosanna in the highest" that we pray at Mass (*Roman Missal*, page 532). "I will bless the LORD at all times; / his praise shall be always in my mouth" (Psalm 34:1) is a blessing from the Psalms. It is because God has bestowed blessings on us that "the human heart can in return bless the One who is the source of every blessing" (*CCC*, number 2626).

---

blessing ➤ A prayer asking God to care for a particular person, place, or activity.

Adoration is a prayer form closely related to blessing. Imagine parents adoring their first newborn child. They are amazed at this lovely creature and are overwhelmed with a deep reverence for God's gift of life. This example provides a sense of what adoration is: the prayerful acknowledgment that God is God and Creator of all that is. It's a recognition of the awesome power of God. Sometimes prayers of adoration are expressed in respectful silence because words won't do justice to express adoration. Sometimes they can take the form of joyful songs that speak of the grandeur of our Creator. Adoration can even come spontaneously as you look up into the infinite space of the night sky.

Looking up at the night sky in awe, acknowledging the vastness of space and the beauty of all that God has created, is a form of adoration.

Prayers of Petition

Petition is a prayer form in which you ask God for something you need. We offer petitions all of the time. Perhaps when your teacher hands you the exam, you silently say, "Please, Lord, help me pass this test!" In a difficult situation when the right thing to do is not clear, you may have asked, "Jesus, please show me the way." When you were in some type of trouble, your petition might have been as simple as "Help me, God."

---

adoration ➤ The prayerful acknowledgment that God is God and Creator of all that is.

petition ➤ A prayer form in which one asks God for help and forgiveness.

Petition is the probably the most familiar of all the prayer forms because it is the most spontaneous. It arises naturally from the depths of our hearts, where we are aware of our relationship with God, where we know we depend on our Creator. Jesus promised the disciples that God would respond favorably to their petitions:

> Ask and it will be given to you; seek and you will find; knock and the door will be opened to you. For everyone who asks, receives; and the one who seeks, finds; and to the one who knocks, the door will be opened. Which one of you would hand his son a stone when he asks for a loaf of bread, or a snake when he asks for a fish? (Matthew 7:7-10)

This passage might be confusing, especially if you have ever offered a petition to God that was not "answered." God does not necessarily respond to our prayers in the way we want. Even when we ask for things that are undeniably good, it does not mean that things will go exactly as we asked. We do not always understand God's ways, but we can be assured that he desires the best for all of us. We offer our petitions up to God knowing that he continually cares for us.

Of the different types of prayers—blessing and adoration, petition, thanksgiving, intercession, praise—which is your favorite and why?

© Dream Perfection / Shutterstock.com

UNIT 5

Prayers of Intercession

"Would you put in a good word for me?" In the ordinary circumstances of life, it is often helpful to have a friend recommend you for a role in student government, a position on a team, or a job at the grocery store. We do something similar in prayer when we offer petitions for others instead of for ourselves. **Intercession** is a prayer on behalf of another person or group. When we offer intercessions, we join our love with God's love in prayerful concern for someone else.

Intercessions not only aim to support the person who is the focus of our prayers but also help us and the entire Church. Offering prayers for others helps us avoid self-centeredness and allows us to broaden our circle of concern. We can pray for loved ones, acquaintances, people we see on the local news, and communities and events that are on the other side of the world. This helps us see and participate in the interconnectedness of our world.

But what about Jesus' command to pray for our enemies and those who persecute us (see Matthew 5:43–44)? These can be the hardest prayers to offer with a sincere heart. Stretching ourselves to pray for someone we are in conflict with or for someone who has hurt us can powerfully change our hearts; we may even find that they cease to be enemies.

Prayers of Thanksgiving

"Don't forget to say 'thank you.'" You have probably heard your parents tell you this a thousand times. Maybe they have also said things like, "Be thankful; there are people in other countries who don't have half of what you have." Even though it might feel like a guilt trip, your parents just want you to know that gratitude is important.

When we pray in **thanksgiving**, we grow in awareness that all we have comes to us as a gift from God's abundant love. It is a prayer of gratitude for the gift of life and the gifts of life. Think back to a joyful moment in your life. It could be a time when you won the big game and the team jumped all over one another. Or maybe it was when you and your friends were laughing so hard that your friend's drink shot out of his nose. It could have been a vacation spent having lots of fun with good friends or family. Remembering these times can be prayerful. It is moments like these that make us happy to be alive.

UNIT 5

intercession ➤ A prayer on behalf of another person or group.

thanksgiving ➤ A prayer of gratitude for the gift of life and the gifts of life. Thanksgiving characterizes the prayer of the Church which, in celebrating the Eucharist, offers perfect thanks to the Father through, with, and in Christ, in the unity of the Holy Spirit.

Offering personal prayers of thanksgiving is important, but prayers of thanksgiving are also an essential aspect of our communal prayer. *Eucharist* comes from a Greek word meaning "thanksgiving." When we gather to celebrate Mass, all the people gathered are expressing their thanks for the gifts God has given us, especially the gift of his Son as we recall the events of his Paschal Mystery.

Saint Paul tells us the real test of a grateful heart is to be thankful in all circumstances (see 1 Thessalonians 5:18). It makes sense to be thankful for the good we experience in life, but why would anyone be grateful for a painful situation? What Paul means here is that we can have confidence that God is loving us, even in the midst of difficulties, even when we can't see the purpose for our suffering, even when no end is in sight. Faith in the Paschal Mystery reminds us that good can come from even the worst circumstances. A prayerful attitude of thankfulness helps us remember this truth and can actually lead us to that goodness.

Take time in your prayers to offer thanks to God. Name the specific things for which you are grateful. Your prayers of gratitude do not have to come at any specific time either. When one of these moments of gratitude happen during the day, just stop long enough to silently say, "God, thank you for this moment. I'm having a great time!"

Scripture offers us a lot of prayer choices. The Bible can be very helpful, especially during those times when we can't seem to find the words to pray.

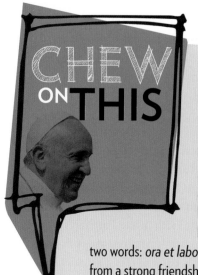

CHEW ON THIS

A prayer that does not lead you to practical action for your brother—the poor, the sick, those in need of help, a brother in difficulty—is a sterile and incomplete prayer. But, in the same way . . . when time is not set aside for dialogue with [God] in prayer, we risk serving ourselves and not God present in our needy brother and sister. St. Benedict sums up the kind of life that indicated for his monks in two words: *ora et labora*, pray and work. It is from contemplation, from a strong friendship with the Lord that the capacity is born in us to live and to bring the love of God, his mercy, his tenderness, to others. And also our work with brothers in need, our charitable works of mercy, lead us to the Lord, because it is in the needy brother and sister that we see the Lord himself. (Pope Francis, *Angelus*, July 21, 2013)

Prayers of Praise

Imagine an elderly couple having dinner at home on a quiet night. After a nice meal and conversation, they sit together in a comfortable silence and eat dessert. When they are done, the husband looks at his wife and says, "I love you so much." He did not say it for anything special she had done or for any specific quality she embodies. He simply expressed his deep and abiding love for her.

In a similar way, when we express our love and appreciation for God, we call it **praise**. Praise is a prayer of acknowledgment that God is God, giving him glory not for what he does, but simply because he *is*. We can find numerous examples of praise in the Book of Psalms (see for example Psalm 149:1,3,5–6).

---

praise ➤ A prayer of acknowledgment that God is God, giving him glory not for what he does, but simply because he is.

The traditional Christian prayer called the Glory Be gives glory and praise to each of the three Persons of the Trinity:

> Glory be to the Father, and to the Son, and to the Holy Spirit;
> as it was in the beginning, is now, and ever shall be,
> world without end.
> Amen.

Most notably, we can find other traditional prayers of praise throughout the Mass, the Church's ultimate prayer of praise. Near the beginning of the Mass, we often sing the Gloria, where we say:

> We praise you,
> we bless you,
> we adore you,
> we glorify you,
> we give you thanks for your great glory
> (*Roman Missal*, page 522)

The Gloria does not praise God for anything except for being who he is. In the Liturgy of the Eucharist, we say, "For the kingdom, the power and the glory are yours now and for ever" (*Roman Missal*, page 337). **Doxology** is a word for the Christian prayers of praise that are usually directed toward the Trinity. ✳

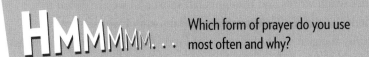

HMMMMM. . . Which form of prayer do you use most often and why?

UNIT 5

---

doxology ➤ Christian prayer that gives glory and praise to God, often calling upon the three Divine Persons of the Trinity.

Article 49
Expressions of Prayer

Along with the forms of prayer, Tradition teaches us about the three major expressions in a life of prayer: vocal prayer, meditation, and contemplation. Expressions of prayer are built upon an open and sincere heart as we deepen our relationship with God.

Vocal Prayer

When you want to get to know someone, you might strike up a conversation. At first, you usually focus on simple things: school, music, sports. As you get to know each other better, you begin to share about topics of greater importance: your beliefs, your worries, your dreams for the future. **Vocal prayer**, which uses words either spoken aloud or recited silently, is similar to this kind of sharing because it focuses on your conversation with God, which grows over time. Memorized prayer is the first way most people learn to pray vocally. Perhaps when you were a child, you memorized prayers such as the Lord's Prayer or the Hail Mary in your family or religious education classes.

Vocal prayer can also be expressed by using your own words to talk to God. Simply talking from the heart and asking God your questions or telling him what you are feeling can be a powerful way to pray.

Contemplation

There are times when words and thoughts fall short and we are called to a deeper experience of prayer. **Contemplation** is a form of wordless prayer in which one is fully focused on the presence of God. This type of prayer is often associated with mysticism, which we discussed in chapter 11. It requires no words, no rational thought, no imagination, no activity. Rather, it is arrived at by love. All you have to do is remember that you are in the holy presence of God and open your heart to him.

Try not to think of contemplation as something to "do." It is God's gift to you, and you can accept it only in humility. Think of it as climbing into God's lap, like a child rests in her mother's arms. It is simply dwelling and resting in God's love.

---

vocal prayer ➤ A prayer that is spoken aloud or silently, such as the Lord's Prayer.

contemplation ➤ A form of wordless prayer in which one is fully focused on the presence of God; sometimes defined as "resting in God."

UNIT 5

Meditation allows us to quietly ponder God's presence in our lives. Have you ever meditated? What was that experience like for you?

Meditation

When people hear the term **meditation**, the image of a person silently sitting cross-legged often comes to mind. This can be a good posture for meditating, but it is not the only way to meditate. Meditation is a prayer expression that uses a variety of methods and techniques. When we meditate, our mind, our imagination, our desires, and our emotions focus on a particular truth, biblical theme, or other spiritual matter. We use these faculties to ponder God's presence and activity in our lives and in the world, to discover the movements that stir our hearts, and to say, "God, I want you to be the focus of my life."

UNIT 5

meditation ➤ A form of prayer involving a variety of methods and techniques, in which one engages the mind, imagination, and emotions to focus on a particular truth, Scripture passage, or other spiritual matter.

There are many and varied methods of meditation. Catholics and other Christians often use Scripture as a springboard to meditation, as in *lectio divina*. *Lectio divina* means "sacred reading" and was introduced in a previous student book in this series, *Revelation and the Old Testament*. Liturgical texts of the day or season, holy writings, the Rosary, icons, Saint Ignatius's *Spiritual Exercises*, and all creation are other doors through which you can enter into meditation—a path to the love of and union with Christ.

CATHOLICS MAKING A DIFFERENCE

© Vladimir Korostyshevskiy / Shutterstock.com

Years before Saint Ignatius of Loyola (1491–1556) formed the Society of Jesus (the Jesuits), he was a Spanish soldier recovering from a serious battle wound. His leg was shattered when he was hit by a cannonball. As he made his slow and painful recovery, he would prayerfully use his imagination to place himself in the scenes of many of the Gospel accounts. He envisioned himself present at Jesus' birth and at his Crucifixion, imagining what all five of his senses would capture. After his recovery, he realized that these practices could be beneficial to others, so he wrote the *Spiritual Exercises*, designed to help Christians deepen their experience of God in their daily lives. Today, people all over the world use Saint Ignatius's methods to bring them closer to God.

---

lectio divina ➤ A Latin term meaning "divine reading." *Lectio divina* is a form of meditative prayer focused on a Scripture passage. It involves repetitive readings and periods of reflection and can serve as either private or communal prayer.

Ignatian Gospel Meditation

To help you understand better how meditation works as an expression of prayer, let's look at a prayer called Ignatian Gospel meditation. In his *Spiritual Exercises,* Saint Ignatius of Loyola (1491–1556) developed a method of prayer in which you use your imagination to immerse yourself in a story from the Bible. With this method, you visualize in your mind the details of a specific Gospel account. As the story comes to life in your imagination, you are brought to a personal and real encounter with Jesus in the present moment. Here is a suggested format to follow for Ignatian Gospel meditation:

1. Prepare yourself for prayer by assuming a comfortable position and allowing yourself to become silent. Select a passage from Sacred Scripture with which to pray. It is usually best to begin with an account from the Gospels, because the details and storyline are especially suited to this method. With some experience you will be able to spot other passages in Sacred Scripture that also work well.

2. Read the passage through once, paying special attention to the characters and the concrete details: What does this place look, feel, smell, and sound like? Who is there? What action unfolds? What words are spoken? You may wish to reread the passage several times to absorb all the details.

3. Next, enter the story in your imagination, just as if you were there. Employ your senses to allow the details of the story to come alive. Hear, taste, feel, smell, and see all you can. You can be yourself, or you can imagine yourself as one of the people in the story. Converse and interact with the people in the account. Allow the experience to unfold in your imagination without changing any of the essential details from the Bible passage.

4. As you experience the story, pay careful attention to all your reactions, all that you are feeling and thinking.

5. Respond to this experience in prayerful conversation with Jesus.

You might be thinking, "This is all just imagination. It isn't real!" Recall that Sacred Scripture is the living Word. When you pray with this method, you will have very real encounters with Jesus and will find that in the experience, God touches you. You can be comforted, healed, and challenged by the living Christ as you meet him through the doorway of your imagination. You may find meaning in the story that perhaps you overlooked before. ✳

UNIT 5

Dedicate 10–15 minutes one morning a week to sit with the Bible and allow God's Word to speak to you. Below is a list of suggested passages from Sacred Scripture that you can use—or choose your own!

- Luke 2:1–20 (the birth of Jesus)
- Matthew 4:18–22 (the call of the first disciples)
- Mark 8:27–30 (Peter recognizes that Jesus is the Messiah)
- John 13:1–17 (Jesus washes the disciples' feet)
- Matthew 26:57–75 (Jesus before the Sanhedrin, Peter's denial of Jesus)
- Mark 15:15–41 (the death of Jesus)
- Luke 24:13–32 (the Risen Jesus appears to two disciples)
- John 20:24–29 (Jesus appears to Thomas)

HMMMMM...

Try Ignatian meditation with a Gospel story that particularly appeals to you. What new insights did you gain during this experience?

Article 50

Scripture: A Source and Guide

Sacred Scripture gives us many role models who guide us and teach us about prayer through both their words and their actions. Moses had an intimate relationship with the Lord, and he would enter the meeting tent to listen to God (see Exodus 33:7–9). Hannah, who petitioned God unceasingly for a son, gave birth to the prophet and judge, Samuel (see 1 Samuel 1:19–20). King David would confess his sins and ask for God's forgiveness (see 2 Samuel 24:10). The widow and prophetess Anna persistently prayed for the coming of the Messiah (see Luke 2:36–38). Saint James provided guidance on the power of prayer for those suffering from illness and guilt (see James 5:13–16).

Most important, the supreme model of prayer was Jesus. He often withdrew alone to deserted places to be alone with God (see Luke 5:16). He taught the importance of prayer and humility (see Matthew 6:5–8). In his last words on the cross, Jesus quoted the Psalms in a prayer to his Father (see 27:46). Jesus both taught and lived a life of prayer.

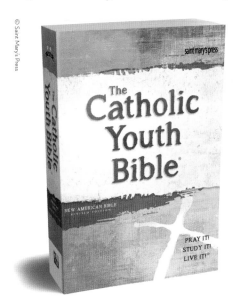

Many of our formal prayers, like the Lord's Prayer and the Hail Mary, are based on passages found in the Gospels.

Sacred Scripture is an importance source for prayer. Many of our formal prayers come directly from or are based on passages from the Bible. For example, the Hail Mary is based on the angel Gabriel's announcement to Mary that she will become the Mother of God, and the words of her cousin Elizabeth in the Gospel of Luke (see 1:28,42). Another traditional Marian prayer, the *Angelus*, is also based on these and other passages from Scripture. Psalms and canticles from the Bible are used in many of the Church's liturgical prayers. This is especially true when we celebrate Mass, as much of the Liturgy of the Eucharist is taken from Sacred Scripture. The Lord's Prayer is taken from both the Gospel of Matthew and the Gospel of Luke (see Matthew 6:9–13, Luke 11:2–4).

UNIT 5

The Lord's Prayer

It has been said that the Lord's Prayer "is truly the summary of the whole gospel"[1] (*CCC*, number 2761). It is an essential prayer for Christians because it was taught to us by the Son of God. In giving us this model for praying, Jesus teaches us about the value of prayer—so important it should be part of every Christian's life.

The Lord's Prayer is focused on "seven petitions, seven blessings. The first three, more theological, draw us toward the glory of the Father; the last four, as ways toward him, commend our wretchedness to his grace" (number 2803). The first three are listed below in red, and the last four are in blue. The prayer ends with **Amen**, a Hebrew word that means "so be it." It expresses agreement with what has just been said.

> Our Father, who art in Heaven,
>
> hallowed be your name,
>
> your kingdom come,
>
> your will be done, on earth as it is in Heaven.
>
> Give us this day our daily bread,
>
> and forgive us our trespasses as we forgive those who trespass against us.
>
> And lead us not into temptation
>
> but deliver us from evil.
>
> Amen.

Though it is certainly good and acceptable to say the Lord's Prayer privately on your own, it is essentially a communal prayer because it begins with "*Our* Father." Even when we do say it alone, we pray on behalf of the whole Church. It is the ultimate prayer of our community. We say it at every Eucharistic celebration, and it is an integral part in the rites of every Sacrament of Initiation: Baptism, Confirmation, and the Eucharist. ❋

Amen ➤ A Hebrew word that expresses agreement. The word adds authority when Jesus uses it to introduce a teaching, because he is teaching divine truth.

I DIDN'T KNOW THAT!

The Lord's Prayer probably sounded a little familiar to those who first heard it. There are a number of lines in it that are similar to a Jewish prayer called the Kaddish. The Kaddish is a prayer used in various Jewish liturgies, especially in their prayers mourning the death of a loved one. It begins with the lines: "Exalted and hallowed be His great Name. Throughout the world which He has created according to His Will. May He establish His kingship, bring forth His redemption" (www.chabad.org). Jesus' prayer was certainly different from the Kaddish, but it's clear that Jesus' love and trust is rooted in his faith in God.

© david leda / Shutterstock.com

It is a common practice in Judaism for mourners to place a stone on the gravestone when visiting a loved one's grave.

UNIT 5

HMMMMM. . .

How would you explain to a friend why Scripture is an important source for prayer?

1. What is prayer?

2. What obstacles can get in the way of prayer?

3. Why is listening to God as important as talking to God?

4. Briefly describe the different forms of prayer.

5. What is vocal prayer? Give an example.

6. What is Ignatian Gospel meditation?

7. Why is Sacred Scripture an important source for prayer?

8. Why is the Lord's Prayer such an important prayer for Christians?

UNIT 5

1. *Prayer II* is an abstract and surrealist painting by Angu Walters of Cameroon, depicting African Christians in prayer. What is your first reaction to this artwork? Why do you think you had this reaction?

2. Which area of the artwork is most important? Why?

3. Which form(s) of prayer does the painting depict? How do you know?

CHAPTER 13
Praying with the Triduum

HOW WILL CELEBRATING THE TRIDUUM HELP US UNDERSTAND THE PASCHAL MYSTERY?

SNAPSHOT

Article 51   Page 361
The Paschal Mystery and the Triduum
• Pre-read: Matthew 12:38–42

Article 52   Page 365
Holy Thursday
• Pre-read: Matthew 26:17–56
• Pre-read: Luke 22:7–46

Article 53   Page 371
Good Friday
• Pre-read: Mark 14:43–15:47
• Pre-read: John 18:1–19:42

Article 54   Page 375
Easter Vigil
• Pre-read: John 20:1–21:25

Article 51
The Paschal Mystery and the Triduum

Having been in school for most of your life now, you have become accustomed to the flow of the school year. There are many anticipated events and moments that bind and strengthen the school community during that nine-month period. At the beginning of school, there is the sadness of summer vacation ending, mixed with the enthusiasm of seeing friends again. As the year progresses, so does school work. But there is also the excitement of sporting events, dances, plays, and art competitions that add spark to the regular school schedule. Spring brings proms, spring break, and registering for next year's classes. The school year ends with exams; then summer comes and the process starts over.

Like the school year, the Church also commemorates significant events through an annual cycle called the **Liturgical Year.** In our liturgical celebrations on Sundays and holy days throughout the year, the Church recalls God's plan for our salvation, fulfilled in the Paschal Mystery. In this chapter, we will examine how the Church prays and worships together, specifically in the context of the Easter Triduum, the liturgical celebration of the events of the Paschal Mystery.

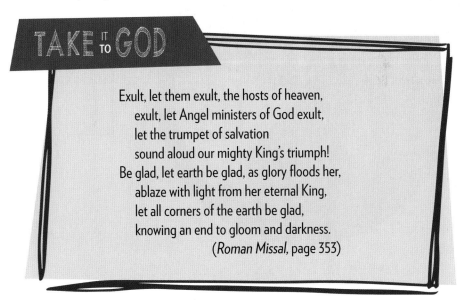

TAKE IT TO GOD

Exult, let them exult, the hosts of heaven,
   exult, let Angel ministers of God exult,
   let the trumpet of salvation
   sound aloud our mighty King's triumph!
Be glad, let earth be glad, as glory floods her,
   ablaze with light from her eternal King,
   let all corners of the earth be glad,
   knowing an end to gloom and darkness.
          (*Roman Missal,* page 353)

UNIT 5

Liturgical Year ➤ The Church's annual cycle of feasts and seasons that celebrates the events and mysteries of Christ's birth, life, death, Resurrection, and Ascension, and forms the context for the Church's worship.

The Liturgical Year

Liturgy is the Church's official, public, communal prayer. The term *liturgy* comes from the Greek word *leiturgia*, which means "work of the people." This has an important implication for us. The liturgy is not just the work of the priests, deacons, and other ministers leading the congregation. It is *our* responsibility too, and our participation is important and required! When it comes to celebrating the Church's most important liturgy, the Eucharist, consider how much of a role you play: singing the hymns, offering prayers and responses, offering the sign of peace, going to Communion, and so on. The Mass needs your conscious and active participation.

As indicated earlier, the Liturgical Year is the Church's annual cycle of feasts and seasons that celebrates the events and mysteries of Christ's birth, life, death, Resurrection, and Ascension, and forms the context for the Church's worship. It is divided up into several seasons that reveal and celebrate the life of Jesus Christ.

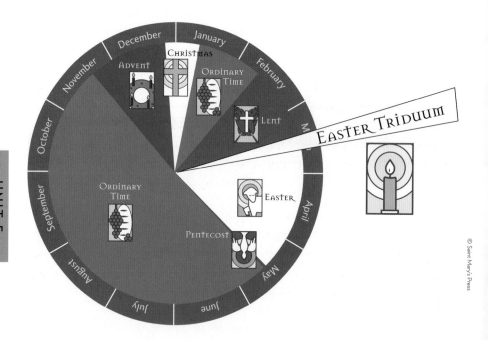

© Saint Mary's Press

UNIT 5

---

liturgy ➤ The Church's official, public, communal prayer. It is God's work, in which the People of God participate. The Church's most important liturgy is the Eucharist, or the Mass.

The liturgies during the Triduum are the most dramatic and unique in all of the Church's celebrations. Next time you have a chance, go to all of the liturgies starting from Holy Thursday through night prayer on Easter Sunday. Not only will you celebrate the most central elements on which our faith rests—the Paschal Mystery—you will also see the priest wash the feet of his parishioners. You will witness adults enter the faith after a year of preparation. You will hear the history of our faith told through a number of Scripture readings. You will participate in emotionally-charged rituals that are not done in any other time of year. Do not let the opportunity pass you by!

The Triduum

Triduum (pronounced TRI-doo-um) is a Latin word that means "three days." The Easter Triduum, then, encompasses the three holy days that are at the center of the Church's Liturgical Year. It begins with the Mass of the Lord's Supper on Holy Thursday night, continues with the Celebration of the Lord's Passion on Good Friday afternoon, reaches its climax with the Easter Vigil on Holy Saturday night, and ends with evening prayer on Easter Sunday. If you add up the number of those days, it might seem like "Easter Triduum" is a bad title. In actuality, the Triduum encompasses three 24–hour periods over four days. The liturgies of the Triduum form one continuous celebration, each liturgy picking up where the previous one leaves off. We follow Jesus' Paschal journey from the Last Supper, through his arrest, torture, and Crucifixion, and finally to the joy of the empty tomb and his Resurrection.

Triduum ➤ The three-day period of the Liturgical Year that begins with the Mass of the Lord's Supper on Holy Thursday and ends with evening prayer on Easter Sunday.

The Triduum liturgies are meant not to reenact these events but to help us to remember them and celebrate them in a sacramental way.

Liturgy	Corresponding Events in Jesus' Life
Holy Thursday	Jesus washes the feet of the Apostles and institutes the Eucharist at the Last Supper.
Good Friday	Jesus' Passion and Death
Easter Vigil and Easter Sunday	Jesus rises from the dead, and his followers discover the empty tomb.

The worshipping community has many opportunities to actively participate and to be drawn into the mystery and drama of the final days of Christ's earthly ministry. Prior to the Triduum, we seek to deepen our participation with his ministry through prayer, fasting, and acts of charity (almsgiving) throughout the forty days of Lent. On Passion (Palm) Sunday, we enter into Holy Week by recalling Christ's suffering and Crucifixion, his sacrifice to save us from sin and death. As Holy Week concludes, the liturgies of the Triduum are filled with special signs and symbolic actions that help us to meditate on the wonder and glory of God's saving plan, culminating with the Resurrection of Christ (Easter). By participating in these liturgies, we hope to make real our own sacrifice and service to others, as well as our own resurrection into God's eternal presence.

It is a shame that many Catholics miss these wonderful liturgies—a gift of the Holy Spirit to renew and strengthen our faith. Try to think of the Easter Triduum as a personal retreat, a time when you can meditate on Christ's suffering, death, and Resurrection and enter more deeply into these great mysteries. You may need to change your ordinary schedule and obligations so you can enter into sacred time and space for these three holy days. Even though you are only obligated to attend the Mass on Easter, make whatever sacrifices necessary to attend all the liturgies of the Easter Triduum too. This chapter will help you to make the most of this opportunity. ✳

UNIT 5

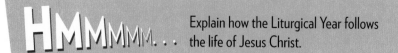

HMMMMM. . . Explain how the Liturgical Year follows the life of Jesus Christ.

Article 52
Holy Thursday

Sabrina and all of her family gathered in her grandmother's house because they knew that the end of her grandmother's life was near. Sabrina always called her *Abuelita*, or "little grandmother," but the only thing "little" about her was her physical stature. Aunts, uncles, cousins, close friends, church members, and neighbors all came by to pay their respects to this matriarch of the community. Most people stayed in her grandmother's bedroom, quietly recalling stories about her gentle strength, kindness, and generosity. Even though her grandmother had been unconscious for two straight days, Sabrina stayed right by her side the whole time she was there.

Right before she died, Sabrina's grandmother woke up and was completely conscious. Sabrina got excited for a minute but then recalled her mom saying that people sometimes gain consciousness briefly before they die. She listened intently to her grandmother talk about a dream where she saw her grandfather, who had died two years before. Abuelita told everybody how much she loved them; then she took hold of Sabrina's hand and looked straight into her eyes. Her grandmother said, "That's all that matters anyway—how much you love them." Then she closed her eyes and peacefully died. Sabrina was so glad to be there at that special time. Her Abuelita's last words would guide her for the rest of her life.

Though not quite the same as Sabrina and her Abuelita, on the day before Jesus died, he gathered his closest friends together and entrusted them with the mission that he started. We recall these events in the Mass of the Lord's Supper on **Holy Thursday**, the first day of the Easter Triduum.

Holy Thursday ➤ The beginning of the Easter Triduum, starting with the evening celebration of the Mass of the Lord's Supper.

UNIT 5

Mass of the Lord's Supper

The Holy Thursday liturgy, which begins the Triduum, recalls how Jesus instituted the Eucharist at the Last Supper.

The first day of the Triduum is filled with anticipation. It begins in the evening with the celebration of the Mass of the Lord's Supper. Here, we recall how Christ instituted the Eucharist at the Last Supper. In the opening prayer, we ask God to grant the fullness of life and love through the sacrifice of the Eucharist:

> O God, who have called us to participate
> in this most sacred Supper,
> in which your Only Begotten Son,
> when about to hand himself over to death,
> entrusted to the Church a sacrifice new for all eternity,
> the banquet of his love,
> grant, we pray,
> that we may draw from so great a mystery,
> the fullness of charity and of life.
> Through our Lord Jesus Christ your Son,
> who lives and reigns with you in the unity of the Holy Spirit,
> one God, for ever and ever.
> Amen.
>
> (*Roman Missal*, page 299)

UNIT 5

Liturgical Highlights

The Mass of the Lord's Supper is unlike your average Sunday Mass. There are a number of rituals that make this liturgy quite unique.

The Presentation of the Oils

At the beginning of the liturgy, members of the parish community process in with three containers of consecrated oil that were recently blessed by the bishop:

- **Oil of the Catechumens:** Blessed olive oil used to anoint those preparing for Baptism.
- **Oil of the Sick:** Used in the Sacrament of Anointing of the Sick to anoint those who are seriously ill or near death.
- **Sacred Chrism:** Perfumed oil used for anointing in the Sacraments of Baptism, Confirmation, and Holy Orders.

These oils represent your parish's connection to the diocese and the worldwide Church.

The Washing of the Feet

In John's Gospel, Jesus tells his disciples, "If I, therefore, the master and teacher, have washed your feet, you ought to wash one another's feet. I have given you a model to follow, so that as I have done for you, you should also do" (13:14–15). After the homily, the priest washes the feet of some of the parishioners in memory of what Jesus did. This also acts as a reminder of his commandment to serve one another.

On Holy Thursday, the priest washes the feet of the parishioners in memory of Jesus' commandment to serve one another.

UNIT 5

© JesusFernandez52 / iStockphoto.com

Oil of the Catechumens ➤ Blessed olive oil used to anoint those preparing for Baptism.

Oil of the Sick ➤ Blessed olive oil used in the Sacrament of Anointing of the Sick to anoint the forehead and hands of people who are seriously ill or near death.

Sacred Chrism ➤ Perfumed olive oil consecrated by the bishop that is used for anointing in the Sacraments of Baptism, Confirmation, and Holy Orders.

The Collection for the Poor

The call to serve that is symbolized in the washing of the feet is further carried out in the collection for the poor. Usually, the money collected at Mass goes toward parish expenses. But on Holy Thursday, many parishes take up separate collections for those in special need. Some parishes participate in Operation Rice Bowl, which is organized by Catholic Relief Services, and that collection is also taken up at this time. Some parishes also encourage people to bring bags of food for the hungry in their community. Encourage your family to participate in these separate collections. Remember that Christ calls us to sacrifice for the needs of others. Make your donation more than just pocket change; make it a sign of your commitment to sacrificial service of those most in need.

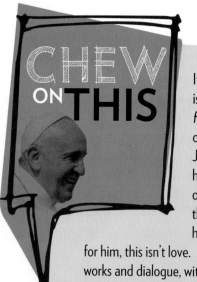

CHEW ON THIS

If love is respectful, if love is in deeds, if love is in communicating, *love makes sacrifices for others. . . . Love is service.* It is serving others. When after the washing of the feet Jesus explained the gesture to the Apostles, he taught that we are made to serve one another, and if I say that I love but I don't serve the other, don't help the other, don't enable him to go forward, don't sacrifice myself for him, this isn't love. . . . That history of God's love involved in works and dialogue, with respect, with forgiveness, with patience during so many centuries of history with his people, ends there—his Son on the Cross, the greatest service, which is giving one's life, sacrificing oneself, helping others. It's not easy to speak of love, it's not easy to experience love. (Pope Francis, "World Youth Day, Meeting with Children and Young People," June 21, 2015)

The Transfer of the Eucharist

Because the Liturgy of the Eucharist is not celebrated on Good Friday, enough bread is consecrated at the Holy Thursday liturgy for both Holy Thursday and Good Friday. At the end of Mass, the remaining consecrated hosts are taken to the chapel where they stay until the Good Friday liturgy. In some parishes, the congregation joins in a procession that follows the priest carrying the Body of Christ. Recall that after the Last Supper, the disciples walked with Jesus to the garden of Gethsemane to be with him and pray. In memory of Jesus' Agony in the Garden, many remain in the chapel to pray in the presence of Jesus.

The Paschal Fast

After the Mass of the Lord's Supper, the Paschal Fast begins. The Church calls for us to fast on Good Friday, meaning that we eat only one full meal, as well as two smaller meals that together are not equal to a full meal. Although those under age eighteen are not required to fast, you may fast with your parents' consent. Everyone over the age of fourteen is also required to abstain from eating meat. Fasting is not simply a trial you have to endure. As a spiritual undertaking, our hunger pains can become a prayerful reminder of what Jesus said after forty days of fasting: "One does not live by bread alone, / but by every word that comes forth from the mouth of God" (Matthew 4:4).

Anointed for Sacrifice

A few days before Jesus was arrested and crucified, his friend Lazarus (whom he raised from the dead) gave a dinner for him. One of his disciples—Mary, the sister of Martha and Lazarus—anointed Jesus' feet with costly oils. Pretending to care about the poor, Judas Iscariot objected to her action, claiming that the money for the oils could have been used to help those in need. Jesus still allowed her to do it because he saw it as a preparation for his sacrifice and death (see John 12:1–8). In the Holy Thursday liturgy, we take both of these steps: we process in with the oils that will anoint those being initiated into Christ's path of service and sacrifice, and we make sacrifices by giving to the collection for the poor. Through all of these rituals, we prepare ourselves for our own death and resurrection into new life.

UNIT 5

Entering into Sacred Time on Holy Thursday

The following suggestions are some ways you can more fully enter into the celebration of the Paschal Mystery, beginning with Holy Thursday:

- If you do nothing else, be sure to attend the Mass of the Lord's Supper. Find out what time it begins and mark it on your calendar. Encourage your family and friends to go too.
- Decide what you are going to contribute to the collection for the poor. Throughout Lent, you might save money you would ordinarily spend on food, clothes, music, or games, and then donate it to the collection. Talk with your family about making this a family effort.
- Before or after the Mass of the Lord's Supper, take time to read and reflect on the readings for the Mass: Exodus 12:1–14, Psalm 116, 1 Corinthians 11:23–26, and John 13:1–15. The Gospel reading is an excellent reading to use for Ignatian Gospel meditation.

One of the ways you can more fully participate in the celebration of the Paschal Mystery is by contributing to the special collection of the poor on Holy Thursday.

- Make a commitment to fast and free yourself of distractions for the next three days. Decide what you will allow yourself to eat, and then stick to your commitment. Commit to not watching television or using the computer or your phone for anything that is not absolutely necessary.
- Spend an hour with the Blessed Sacrament in the reservation chapel on Thursday night. Jesus' presence in his Body is real and substantial. You can talk with him in prayer, read Sacred Scripture (the Church recommends Psalm 22, the Book of Lamentations, and John chapters 14–17), pray the Rosary, or just sit quietly and peacefully in his presence. ✳

HMMMMM. . . How is the Holy Thursday ritual of washing the feet related to the collection for the poor?

Article 53
Good Friday

Good Friday is the second day of the Easter Triduum, on which we commemorate Jesus' Passion and death on the cross. Because it names the day on which Jesus Christ was crucified and died, the name "Good Friday" might seem like an oxymoron. An oxymoron is a figure of speech that seems to contradict itself (like "jumbo shrimp"). How could the execution of an innocent man, the Son of God, ever be described as "good"? True, Good Friday is a day on which we mourn the sins that sent Jesus to the cross, but it is much more than that. By calling that Friday "Good," we are not describing the actions of those who killed Jesus. On the contrary, "Good" is what we call the person who was crucified. "Good" describes the work of salvation that Christ accomplished on that day. Because of the twofold nature of this day, the liturgy reflects both the sorrowful and hopeful nature of this celebration.

The crown of thorns and the nails in Jesus' hands and feet are a stark reminder of his intense suffering for our salvation.

At the beginning of the Good Friday liturgy, the altar is bare, the fonts have been emptied of holy water, there are no candles, and the decorations have been removed. The atmosphere is stark as the priest leads the community in prayer:

Remember your mercies, O Lord,
and with your eternal protection sanctify your servants,
for whom Christ your Son,
by the shedding of his Blood,
established the Paschal Mystery.
Who lives and reigns for ever and ever.
Amen.

(*Roman Missal*, page 315)

UNIT 5

Good Friday ➤ The second day of the Easter Triduum, on which we commemorate Jesus' Passion and death on the cross.

CATHOLICS MAKING A DIFFERENCE

In 1584, the English Parliament passed an act that forced all Roman Catholic priests to leave the country or be punished for high treason. Those who knew of clergy's presence and did not report it could face execution. Margaret Clitherow (1556-1586) was a wife and mother in York, England, who had converted to Catholicism despite it being outlawed. She was jailed several times for not attending the established Church of England, and gave birth to her third child in prison. Margaret risked her life by hiding fugitive priests in her home. When this was discovered, she was arrested and executed by being crushed to death. She was martyred on Good Friday of 1586. Nicknamed "the Pearl of York," Saint Margaret Clitherow was canonized in 1970 by Pope Paul VI.

Liturgical Highlights

The Good Friday liturgy is called the Celebration of the Lord's Passion. It begins in silence, picking up where the Holy Thursday liturgy ended. It is usually held in the afternoon near the time of Christ's death (3:00 p.m.).

The Liturgy of the Word

The first reading is Isaiah 52:13–53:12, one of Isaiah's Songs of the Suffering Servant. It recounts the prophecy of the suffering servant (see Isaiah 53:5,12, *Lectionary for Mass*). The second reading comes from the Book of Hebrews and is a reflection on the meaning of Christ's suffering and death (4:14–16, 5:7–9). The Gospel reading is the account of the Passion in the Gospel of John (18:1–19:42). It is a long reading that covers Jesus' arrest, trial, scourging, and Crucifixion. Parishes often split up the reading duties, giving some parts for the congregation to read.

The Intercessions

The general intercessions on Good Friday are a little different than at the average Mass. They are longer, and instead of being read, they are usually sung. We pray for the Church, the Pope, the clergy and laity, those preparing for Baptism, the unity of Christians, the Jewish people, those who do not believe in Christ, those who do not believe in God, leaders in the world, and those in special need.

© Marmaduke St. John / Alamy Stock Photo

The Veneration of the Cross

After the general intercessions, the priest brings up a cross in a solemn procession. He lifts up the cross three times and sings, "Behold the wood of the Cross, / on which hung the salvation of the world." The people respond, "Come, let us adore" (*Roman Missal*, page 330). The congregation is then invited to come forward and **venerate** the cross, in which we offer some sign of our respect and devotion for Christ's sacrifice. Some people **genuflect** or kneel before the cross, while others kiss or touch it. Cultures and communities have different traditions and ways they show their reverence. While the actions vary, they all come from a heart of gratitude, love, and devotion to Christ.

Communion

The Liturgy of the Eucharist is not celebrated on Good Friday. The congregation prays the Lord's Prayer together and then receives the Eucharist that was consecrated on Holy Thursday. After receiving Communion, the priest offers a

On Good Friday, the cross is venerated: "Behold the wood of the Cross, on which hung the salvation of the world" (*Roman Missal*, page 329).

blessing, and the liturgy ends with everyone leaving in silence. Leaving a silent church brings a sense of incompleteness as well as anticipation for the events celebrated in the Easter Vigil the next night.

UNIT 5

Entering into Sacred Time on Good Friday

The following suggestions are some ways you can more fully enter into the celebration of the Paschal Mystery, continuing into Good Friday:

* Make a plan to attend the Celebration of the Lord's Passion. Find out what time it begins and mark it on your calendar. Encourage your family and friends to go too.

venerate ➤ To show respect and devotion to someone or something.

genuflect ➤ To kneel on one knee as a sign of reverence for the Blessed Sacrament.

- Fasting on this day is especially important, as a way to maintain your focus on Christ's sacrifice and to anticipate the celebration of the Resurrection. The Church requires us to eat two small meals that don't equal one full meal this day (for those between ages eighteen and fifty-nine) and to abstain from eating meat (required of all those over age fourteen). Decide what is possible for you based on your health needs, but make your fast a true sacrifice.

- Some parishes also celebrate the **Stations of the Cross** on Good Friday. In some places, this celebration is conducted very publicly. Sometimes it is even held outdoors, and participants stop at places that symbolize where Christ still suffers in the lives of people today. Find out if the Stations of the Cross will be celebrated in your area and try to attend this very moving remembrance of Christ's Passion.

- In the general intercessions on Good Friday, we pray for the spiritual and physical needs of the whole world. Take some time to pray for the needs of people who are close to you and for those who are in your community. Think especially of those people who are sick, hurting, or without work or who don't know Christ. ✳

© HolyLandPhotos.org

In the Old City of Jerusalem, Christian pilgrims walk the "Via Dolorosa" or "Way of Sorrows," the possible route that Jesus took on his way to his Crucifixion.

HMMMMM...

How does the absence of the Liturgy of the Eucharist reflect the events of Good Friday?

Stations of the Cross ➤ A devotion for prayer and reflection, popular during Lent, that retraces the events of Jesus' Passion and death in fourteen "stations," or events. Most Catholic churches have artistic representations of the fourteen Stations of the Cross. Also called the Way of the Cross.

Article 54
Easter Vigil

If you have ever seen a movie trilogy, you know that the second film usually ends with a cliffhanger of some sort. There might be someone held in captivity, or some ominous situation that poses a threat to a great number of people. In some way, there is unfinished business that needs to be resolved in the final movie.

Good Friday is kind of like that. We do not celebrate a full Liturgy of the Eucharist on Good Friday. In a simple ritual, we receive the Body of Christ that was consecrated on Holy Thursday. Then the liturgy ends, and the people walk out of the church in silence. But we know there is more to come—the Easter Vigil celebration on Holy Saturday.

Beginning with the Easter Vigil, the vestments, banners, and other decor in the church are white, symbolizing light, joy, triumph, and glory.

Liturgical Highlights

Easter begins on Holy Saturday with the celebration of the Easter Vigil. Many consider this liturgy to be the highlight of the Liturgical Year. The Easter Vigil celebrates the light of the Risen Christ coming into the world. It is also the time when adults and older children are received into the Church through the Sacraments of Christian Initiation. The word *vigil* is the term we give to liturgies held on the evening before the feast day. *Vigil* means "to be awake, to be watchful." The Easter Vigil begins sometime after dark on Holy Saturday and must conclude before daybreak on Sunday.

UNIT 5

The Service of Light

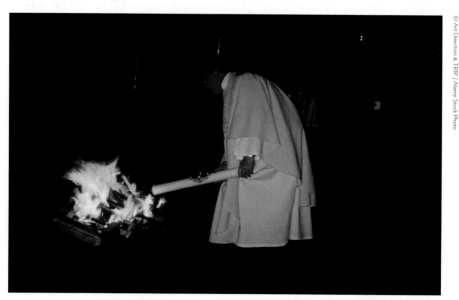

The Easter candle, also called the Paschal candle, symbolizes the light of the Risen Christ who "was the light of the human race; / the light shines in the darkness, / and the darkness has not overcome it" (John 1:4–5).

The Easter Vigil begins in a dramatic darkness, outside the church if possible. A fire is lit, and the priest begins the liturgy:

On this most sacred night,
in which our Lord Jesus Christ
passed over from death to life,
the Church calls upon her sons and daughters,
scattered throughout the world,
to come together to watch and pray.
If we keep the memorial
of the Lord's paschal solemnity in this way,
listening to his word and celebrating his mysteries,
then we shall have the sure hope
of sharing his triumph over death
and living with him in God.

(*Roman Missal*, page 344)

The priest blesses the fire and then lights the Easter candle, or Paschal candle—a large candle symbolizing the light of the Risen Christ. The members of the congregation process by, light their individual candles from the Easter candle flame as they do so, and enter the darkened church. The darkness is slowly overcome by the glow of candles as everyone enters the church. The deacon then sings the Easter Proclamation, or the Exsultet, in which he joyfully pronounces:

> O truly necessary sin of Adam,
> destroyed completely by the Death of Christ!
>
> O happy fault
> that earned so great, so glorious a Redeemer!"
> (*Roman Missal,* page 355)

In the absence of a deacon, it may be sung by the priest or a lay cantor.

Easter eggs did not originally come from the Easter Bunny! The egg has been a natural symbol for new life in various cultures outside of Christianity for centuries. For Christians, there are numerous and varying traditions surrounding the Easter egg. Some early Christians would dye their eggs red in memory of the Crucifixion. In the Middle Ages, the Lenten restrictions on food were stricter than they are today. Besides meat, Christians were also required to abstain from all dairy products, including eggs, for the entire Lenten season. The chickens did not stop producing eggs, though! In order to preserve as many as possible, they would hard-boil the eggs and use them as treats when Easter arrived.

UNIT 5

The Liturgy of the Word

The Liturgy of the Word is an inspiring and unique experience. There are three to seven readings from the Old Testament and two from the New Testament that offer us an overview of salvation history. It is kind of like hearing your family's history. Beginning with the Creation of the world, the scriptural journey then visits Abraham and Isaac, Moses and the Israelites as they escape from slavery through the Red Sea, and the prophets Isaiah, Baruch, and Ezekiel. Next, it travels to the New Testament to hear Saint Paul's proclamation of Jesus' Resurrection and Matthew's account of Jesus' disciples at the empty tomb.

The Celebration of Baptism and Confirmation

After the homily, the **catechumens**—those who have been preparing to join the Body of Christ—receive the first two Sacraments of Initiation: Baptism and Confirmation. First, the **Litany of the Saints** is sung. This is a prayer in the form of a chant or a responsive petition in which the great saints of the Church are asked to pray for us. Then the priest or bishop baptizes the catechumens. Those who were already baptized into another Christian denomination are not baptized again, but make a profession of faith to be received into full communion with the Catholic Church. Finally, both of these groups receive the Sacrament of Confirmation.

© Art Directors & TRIP / Alamy Stock Photo

Catechumens, people age seven and older who have been preparing to join the Catholic Church, are received into full communion with the Church through the Sacraments of Baptism, Confirmation, and the Eucharist.

---

catechumen ➤ An unbaptized person who is preparing for full initiation into the Catholic Church by engaging in formal study, reflection, and prayer.

Litany of the Saints ➤ A prayer in the form of a chant or a responsive petition in which the great saints of the Church are asked to pray for us.

Liturgy of the Eucharist

With the fasting of Good Friday behind us, we participate in the Eucharistic feast by consuming the Body and Blood of Christ, our spiritual food and drink. This is also the First Eucharist for those who were just baptized or were just received into the Church. It is a time to be happy and rejoice! Christ has conquered death and leads us toward eternal life with God. Jesus is the bridge that repairs the separation caused by sin.

Entering into Sacred Time for the Easter Season

The following suggestions are ways you can more fully enter into the celebration of the Paschal Mystery, culminating in the Easter Vigil and Easter Sunday:

- Most parishes have a reception after the Easter Vigil to continue the celebration and to allow you to meet the newly baptized and those received into the Church. Stick around for a few minutes and introduce yourself to these new members of your community.
- Celebrate Easter with your family and friends. If you hunt Easter eggs, remember that eggs, chicks, and bunnies are associated with Easter because they are signs of spring and of new life. Candy can be a sign of the sweetness of God's gift of salvation. A big Easter dinner is a sign that you are breaking the fasting of Lent and the Triduum.
- Your celebration does not have to end with the Easter Vigil. Consider attending Mass again on Easter Sunday, when a different set of readings will be proclaimed. Or attend evening prayer on Easter Sunday, if your parish celebrates that liturgy.
- It is always a good idea to take a few minutes on Easter Sunday for some praise and thanksgiving prayer. You might want to listen to or sing favorite Christian songs or hymns. You might also meditate on passages from Sacred Scripture, especially the Resurrection accounts in the Gospel of John (see chapters 20–21), Paul's reflection on resurrection (see 1 Corinthians, chapter 15), and the reflection on following Jesus found in the Letter to the Hebrews (see chapter 12). ✳

UNIT 5

HMMMMMM. . . What do the symbols of darkness and light in the Easter Vigil liturgy point to?

1. What is a liturgy?

2. What are the six seasons of the Liturgical Year?

3. What is the Triduum? What does the word mean?

4. What is celebrated at the Holy Thursday liturgy?

5. What are the unique rituals of the Holy Thursday liturgy?

6. What does Good Friday commemorate?

7. What is the veneration of the cross?

8. What is the Easter Vigil?

9. Describe the use of darkness and light in the Easter Vigil.

10. Describe the Liturgy of the Word in the Easter Vigil.

UNIT 5

Celebrating the Triduum

UNIT 5

1. How do these images from the Triduum liturgies reflect the life of Christ?

2. Which of these symbolic actions feels the most powerful to you? Why?

UNIT 5 HIGHLIGHTS

CHAPTER 11 The Path to Holiness

HOLINESS

Service and Sacrifice

LOVE

Be Humble

Dedicate Yourself to God

Ju/ge

Don' Money You A

Aids to Holiness

Church

Intellect

Free Will

Self-Reflection

Grace

Seeking Union with God

Prayer/Mysticism

An intense experience of the presence and power of God, resulting in a deeper sense of union with God; those who regularly experience such union are called mystics.

The Sacraments

Sacraments connect us with God.

BAPTISM   EUCHARIST   CONFIRMATION

Initiation
Baptism, the Eucharist, Confirmation

UNIT 5

MATRIMONY   HOLY ORDERS

In Service of Communion
Marriage, Holy Orders

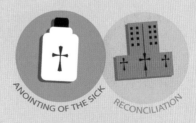

ANOINTING OF THE SICK   RECONCILIATION

Healing
Anointing of the Sick,
Penance and Reconciliation

CHAPTER 12   Communing with God

The Forms and Expressions of Prayer

Prayer
The lifting up of one's mind and heart to God
or the requesting of good things from him

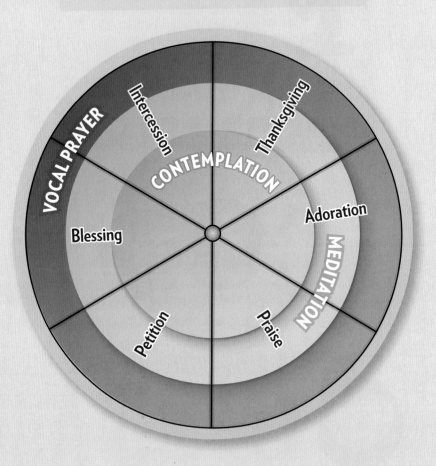

CHAPTER 13   Praying with the Triduum

Holy Days	TRIDUUM		
	Holy Thursday	Good Friday	Easter Vigil

Events in Jesus' Life	TRIDUUM		
	The Last Supper / Jesus Washes Apostles' Feet	Jesus' Passion and Death	Jesus' Resurrection

Liturgical Celebrations	TRIDUUM		
	Mass of the Lord's Supper	Celebration of the Lord's Passion	Easter Vigil / Sacraments of Christian Initiation

• Washing of the feet	• Reading of the Passion from the Gospel of John	• Service of Light
• Collection for the poor	• The General Intercessions	• Nine Scripture readings
• Reservation of the Eucharist for Adoration	• Veneration of the cross	• Celebration of Baptism and Confirmation

UNIT 5
BRING IT HOME

HOW DOES PRAYER BRING US CLOSER TO GOD AND ONE ANOTHER?

FOCUS QUESTIONS

CHAPTER 11   What does it mean to be holy?

CHAPTER 12   How does prayer bring us closer to God?

CHAPTER 13   How will celebrating the Triduum help us understand the Paschal Mystery?

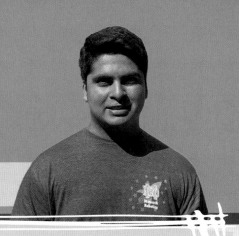

When I was younger, I thought prayer was only about asking God for help. I guess when all you are doing is asking for things, and many times not getting what you want or thinking you haven't been answered, it is kind of boring. But this unit helped me to see that we can actually connect with one another through prayer. When we pray together, we are all in communion with one another. We bond by sharing the same intentions or thoughts through prayer, especially at Mass.

UNIT 5

REFLECT

Take some time to read and reflect on the unit and chapter focus questions listed on the facing page.

- What question or section did you identify most closely with?

- What did you find within the unit that was comforting or challenging?

APPENDIX
Challenge Questions

The content of this course will raise some important questions for those who think seriously about their faith. This is especially true today when many people are asking hard questions about religious beliefs. We are not afraid of these hard questions because an honest search for answers will deepen our faith and understanding of what God has revealed. Here are some common questions with some key points to help answer them. The references to paragraphs in the *Catechism of the Catholic Church (CCC)* are for further reading if you want to explore these questions more deeply.

QUESTION 1. Why would God the Father allow his Son, Jesus, to suffer and die the way he did?
(*CCC*, numbers 599–609)

When confronted with this type of question, you might find it helpful to remember that God loves all human beings and wants us to live eternally with him in Heaven. Jesus' Passion reveals the depth of God's love in helping all people to not be overcome by the magnitude of evil, sin, and death. Jesus' suffering and death also show the gravity and seriousness of sin, as such a great sacrifice was fitting to overcome the power of sin.

No action on God's part *required* Jesus' redeeming death. It is actually Original Sin that necessitated Jesus' sacrifice. Original Sin is a result of the sin of Adam and Eve. Because of their sin, all human beings are born with a wounded human nature due to the absence of Christ's grace. Therefore, we cannot live eternally with God unless we are redeemed (*CCC*, numbers 402–406).

The Father did not force the Son's death; Jesus Christ freely accepted the sacrifice of his Passion and death. As Christ was without sin, he was a completely innocent victim, yet he took upon himself all the sins and injustices of humanity to overcome them. As true God and true man, he was the perfect mediator to bring us back to full communion with the Holy Trinity. So, God the Father allowed his Son, Jesus, to suffer and die because Jesus' sacrifice destroyed the power of sin and restored us to friendship with God. Christ's suffering and death brought about our redemption. Indeed, he paid the price for our sinfulness with his willing sacrifice.

QUESTION 2. Why are followers of Jesus Christ sometimes so willing to make sacrifices and to accept pain and suffering, especially in witness to Christ and their faith?

Christians are willing to make sacrifices and undergo suffering patiently for a number of reasons. Here are some examples:

- Christians willingly undergo sacrifice and suffering because they are following the example of Jesus Christ, who through his suffering and death gained salvation for us (*CCC*, number 1505). Sacrifice is simply suffering that we freely accept. You may have heard the saying "No pain, no gain." In one way, this reflects a deep spiritual truth: God can and will transform our freely offered suffering and sacrifice into healing and new life.
- Followers of Jesus Christ know that suffering is never in vain, because it can help us move toward Heaven and eternal life. In our suffering, we can help make up to some degree for the hurt and harm we cause by our sin.
- Jesus Christ also predicted that people would suffer for their faith and promised that he would be with them in their suffering. Knowing this, believers try to accept suffering patiently, to trust in God, and to pray for his grace to sustain them. So, we rely on the Holy Spirit's gift of fortitude to grow in the virtue of fortitude (*CCC*, numbers 1808, 1831). Fortitude, or courage, is a key to finding hope and strength in times of suffering. Fortitude is one of the seven Gifts of the Holy Spirit that we receive through Baptism and that are strengthened at our Confirmation. You have only to ask for fortitude when you need it, so ask often!
- The suffering, death, Resurrection, and Ascension of Jesus teaches us to look beyond the sufferings of this world to the promise of eternal life with God in Heaven (*CCC*, number 1521). We know the Paschal Mystery ends with Christ's Resurrection and Ascension into Heaven. The Paschal Mystery is God's promise that we too shall experience resurrection and eternal life with God in Heaven if we are faithful in following Christ. The joy and peace of Heaven will be ours for all eternity.
- In order for us to experience the joy and peace of Heaven, Christ strengthens us to undergo suffering and thereby become more like himself. Our suffering, when united with his own, can become a means of purification and of salvation for us and for others (*CCC*, numbers 618, 1505).

This isn't meant in any way to minimize the sacrifice and suffering that many people experience. In fact, we have a responsibility to help wherever and however we can to lessen and eliminate suffering.

QUESTION 3. Isn't making sacrifices and putting up with suffering a sign of weakness?

(*CCC*, numbers 1808, 1831)

By this point in your life, you probably know firsthand that our most common reaction to suffering is to try to avoid it. In fact, many people would consider the willingness to sacrifice time, money, and worldly success to be foolish, a sign of personal weakness. Yet the example of Jesus shows us that the willingness to accept suffering takes a great deal of courage and strength. It takes grace and personal holiness to live as Jesus Christ taught us. Jesus shows us through the whole Paschal Mystery (his suffering, death, Resurrection, and Ascension) that giving of ourselves is the path to eternal life and happiness (*CCC*, numbers 571–655). We see this most clearly in Jesus' last days. He could have avoided his torturous death if he had chosen to. He prayed to his Father to allow him to avoid this suffering if possible. But in the end, Jesus accepted the necessity of doing his Father's will with courage and strength. All four Gospels testify to Jesus' struggle and his ultimate acceptance of the Father's will.

Jesus' Passion and death are not the only times he demonstrated the strength and courage required for sacrificial love. He teaches us both in word and by example to refrain from revenge and to forgive those who hurt or sin against us (*CCC*, numbers 2842–2845). He taught it in his Parable of the Prodigal Son and his Parable of the Lost Sheep. He taught it in his sayings about forgiveness and love of enemies. He demonstrated it by embracing a life of poverty and simplicity. He asked others to exercise moral courage by challenging wealthy and powerful people to give away their wealth and serve those in need.

Deep down, every human heart knows that it is only through courage and sacrifice that we can truly achieve something worthwhile. Therefore, suffering is necessary to develop our maturity in Christ and to love our neighbor as Christ loves him (see Colossians 1:24; *CCC*, numbers 1808, 1831). Some people make tremendous sacrifices to achieve personal fame and fortune. But when they have achieved their success, they still feel like they are missing something. And they are! We must sacrifice for the right thing: to build the Kingdom of God. Only then will we experience the love and joy that come from letting Christ live in our heart, from participating in his mission to bring God's love to others.

QUESTION 4. In the end, isn't it really only the final result that matters?

Every moral choice that a person makes has an effect on that person and on society (*CCC*, numbers 1749–1756). So it is not only the final result of our actions that matters. For instance, if we choose to buy products that are made by manufacturers who pay their employees substandard wages and force them to work in unsafe conditions, we are a very real part of the process that demeans the employees' dignity. We often purchase goods based on their low prices, not realizing that the price point is low because the people manufacturing the goods are not paid much at all.

Even if something good comes from our actions, in no way does the good outcome justify an evil means (*CCC*, number 1753). For example, testing new medicines is crucial to their approval as safe for humans. However, performing medical or scientific experiments on human beings against their will or for immoral purposes, such as was done by the Nazis or Tuskegee studies, is not justifiable treating all of God's creation with dignity and respect is our vocation. One must never do evil just so that good may come of it (*CCC*, number 1789).

GLOSSARY

A

adoration ➤ The prayerful acknowledgment that God is God and Creator of all that is.

Amen ➤ A Hebrew word that expresses agreement. The word adds authority when Jesus uses it to introduce a teaching, because he is teaching Divine Truth.

angel ➤ Based on a Greek word meaning "messenger," a personal and immortal creature with intelligence and free will who constantly glorifies God and serves as a messenger of God to humans to carry out God's saving plan.

Ascension ➤ The "going up" into Heaven of the Risen Christ forty days after his Resurrection.

asceticism ➤ The spiritual discipline in which a person leads a strict life of simplicity and self-denial.

Assumption of Mary ➤ The dogma that recognizes that the body of the Blessed Virgin Mary was taken directly to Heaven after her life on earth had ended.

atonement ➤ Reparation for wrongdoing or sin and reconciliation with God, accomplished for mankind by Christ's sacrifice.

B

blasphemy ➤ Speaking, acting, or thinking about God in a way that is irreverent, mocking, or offensive. It is a sin against the Second Commandment.

blessing ➤ A prayer asking God to care for a particular person, place, or activity.

Body of Christ ➤ A term that when capitalized designates Jesus' Body in the Eucharist, or the entire Church, which is also referred to as the Mystical Body of Christ.

C

Cardinal Virtues ➤ Based on the Latin word *cardo*, meaning "pivot," four virtues that are viewed as pivotal or essential for full Christian living: prudence, justice, fortitude, and temperance.

catechumen ➤ An unbaptized person who is preparing for full initiation into the Catholic Church by engaging in formal study, reflection, and prayer.

chalice ➤ The cup used during the Mass that holds the wine before the Consecration and the Blood of Christ after the Consecration. It represents the cup used at the Last Supper and is a symbol of Jesus' sacrifice and eternal life.

charism ➤ A special grace of the Holy Spirit given to an individual Christian or community, for the benefit and building up of the entire Church.

chief priests ➤ These were Jewish priests of high rank in the Temple. They had administrative authority and presided over important Temple functions and were probably leaders in the Sanhedrin.

ciborium ➤ From a Latin word for *cup*, a cup-shaped vessel for holding the consecrated hosts, the Body of Christ, at the Mass.

communal sin ➤ The negative influence exerted on people by communal situations and social structures that are the fruit of man's sins; also refers to the collective effect of many people's sins over time, which corrupts society and its institutions by creating "structures of sin."

concupiscence ➤ The tendency of all human beings toward sin, as a result of Original Sin.

conditional ➤ Used to describe something (such as an agreement) that will happen only if something else will happen.

consecrate ➤ To declare or set apart as sacred or solemnly dedicated to God's service; to make holy.

contemplation ➤ A form of wordless prayer in which one is fully focused on the presence of God; sometimes defined as "resting in God."

corrupt ➤ Having or showing a willingness to act dishonestly in return for money or personal gain.

corruptible ➤ Something that can be spoiled, contaminated, or made rotten, especially to be made morally perverted.

covenant ➤ A solemn agreement between human beings or between God and a human being in which mutual commitments are made.

D

Davidic Covenant ➤ The unconditional covenant made between God and David in which God promised David that he would establish an everlasting kingdom through David's descendants, and that the Messiah would come from David's lineage.

Devil ➤ From the Greek *diabolus*, meaning "slanderer" or "accuser"; refers in general to the fallen angels, those spiritual beings who sinned against God.

divine retributive justice ➤ The belief that God punishes people for their sins during this lifetime.

dogma ➤ Teachings recognized as central to Church teaching, defined by the Magisterium and considered definitive and authoritative.

doxology ➤ Christian prayer that gives glory and praise to God, often calling upon the three Divine Persons of the Trinity.

E

Easter Vigil ➤ The liturgy celebrated on Holy Saturday night. It celebrates the coming of the light of Christ into the world and is also the time when adults and older children are received into the Church through the Sacraments of Christian Initiation.

Emmanuel ➤ A Hebrew word meaning "God is with us."

etiology ➤ A story that explains something's cause or origin.

Eucharist, the ➤ The celebration of the entire Mass. The term can also refer specifically to the consecrated bread and wine that have become the Body and Blood of Christ.

Exsultet ➤ Sung during the Easter Vigil, this triumphant hymn of praise proclaims, "Christ is Risen!" It announces that on this night, humanity and all creation receive the Good News of salvation. Also called the Easter Proclamation.

F

Fall, the ➤ Also called the Fall from Grace, the biblical Revelation about the origins of sin and evil in the world, expressed figuratively in the account of Adam and Eve in Genesis.

figurative language ➤ A literary form that uses symbolic images, stories, and names to point to a deeper truth.

G

genuflect ➤ To kneel on one knee as a sign of reverence for the Blessed Sacrament.

Golgotha ➤ A Hebrew word meaning "place of the skull," referring to the place where Jesus was crucified.

Good Friday ➤ The second day of the Easter Triduum, on which we commemorate Jesus' Passion and death on the cross.

grace ➤ The free and undeserved gift that God gives us to empower us to respond to his call and to live as his adopted sons and daughters. Grace restores our loving communion with the Holy Trinity, lost through sin.

H

Heaven ➤ A state of eternal life and union with God, in which one experiences full happiness and the satisfaction of the deepest human longings.

Hell ➤ Refers to the state of definitive separation from God and the saints, and so is a state of eternal punishment.

hesed ➤ A Hebrew word for *mercy* that expresses God's loving forgiveness for the Chosen People.

holiness ➤ The state of being holy. This means to be set apart for God's service, to be devoted to God and united with him and his Church, to live a morally good life, to be a person of prayer, and to reveal God's love to the world through acts of loving service.

Holy Spirit ➤ The Third Person of the Blessed Trinity, the perfect personal love between the Father and the Son, who inspires, guides, and sanctifies the life of believers.

Holy Thursday ➤ The beginning of the Easter Triduum, starting with the evening celebration of the Mass of the Lord's Supper.

hyperbole ➤ Exaggerated statements or claims not meant to be taken literally.

I

immortality ➤ The state of never having to experience death.

Incarnation ➤ From the Latin, meaning "to become flesh," referring to the mystery of Jesus Christ, the Divine Son of God, becoming man. In the Incarnation, Jesus Christ became truly man while remaining truly God.

infancy narratives ➤ The accounts of Jesus' birth and early childhood.

intercession ➤ A prayer on behalf of another person or group.

interiority ➤ The practice of developing a life of self-reflection and self-examination to attend to our spiritual life and call to holiness.

J

judges ➤ The eleven men and one woman who served the Hebrew people as tribal leaders, military commanders, arbiters of disputes, and enliveners of faith.

justification ➤ God's act of bringing a sinful human being into right relationship with him. It involves removal of sin and the gift of God's sanctifying grace to renew holiness.

L

Last Judgment ➤ The judgment of the human race by Jesus Christ at his second coming. It is also called the Final Judgment.

lectio divina ➤ A Latin term meaning "divine reading." *Lectio divina* is a form of meditative prayer focused on a Scripture passage. It involves repetitive readings and periods of reflection and can serve as either private or communal prayer.

Litany of the Saints ➤ A prayer in the form of a chant or a responsive petition in which the great saints of the Church are asked to pray for us.

Liturgical Year ➤ The Church's annual cycle of feasts and seasons that celebrates the events and mysteries of Christ's birth, life, death, Resurrection, and Ascension, and forms the context for the Church's worship.

liturgy ➤ The Church's official, public, communal prayer. It is God's work, in which the People of God participate. The Church's most important liturgy is the Eucharist, or the Mass.

love ➤ Also called "charity," the Theological Virtue by which we love God above all things and, out of that love of God, love our neighbors as ourselves.

mediator ➤ Someone who acts as a go-between between separate or opposing parties in order to connect or reconcile them. Jesus Christ is the unique mediator between God and humanity; through his death and Resurrection, we have gained access to God's saving grace.

meditation ➤ A form of prayer involving a variety of methods and techniques, in which one engages the mind, imagination, and emotions to focus on a particular truth, Scripture passage, or other spiritual matter.

Messiah ➤ Hebrew word for "anointed one." The equivalent Greek term is *Christos*. Jesus is the Christ and the Messiah because he is the Anointed One who brings salvation through his life, death, and Resurrection.

messianic hope ➤ The Jewish belief and expectation that a messiah would come to protect and unite Israel and lead the nation to freedom.

miracles ➤ Signs or wonders, such as healing or the control of nature, that can be attributed to divine power only.

monotheism ➤ The belief in and worship of only one God.

Mysteries of the Rosary ➤ The sacred events in the lives of Jesus and Mary that are meditated on when praying the Rosary. They are called mysteries because they are beyond our understanding. There are four groups of mysteries: Joyful, Sorrowful, Glorious, and Luminous.

mystical ➤ Having a spiritual meaning or reality that is neither apparent to the senses nor obvious to the intelligence; the visible sign of the hidden reality of salvation.

mysticism ➤ An intense experience of the presence and power of God, resulting in a deeper sense of union with God; those who regularly experience such union are called mystics.

Oil of the Catechumens ➤ Blessed olive oil used to anoint those preparing for Baptism.

Oil of the Sick ➤ Blessed olive oil used in the Sacrament of Anointing of the Sick to anoint the forehead and hands of people who are seriously ill or near death.

omnipotent ➤ From the Latin *omnia*, meaning "all," and *potens*, meaning "powerful"; refers to the divine attribute that God is almighty and so has unlimited authority and power.

omniscient ➤ From the Latin *omnia*, meaning "all" and *scientia*, meaning "knowledge." Refers to the divine attribute that God is able to know everything past, present, and future.

original holiness ➤ The original state of human beings in their relationship with God, sharing in the divine life in full communion with him.

original justice ➤ The original state of Adam and Eve before the Fall; sharing in the divine life, they were in a state of complete harmony with God, with themselves, with each other, and with all of creation.

Original Sin ➤ From the Latin *origo*, meaning "beginning" or "birth." The term has two meanings: (1) the sin of the first human beings, who disobeyed God's command by choosing to follow their own will and thus lost their original holiness and became subject to death, (2) the fallen state of human nature that affects every person born into the world, except Jesus and Mary.

P

paradox ➤ A statement that seems contradictory or opposed to common sense and yet is true.

parity treaty ➤ An agreement made between two equal parties binding them in mutual respect and cooperation.

Parousia ➤ The second coming of Christ as judge of all the living and the dead, at the end of time, when the Kingdom of God will be fulfilled.

Particular Judgment ➤ The judgment that occurs immediately at the time of our death, when our immortal souls will be judged as worthy or unworthy of Heaven.

Paschal candle ➤ Also called Easter candle, this is the large, tall candle lit at the Easter Vigil by a flame from the new fire; the symbol of the Risen Christ.

Paschal Lamb ➤ In the Old Testament, the sacrificial lamb shared at the Seder meal of the Passover on the night the Israelites escaped from Egypt; in the New Testament, the Paschal Lamb is Jesus, the Incarnate Son of God who dies on a cross to take away sin (see John 1:29).

Paschal Mystery ➤ The work of salvation accomplished by Jesus Christ mainly through his Passion, death, Resurrection, and Ascension.

Passover ➤ The night the Lord passed over the houses of the Israelites marked by the blood of the lamb, and spared the firstborn sons from death. It also is the feast that celebrates the deliverance of the Chosen People from bondage in Egypt and the Exodus from Egypt to the Promised Land.

patriarchy ➤ The familial, social, cultural, and political worldview that claims that men are destined to hold positions of power over, and make decisions for, women and children.

Penitential Act ➤ The invitation by the priest at Mass, after the opening greeting, to have the congregation acknowledge their sins and place their trust in God's mercy.

Pentecost ➤ The fiftieth day following Easter, which commemorates the descent of the Holy Spirit on the Apostles and disciples.

petition ➤ A prayer form in which one asks God for help and forgiveness.

Pharisees ➤ This group of Jews was well-known for its strict interpretation of all the laws of the Old Testament. The Pharisees believed in the resurrection of the dead.

polytheistic ➤ Believing in many gods.

praise ➤ A prayer of acknowledgment that God is God, giving him glory not for what he does, but simply because he is.

prayer ➤ Lifting up of one's mind and heart to God or the requesting of good things from him. The six basic forms of prayer are blessing, adoration, praise, petition, thanksgiving, and intercession. In prayer, we communicate with God in a relationship of love.

prophet ➤ A person God chooses to speak his message of salvation. In the Bible, primarily a communicator of a divine message of repentance to the Chosen People, not necessarily a person who predicted the future.

Protoevangelium ➤ From the Greek *protos*, meaning "first," and *euangelion*, meaning "good news." It refers to the passage in the Book of Genesis (see 3:15) that announces the future coming of a messiah and savior: the first announcement of the Good News.

providence ➤ God's divine care and protection.

Purgatory ➤ A state of final purification or cleansing, which one may need to enter following death and before entering Heaven.

R

redemption ➤ From the Latin *redemptio*, meaning "a buying back," referring, in the Old Testament, to Yahweh's deliverance of Israel and, in the New Testament, to Christ's deliverance of all Christians from the forces of sin. As the agent of redemption, Jesus is called the Redeemer.

reincarnation ➤ The belief that our soul can be reborn into a new human body.

reparation ➤ The act of making amends for something one did wrong that caused physical, emotional, or material harm to another person.

Resurrection ➤ The passage of Jesus from death to life on the third day after his death on the cross; the heart of the Paschal Mystery and the basis of our hope in the resurrection of the dead.

resurrection of the dead ➤ The raising of the righteous on the last day, to live forever with the Risen Christ. The resurrection of the dead means that not only will our immortal souls live on after death but also our transformed bodies.

resuscitation ➤ When someone's heart quits beating and then, perhaps due to some intervention like CPR, the person is revived.

S

sacrament ➤ An efficacious and visible sign of God's grace, instituted by Christ and entrusted to the Church, by which divine life is dispensed to us. The Seven Sacraments are Baptism, the Eucharist, Confirmation, Penance and Reconciliation, Anointing of the Sick, Matrimony, and Holy Orders.

Sacred Chrism ➤ Perfumed olive oil consecrated by the bishop that is used for anointing in the Sacraments of Baptism, Confirmation, and Holy Orders.

sanctifying grace ➤ The grace that heals our human nature wounded by sin and restores us to friendship with God by giving us a share in the divine life of the Trinity. It is a supernatural gift of God, infused into our souls by the Holy Spirit, that continues the work of making us holy.

Sanhedrin ➤ The highest council of ancient Jews, consisting of seventy-one members exercising authority in religious matters.

Satan ➤ The fallen angel or spirit of evil who is the enemy of God and a continuing instigator of temptation and sin in the world.

scapegoat ➤ This term refers to the ritual in the Old Testament of symbolically placing the sins of the Chose People on a goat and then driving the goat into the desert (see Leviticus, chapter 16).

scribe ➤ A scholar and teacher of the Jewish Law and Scripture. Scribes were associated with both the chief priests and the Pharisees.

Sinai Covenant ➤ The covenant established with the Israelites at Mount Sinai that renewed God's covenant with Abraham's descendants. The Sinai Covenant established the Israelites as God's Chosen People.

soul ➤ Our spiritual principle; it is immortal, and it is what makes us most like God. Our soul is created by God at the moment of our conception. It is the seat of human consciousness and freedom.

Stations of the Cross ➤ A devotion for prayer and reflection, popular during Lent, that retraces the events of Jesus' Passion and death in fourteen "stations," represented by artistic depictions. Most Catholic churches have artistic representations of the fourteen Stations of the Cross. Also called the Way of the Cross.

stewardship ➤ The careful and responsible management of someone or something that has been entrusted to a person's care. This includes responsibly using and caring for the gifts of creation that God has given us.

synoptic Gospels ➤ From the Greek for "seeing the whole together," the name given to the Gospels of Matthew, Mark, and Luke, because they are similar in style and content.

T

thanksgiving ➤ A prayer of gratitude for the gift of life and the gifts of life. Thanksgiving characterizes the prayer of the Church which, in celebrating the Eucharist, offers perfect thanks to the Father through, with, and in Christ, in the unity of the Holy Spirit.

Theology of the Body ➤ The name given to Pope Saint John Paul II's teachings on the human body and sexuality.

Theological Virtues ➤ The name given for the God-given virtues of faith, hope, and love. These virtues enable us to know God as God and lead us to union with God in mind and heart.

Theotokos ➤ A Greek title for Mary meaning "God-bearer."

transgression ➤ An act that goes against a law, rule, or code of conduct; sin.

Triduum ➤ The three-day period of the Liturgical Year that begins with the Mass of the Lord's Supper on Holy Thursday and ends with evening prayer on Easter Sunday.

typology ➤ The discernment of God's work in the Old Testament as a prefiguration of what he accomplished through Jesus Christ in the fullness of time. Typology illuminates the unity of God's plan in the two Testaments but does not devalue the Old Covenant or its ongoing relevance and value for the Jewish people.

V

vassal treaty ➤ An agreement made by two unequal parties. The superior power received absolute loyalty, service, and submission from the lesser party, the vassal.

venerate ➤ To show respect and devotion to someone or something.

virtue ➤ A habitual and firm disposition to do good.

vocal prayer ➤ A prayer that is spoken aloud or silently, such as the Lord's Prayer.

Y

Yom Kippur ➤ This Hebrew term refers to the Day of Atonement, a Jewish holy day that is observed with prayer and fasting in accordance with Leviticus, chapter 16.

INDEX

Note: Charts and maps are indicated with "C" and "M," respectively.

A

Abel, 33, 87, 290
abortion, 301
Abraham, 57–59, 58C, 72–75, 74–75C
Acts of the Apostles, 160, 192, 197, 227
actual grace, 321C
Adam
  creation of, 15
  Fall and Original Sin, 24–25, 29–31, 47
  God's love, 47
  Jesus as New, 90, 120–121, 121C
  name of, 18
  original holiness of, 16
  unity with Eve, 15, 20–21, 233
addiction, 41, 241
adoration prayers, 344
afterlife, 227, 250–253
Alcoholics Anonymous (AA), 41, 283
Amen, 356
Amos, 92
angels, 13–14
animals, 51, 57, 58C, 83–84, 88
anointing, 143–144, 369
Anointing of the Sick, 334C
Arche, L', 71–72
Ascension, 191–197
Ascent to Mount Carmel, The
  (John of the Cross), 332
ascetism, 332
Assumption, 195
Athanasius, 122
atonement, 82–84, 86

B

Baptism, 35, 168, 245, 278, 320, 334C
beloved disciple, 187
Benedict XVI, 276, 304
Berrigan, Daniel, 92
Bible, 17–18, 55, 128, 355–356. See also
  Gospels; New Testament; Old Testament;
  specific books and Gospels
blasphemy, 151
blessings, 343
blood, 51, 76, 77, 79, 83, 84, 134, 168
body and soul, 226
Body of Christ, 197, 231, 232–233
Book of Signs, The, 136
Bridges to Life, 164, 283
burning hearts, 185–186

C

Cain, 33, 87, 290
Cardinal Virtues, 221–222, 222C
catechumens, 378
Catholic Relief Services, 368
Celebration of the Lord's Passion, 363,
  372–374
chalices, 320
charism, 330
charity. See love
chief priests, 143–145, 149, 150, 152, 176, 298
Church
  Apostolic mission, 197
  Ascension and, 197
  as Body of Christ, 197, 231, 232–233
  as community, 230–235
  as holiness aid, 322, 333–335, 334C
  Liturgical Year of, 361–362
ciborium, 320
Communion, 373
community, 15, 20, 230–235, 278–280
concupiscence, 33–34, 78, 164, 223
Confirmation, 334C, 356, 367, 378
Consecration, 320
contemplation, 350

Corinthians, Letters to the
  Church community, 232
  geographic location, 220M
  love, 325
  New Adam, 120–121
  Resurrection, 179–183
  resurrection from the body, 227–229
  Theology of the Cross, 219
  weakness as strength, 278
corruptible, 229
corruption, 297–298
covenants
  with Abraham, 57–59, 58C
  with David, 66–67
  definition and descriptions, 50–52
  history of, 61
  of Jesus, 77
  with Moses, 60, 62–65
  with Noah, 55–57
  purpose, 45, 53
Creation
  biblical accounts of, 17–21
  environmental crisis, 300, 302–307
  goodness of, 12
  of humans, 15–17
  invisible categories of, 13–14
  medical interventions and respect
    for, 300–301
  vegetarianism, 57
Crucifixion
  death of Jesus, 159–165 161–162C
  descriptions, 160–161
  liturgies on, 364
  theologies on, 218–221, 223
  violence of, 289, 292

D

Damien of Molokai, 275–276
"Dark Night of the Soul"
  (John of the Cross), 332
Davidic Covenant, 66–67
Day of Atonement, 82–84, 86
death
  as consequence of sin, 29, 31, 241
  of Jesus, 159–166, 161–162C
  judgment after, 247–248
  miracles and raising from, 133–134,
    135–137
  resurrection from, 184, 190, 226–229
Deuteronomy, 63, 175
Devil, 14, 48–49, 48C, 145
discipleship
  burning hearts of, 185–186
  challenges of, 148
  evangelization missions of, 325
  expectation of, 157
  Jesus' teachings on, 128–131, 319,
    323–325, 324C
divine retributive justice, 268–269, 290
dogma, 195
dominion, 303
doxology, 349

E

Earth, 192–194, 197
Easter Proclamation, 43, 377
Easter Vigil, 35, 42–43, 363, 375–379
Ebo, Antona, 292
Elijah, 94
Emmaus, road to, 180, 185, 186M
environment, 300, 302–307
eternal life, 84, 125, 192, 244
etiology, 23, 30C, 36

Eucharist
    as communal prayer, 346–347
    definition, 77
    at Easter Vigil, 379
    Jesus modeling, 185–186
    Jesus' presence in, 186, 197, 235
    origins, 77, 79
    participation during, 362
    as sacrament, 333, 334C
    symbolism of, 168
    Triduum and Liturgy of the, 349, 366, 369, 379
    word origins, 347
evangelization, 325
Eve
    creation of, 15
    Fall and Original Sin, 24–25, 29–31, 47
    God's love, 47
    name of, 18
    original holiness of, 16
    symbolism of, 48C
    unity with Adam, 15, 20–21, 233
evil, 24–25, 32. See also sin
Exodus, 44, 44C, 67, 76–79, 80C, 192
Exsultet, 43, 377
Ezekiel, 44–45, 44C, 92, 93, 378

F

faith, 187–188, 222C
Fall, 24–26, 29–31, 30C, 48–49, 48C
fasting, 369, 374
feet washing, 367
figurative language, 17–18
Final Judgment, 248–249
Flood, 35, 55–56, 290
Food Empowerment Project, 300
forgiveness, 164–165, 243, 297, 324
fortitude, 219, 222C, 272, 277–280
Francis, 191, 285, 301, 303
Francis of Assisi, 47, 301
freedom, 244
free will, 14, 28, 32, 321

G

Ganci, Peter, Jr., 141
Garden of Eden, 19–20, 19M, 24
Genesis
    covenants in, 55–59, 58C
    Creation, 15–21
    etiologies of, 23
    Fall and Original Sin, 24–26, 29–31, 30C, 48–49, 48C
    Noah and the Flood, 35, 55–57
    overview, 21
    sacrifice of Isaac, 72–75, 74–75C
    sacrifice requirements, 87
    sin cycles, 33–36
    violence in, 290
Gentiles, 57, 113, 116, 118, 177, 227
genuflect, 373
"Glory Be," 349
God
    abandonment vs. trust in, 165
    afterlife and relationship with, 251–252
    Bible as revelation of, 17, 18
    communication style of, 44
    covenants with, 50–67
    as Creator, 12–15
    divine retributive justice, 268–269, 290
    Easter Vigil and gratitude to, 43
    evil allowed by, 32
    guidance of, 37
    human creation, 15, 19–20
    image of, 14, 34, 318
    Incarnation, 90, 119–122, 191
    love of, 14, 27, 37, 47, 64–66, 90
    names of, 151
    obedience to, 52, 53, 90, 147
    Old Testament perceptions of, 64
    as omnipotent, 279
    personal encounters with, 327–332
    prayer as relationship with, 339–341
    presence of, 116, 191
    providence of, 281
    sin and separation from, 24–26, 31
    suffering and, 119, 267, 283–284
    violence of, 290

Good Friday, 363, 364C, 369, 371–374
goodness, 12, 24–25, 32
Gospels. *See also specific Gospels*
  agony in the garden, 147
  anointing at Bethany, 143–144
  Ascension, 192, 194–195
  burial of Jesus, 174–176
  cleansing of the Temple, 95, 142
  corruption, 298
  crucifixion of Jesus, 159–168, 161–162C
  discipleship, 148, 319, 323
  feet washing, 367
  God's love, 47
  greed, 299
  infancy narratives, 112–118
  Jesus as prayer model, 355
  Jesus' death responsibility, 149, 152–153
  Judas' betrayal, 144–145
  Last Judgment, 248–249
  Last Supper, 77
  Messiah, 111
  miracles, 132–137, 134C
  parables in, 246–247, 299
  Passion, 156–157
  prophetic role of Jesus, 93, 95
  Resurrection, 179–180, 185–190
  synoptic, definition, 77
  wealth, 126–127
grace, 29, 35, 245, 321, 321C
Greatest Commandment, 325
greed, 78, 87, 126–127, 293, 299–300
Gregory of Nyssa, 122
guilt, 81–84, 240

H

Hail Mary, 355
Heaven
  afterlife in, 250–251
  ascending to, 192, 194–197
  Jewish concept of, 192–194
  judgment for entrance to, 247–248
  purification prior to entering, 253
Hell, 177, 252
Herman, Nicolas, 331
Herod Antipas, 152, 153
hesed, 64–66
holiness
  aids to, 321–322, 321C
  behaviors for, 220–221
  definition and descriptions, 317–320
  discipleship for, 319, 323–325, 324C
  mysticism for, 327–332
  original, 20
  sacramental life for, 333–335, 334C
Holy of Holies, 83, 116, 166
Holy Orders, 334C
Holy Saturday, 375
Holy Spirit, 196–197, 245, 321, 321C
Holy Thursday, 363, 364C, 365–370
hope, as virtue, 222C
Hosea, 92, 93
Human Thread, The, 299
hyperbole, 128

I

"I AM," 151
Ignatius of Loyola, 352–353
image of God, 14, 34, 318
Incarnation, 90, 119–122, 191
infancy narratives, 112–118, 113–114C
INRI, 162
intellect, 321
intercessions, 346, 372, 374
interiority, 322
Isaac, 72–75, 74–75C
Isaiah, 96, 97–99C, 99, 142, 156

J

Jairus's daughter, 133

Jeremiah, 93, 94, 142

Jesus Christ. *See also* Resurrection

anointing for sacrifice, 369

Ascension of, 191–197

authorities' perception of, 95, 141–147

Baptism of, 35

birth and infancy narratives, 112–118

burial of, 174–176

cleansing at Temple, 95, 142

as covenant fulfillment, 65

crucifixion and death, 148–154, 159–165, 161–162C, 289, 292, 298

discipleship teachings, 128–131, 325

on greed, 126–127, 299

in hell, 177

on holiness, 324–325, 324C

Incarnation, 90, 119–122, 191

on justice, 92

Last Supper, 77, 79, 145–146, 145C, 168, 366

on love, 153, 154, 325

as Messiah, 67, 96, 111, 143, 152, 189

miracles of, 132–137, 134C

as New Adam, 90, 120–121, 121C

Passion of, 155–158

power of, 215–216

as prayer model, 355–356

prefigurations, 73–75, 74–75C, 136–137

presence of, 197, 235

prophetic role of, 93, 95

redemption through sacrifice of, 43, 78, 79, 80C, 81, 84–86, 87, 90, 269–270

as Savior, 239

second coming of, 249

selflessness of, 169, 224

sin as gratitude for relationship with, 41, 43

suffering and, 45, 269, 273

as Suffering Servant, 96, 97–99C

teachings of, 43, 125, 214

on violence response, 291–292

on wealth, 126–127

as Word of God, 92

Job, 272

John, Gospel of

agony in the garden, 147

anointing at Bethany, 143–144

Ascension, 195

burial of Jesus, 174

cleansing the Temple, 142

corruption, 298

crucifixion of Jesus, 161–162C, 162, 166, 167–168, 167C

feet washing, 367

God's love, 47

greed, 299

Jesus' death responsibility, 150, 151

Judas' betrayal, 144–145

Last Supper, 77, 145–146, 145C

miracles, 132, 136–137

Paschal Lamb, 79, 80C

Passion, 156–157

Resurrection, 179–180, 187–189

sin as slavery, 78

suffering, 45

unity in Church, 231

John of the Cross, 331

John Paul II, 16, 248, 301

Jonah, sign of, 173, 177

Joseph of Arimathea, 174, 299

joy, 244

Judaism, 82–84, 86, 227, 250

Judas Iscariot, 144–145, 298, 369

judges, 65

judgment, 247–249, 324C

justice, 20, 92, 148, 222C, 268–269, 290, 295–296

justification, 220

K

King, Martin Luther, Jr., 85–86

Kingdom of Heaven, 143, 152, 194, 197, 231, 248

L

Last Judgment, 248–249
Last Supper, 79, 145–146, 145C, 168, 366
Lawrence, Brother, 331
Lazarus, 136–137, 299, 369
lectio divina, 352
leprosy, 275–276
Leviticus, 83, 151, 297
light, 111, 122
Litany of the Saints, 378
Liturgical Year, 361–362
liturgies, 362, 363–364, 372–374, 378
Liturgy of the Eucharist, 379
Liturgy of the Word, 372, 378
Lord's Prayer, 355–356, 373
love (charity)
  definition, 87
  of enemies, 291, 292
  God's, 14, 27, 37, 47, 64–66, 90
  for holiness, 324C
  human creation and unity in, 15
  Jesus' teachings on, 153, 154, 325
  power of authentic, 217
  requirements of, 87, 89
  salvation through, 122
  as Theological Virtue, 222C
Luke, Gospel of
  agony in the garden, 147
  anointing at Bethany, 143–144
  Ascension, 192
  audience of, 118
  burial of Jesus, 174, 175
  cleansing the Temple, 142
  crucifixion of Jesus, 161–162C,
    162–163, 164
  dating, 113
  discipleship and holiness, 319
  greed, 299
  infancy narratives, 112–113, 113–114C,
    117–118
  Jesus as prayer model, 355
  Jesus' death responsibility, 149, 151,
    152–153

Jesus' use of power, 215
Judas' betrayal, 144–145
Last Supper, 145–146, 145C
miracles, 132
parables of, 246–247
Passion, 156–157
Passover and Last Supper, 79
Resurrection, 179–180, 185–186
suffering causes, 269
unity in Church, 231
wealth, 127
lust, 16, 78

M

Mark, Gospel of
  abandonment of God, 165
  agony in the garden, 147
  anointing at Bethany, 143–144
  Ascension, 192
  burial of Jesus, 174
  cleansing the Temple, 142
  crucifixion of Jesus, 159, 161–162,
    161–162C, 162–163, 165, 166
  discipleship, 319
  infancy narratives, 112
  Jesus' death responsibility, 149, 151
  Jesus' use of power, 215
  Judas' betrayal, 144–145
  Last Supper, 145–146, 145C
  miracles, 132, 133–135
  Passion, 156–157
  prophetic role of Jesus, 93, 95
  Resurrection, 181, 185–186
marriage, 16, 60, 334C
Martha, 136
Mary (Lazarus' sister), 136, 369
Mary (Mother of Jesus), 123–124, 195, 303
Mass, 77, 197, 347, 362
Mass of the Lord's Supper, 363, 364–369
mass shootings, 289
Matrimony, 334C

Matthew, Gospel of
  abandonment of God, 165
  agony in the garden, 147
  anointing at Bethany, 143–144
  Ascension, 194
  audience of, 146
  burial of Jesus, 174, 176
  Church community, 234
  cleansing the Temple, 142
  corruption, 298
  crucifixion of Jesus, 161–162C, 162–163,
    165, 166
  dating, 113
  discipleship, 148, 323
  greed, 299
  infancy narratives, 112–116, 113–114C
  Jesus as prayer model, 355
  Jesus' death responsibility, 149, 151, 152
  Jesus' use of power, 215, 216
  Judas' betrayal, 144–145
  Kingdom of Heaven, 194
  Last Judgment, 248
  Last Supper, 145–146, 145C
  miracles, 135
  Passion, 156–157
  prophetic role of Jesus, 93, 95
  Resurrection, 181
  violence, 291
  wealth, 126
medical interventions, 300–301
meditation, 351
Merton, Thomas, 191, 327
Messiah, 67, 96, 97–99C, 111, 143, 152, 189
messianic hope, 96
miracles, 132–137, 134C
monotheism, 59
Moses, 60, 62–65, 192, 355
Mosiac (Sinai) Covenant, 60, 62–65
Mosiac Law, 60, 297
Mysteries of the Rosary, 121
mysticism, 327–332

N

New Adam, 90, 120–121, 121C
Newman, John Henry, 285
New Testament. *See also* Gospels; *specific
  Gospels: Matthew, Mark, Luke, John*
  abandonment of God, 165
  afterlife beliefs, 227
  Ascension, 192, 194–195
  burial of Jesus, 174–176
  Church community, 232
  corruption, 298
  crucifixion, 159–168, 161–162C
  God's love, 47
  Jesus' death responsibility, 149, 152–153
  Jesus' use of power, 215–216
  Kingdom of Heaven, 194
  literary forms in, 55, 128
  messianic hope and fulfillment in, 96,
    97–99C
  miracles, 132–137, 134C
  New Adam, 120–121, 121C
  Old Testament typology, 55
  parables in, 246–247, 299
  Paschal Mystery redemption, 78
  Passion, 155–157
  prophecy fulfillment in, 96, 97–99C
  prophetic roles of Jesus, 93, 95
  purification, 253
  Resurrection, 179–183, 185–189
  resurrection from the body, 227–229
  selflessness models, 169, 224
  sin as slavery, 78
  suffering causes, 44C, 45, 269
  Theology of the Cross, 218–221, 223
  violence, 291–292
  weakness as strength, 278
  wealth, 126–127
  Yom Kippur in, 84
9-11, 141
Noah, 35, 55–57

O

obedience, 52, 53, 62, 90, 147
Oil of Catechumens, 367
Oil of the Sick, 367
Old Testament
  abandonment of God, 165
  atonement rituals, 83–84
  blasphemy punishment, 151
  burial laws, 175
  clouds, 192
  covenants in, 55–67
  Creation accounts in, 17–21
  creation and dominion, 303
  Earth, concepts of, 193
  Exodus, 78
  Fall and Original Sin, 24–26, 29–31, 30C
  messianic hope, 96, 97–99C, 111
  Passover and Exodus from Egypt, 76–79, 80C
  perception of God, 64
  prophets of, 65, 91–94, 95, 97–99C
  purification, 253
  sacrifice of Isaac, 72–75, 74–75C
  sin cycles and concepts, 33–36, 44–45, 44C
  temple sacrifices, 88
  tree of knowledge, 24–25, 29
  typology of, 55
  violence in, 290
"On Care of Our Common Home" (Francis), 303
Operation Rice Bowl, 368
Original Sin
  consequences of, 24–26, 29–31, 30C
  definition, 25
  redemption of, 35, 43
  symbolism of, 47–48, 48C
  transmission of, 33–34, 78

P

Palm Sunday, 364
Parable of the Lost Son, 246–247
Parable of the Rich Man and Lazarus, 299
parity treaties, 61
Parousia, 249

Particular Judgment, 247–248
Paschal candles, 42
Paschal Fast, 369
Paschal Lamb, 79, 80C, 168
Paschal Mystery
  definition, 11, 72
  Old Testament prefiguration of, 72–75, 74–75C, 76–79, 80C
  salvation and redemption through, 78, 81, 84–86, 240, 242–244, 269–270
Passion
  liturgies commemorating, 363, 364, 371–373
  Old Testament prefiguration of, 79, 80C
  path to crucifixion, 155–157
  prayers on, 158, 226
Passover, 76–79
patriarchy, 20, 144, 181
Paul
  Church community, 232, 234
  communal sin awareness, 297
  consequences of sin, 29, 31
  God's love, 27
  Jesus as New Adam, 90
  Last Judgment and second coming, 249
  New Adam, 120–121
  purification, 253
  Resurrection, 180, 181–183
  resurrection from the body, 227
  salvation and redemption, 78, 243
  selflessness models, 169, 224
  students of, 146
  Theology of the Cross, 218–221, 223–224
  violence, response to, 291–292
  weakness as strength, 278
  wealth, 299
Penance and Reconciliation, 82, 243, 334C
Penitential Act, 297
Pentecost, 196
Peter, 14, 128, 160, 188–189
petitions, 344–345
Pharisees, 149, 176
Philippians, Letter to the, 169, 224
Pilate, Pontius, 149, 152–153, 154, 156, 174, 176

polytheism, 219

poverty, 126–127, 304, 368

power, 214–215C, 214–216

Practice of the Presence of God, The (Brother Lawrence), 331

praise, 348–349, 379

prayer
communal, 362
definition, 340
expressions of, 350–353
forms of, 343–349
friendship comparisons, 339
for holiness, 324C
instructions for, 340–341
for mystical experiences, 332
overcoming obstacles to, 341–342
for Passion reflection, 158, 374

Prejean, Helen, 26

Presentation of the Oils, 367

prophets, 65, 91–94, 96, 97–99C

Protoevangelium, 48–49, 48C

providence, 281

prudence, 222C

Psalms, 162, 165

Purgatory, 253

purification, 83, 88, 253

R

racism, 31, 85–86, 292

redemption
definition, 270
Jewish atonement rituals for, 83–84, 88
from sin, 43, 78, 79, 80C, 81, 84–86, 87, 90, 269–270
suffering for, 269–270

reparations, 83, 270

Resurrection
descriptions, 173, 178–183
faith responses to, 187–189
Jesus' appearances after, 184–186
liturgies on, 364
Old Testament comparisons, 173, 177
resurrection from the dead based on, 228
significance of, 43, 120, 189–190

resurrection from the dead, 184, 190, 226–229

Roman Empire
burial of Jesus, 174
communal sins of, 296
crucifixion practices, 160
Jesus' death and leadership of, 149, 151, 152–153, 154
Passion, 156

Romans, Letter to the, 220, 223, 291–292

Rosary, 121

S

sacraments, 333–335, 334C

Sacred Chrism, 367

sacrifice
animal, 51, 58C, 83–84, 88
in discipleship, 128–131
heroism and, 141
for holiness, 324C
of Isaac, 73–75, 74–75C
of Jesus, 43, 78, 79, 80C, 81, 84–86, 87, 90, 217, 269–270
practical examples of, 271–272
as requirement of love, 87, 89
for salvation, 274
temple, 88

Sadducees, 227

Sage, John, 164

salvation
personal role in, 220–223
purpose of, 242–244
sacrifice and suffering for, 274
from slavery of sin, 78, 79, 86, 223
through Jesus' sacrifice, 78, 81, 84–86, 242–244

Samuel, First Book of, 290

Samuel, Second Book of, 142

sanctifying grace, 245, 321C

Sanhedrin, 95, 137, 150–151, 174

Satan, 14, 48–49, 48C, 145

scapegoats, 83–84

scribes, 149

second coming, 249

selflessness, 169, 224

self-reflection, 322

Sendler, Irena, 323

Servant Songs, 96, 97–99C

service, 14, 324C
Seven Storey Mountain (Merton), 191, 327
sexuality, 16, 78
shame, 16, 24, 81, 82, 240
Simeon Salus, 223
Simon the Cyrenian, 157
sin
    communal (social), 35, 296–297
    consequences of, 24–26, 29, 30C, 31, 81, 240–242
    corruption, 297–298
    covenants as remedies to, 53
    cycle of, 33–36, 44–45, 44C
    free will and choosing, 32
    gratitude for, 41, 43
    as human limitation, 26–27
    human tendency toward, 33, 78, 145, 164, 223
    redemption from, 43, 78, 79, 80C, 81, 84–86, 87, 90, 166, 242–244, 269–270
    violence as effect of, 289–293
Sinai (Mosiac) Covenant, 60, 62–65
slavery, 78, 223, 300
snakes, 48–49, 48C
souls, 14, 31, 226
Spiritual Exercises (Ignatius of Loyola), 353
St. Joseph of Arimathea Society, 176
Stations of the Cross, 158, 374
stewardship, 307
strength, 219, 222C, 272, 277–280
suffering
    benefits of, 270
    cause of, 44–45, 44C, 268–269
    coping with, 281–285, 282C
    God allowing, 119, 267, 283
    of saints, 275–276
    for salvation, 267
    salvation from, 269–270
    strength in, 273–280

technological advancements, 300
temperance, 222C
Temple, 95, 142, 166
temptation, 145
Teresa, Mother, 244, 341
Teresa of Ávila, 330, 340

thanksgiving prayers, 346–347, 379
Theological Virtues, 221–222, 222C
Theology of the Body, 16
Theology of the Cross, 218–221, 223–224
Thérèse of Lisieux, 271
Thomas, 187
Tower of Babel, 36
transgressions, 220
treaties, 61
tree of knowledge, 24–25
Triduum
    definition and description, 363–364, 364C
    Easter Vigil, 375–379
    Good Friday, 369, 371–374
    Holy Thursday, 365–370
Trinity, 230, 245, 349
typology, 55

U

unity, 15, 20–21, 230–235, 278–280

V

Vanier, George and Pauline, 72
Vanier, Jean, 71–72, 75
vassal treaties, 61
vegetarianism, 57
veneration, 373
Veneration of the Cross, 373
violence, 289–293
virtues, 221–222, 222C

W

water, 35, 168
weakness, 164, 273, 277–280
wealth
    environment and, 304
    greed, 78, 87, 127, 293, 299–300
    holiness and, 324
    Jesus' teachings on, 126–127, 299–300
women
    equality of, 144
    gender relationships, 20–21
    patriarchy and roles of, 20, 144, 181
    as prophets, 65

Y

Yom Kippur, 82–84, 86

ACKNOWLEDGMENTS

The scriptural quotations in this publication are taken from the *New American Bible, revised edition* © 2010, 1991, 1986, 1970 Confraternity of Christian Doctrine, Inc., Washington, D.C. All Rights Reserved. No part of this work may be reproduced or transmitted in any form or by any means, electronic or mechanical, including photocopying, recording, or by any information storage and retrieval system, without permission in writing from the copyright owner.

The excerpts throughout this publication marked *CCC* are from the English translation of the *Catechism of the Catholic Church* for use in the United States of America, second edition. Copyright © 1994 by the United States Catholic Conference, Inc.—Libreria Editrice Vaticana (LEV). English translation of the *Catechism of the Catholic Church: Modifications from the Editio Typica* copyright © 1997 by the United States Catholic Conference, Inc.—LEV.

The excerpt on page 28 is from *The Works of Mercy*, by Pope Francis (Maryknoll, NY: 2017). English language edition copyright © 2017 by Orbis Books.

The excerpts on pages 43, 349, 361, 366, 371, 376, and 377, and the quotations on pages 343 and 373 are from the English translation of *The Roman Missal* © 2010, International Commission on English in the Liturgy Corporation (ICEL) (Washington, DC: United States Conference of Catholic Bishops, 2011), Easter Vigil and pages 337, 522, 353, 299, 315, 344, 355, 532, and 330 and 329, respectively. Copyright © 2011, USCCB, Washington, D.C. All rights reserved. Used with permission of the ICEL. Texts contained in this work derived whole or in part from liturgical texts copyrighted by the International Commission on English in the Liturgy (ICEL) have been published here with the confirmation of the Committee on Divine Worship, United States Conference of Catholic Bishops. No other texts in this work have been formally reviewed or approved by the United States Conference of Catholic Bishops.

The quotations on page 56 are from "The Gifts and the Calling of God are Irrevocable," Vatican Commission for Religious Relations with the Jews, 2015, at *www.vatican.va/roman_curia /pontifical_councils/chrstuni/relations-jews-docs/rc_pc _chrstuni_doc_20151210_ebraismo-nostra-aetate_en.html.* Copyright © LEV.

The excerpt by Pope Francis on page 63 is from "Homily of His Holiness Pope Francis," Vatican Basilica, November 19, 2016, at *https://w2.vatican.va /content/francesco/en/homilies/2016/documents/papa -francesco_20161119_omelia-concistoro-nuovi-cardinali .html.* Copyright © LEV.

The first quotation on page 71 is from Jean Vanier's essay "What Have People with Disabilities Taught Me?" in *The Paradox of Disability: Responses to Jean Vanier and L'Arche Communities from Theology and the Sciences*, edited by Hans S. Reinders (Grand Rapids, MN: William B. Eerdmans, 2010).

The second quotation on page 71 is from L'Arche, USA, Jean Vanier, founder. For more information, go to *www.larcheusa.org/who-we-are/charter.*

The quotation on page 72 is from the Vanier Institute of the Family, Georges and Pauline Vanier, founders. © 2019 The Vanier Institute of the Family. For more information, go to *http://vanierinstitute.ca /about-us/our-founders.*

The excerpts by Pope Francis on page 88 and 368 are from "World Youth Day, Meeting with Children and Young People," Turin, Italy, June 21, 2015, at *https://w2.vatican.va/content/francesco/en/speeches/2015 /june/documents/papa-francesco_20150621 _torino-giovani.html.* Copyright © LEV.

The quotation on page 121 is from Pope John Paul II's apostolic letter "On the Most Holy Rosary" ("*Rosarium Virginus Marias*"), number 19, at *https:// w2.vatican.va/content/john-paul-ii/en/apost_letters/2002 /documents/hf_jp-ii_apl_20021016_rosarium -virginis -mariae.html.* Copyright © LEV.

The excerpt by Pope Francis on page 137 is from "General Audience," Saint Peter's Square, September 7, 2016, at *https://w2.vatican.va/content/francesco/en /audiences/2016/documents/papa-francesco_20160907 _udienza-generale.html.* Copyright © LEV.

The excerpt by Pope Francis on page 158 is from "Extraordinary Jubilee of Mercy, Jubilee Audience," March 12, 2016, at *http://w2.vatican.va/content /francesco/en/audiences/2016/documents /papa-francesco_20160312_udienza-giubilare.html.* Copyright © LEV.

The excerpt by Pope Francis on page 196 is from World Youth Day, "Prayer Vigil with the Young People," Kraków, July 30, 2016, at *http://w2.vatican.va /content/francesco/en/speeches/2016/july/documents /papa-francesco_20160730_polonia-veglia-giovani.html.* Copyright © LEV.

The excerpt by Pope Francis on page 235 is from "Way of the Cross with the Young People, Address of the Holy Father," Poland, July 29, 2016, at *http:// w2.vatican.va/content/francesco/en/speeches/2016/july /documents/papa-francesco_20160729_polonia-via-crucis .html.* Copyright © LEV.

The excerpt by Saint Pope John Paul II on page 248 is from "General Audience," Saint Peter's Square July 28, 1999, at *http://w2.vatican.va/content /john-paul-ii/en/audiences/1999/documents /hf_jp-ii_aud_28071999.html.* Copyright © LEV.

The excerpt by Pope Francis on page 252 is from *Angelus* on the Solemnity of All Saints, November 1, 2013, at *http://w2.vatican.va/content/francesco/en /angelus/2013/documents/papa-francesco _angelus_20131101.html.* Copyright © LEV.

The excerpt on page 273 is from *Pastoral Constitution on the Church in the Modern World (Gaudium et Spes*, 1965), number 22, Vatican Council II, at *www .vatican.va/archive/hist_councils/ii_vatican_council /documents/vat-ii_const_19651207_gaudium-et-spes _en.html.* Copyright © LEV.

The excerpt by Pope Francis on page 275 is from "Prayer Vigil to 'Dry the Tears,'" Meditation of His Holiness Pope Francis, May 5, 2016, at *https://w2 .vatican.va/content/francesco/en/speeches/2016/may /documents/papa-francesco_20160505_veglia-asciug- are-lacrime.html*. Copyright © LEV.

The first quotation on page 301 is from "The Charter for Health Care Workers: A Synthesis of Hippocratic Ethics and Christian Morality," number 3.1, at *www.vatican.va/roman_curia/pontifical_councils /hlthwork/documents/rc_pc_hlthwork_doc_30061997 _honings_en.html*. Copyright © LEV.

The second quotation on page 301 is from "Pastoral Visit to Assisi, Homily of His Holiness Pope Francis," October 4, 2013, at *https://w2.vatican.va /content/francesco/en/homilies/2013/documents/papa -francesco_20131004_omelia-visita-assisi.html*. Copyright © LEV.

The quotation by Pope Francis on page 303 is from his encyclical "On Care for Our Common Home" *("Laudato Si'")*, number 241, at *http://w2 .vatican.va/content/francesco/en/encyclicals/documents /papa-francesco_20150524_enciclica-laudato-si.html*. Copyright © LEV.

The quotation on page 304 is from Pope Benedict XVI's "Message for the Celebration of the World Day of Peace," number 1, January 1, 2010, at *http://w2 .vatican.va/content/benedict-xvi/en/messages/peace /documents/hf_ben-xvi_mes_20091208_xliii-world -day-peace.html*. Copyright © LEV.

The excerpt by Pope Francis on page 306 is from "Message of His Holiness Pope Francis on the Occasion of the World Meeting of Popular Movements," Modesto, California," February 10, 2017, at *https:// w2.vatican.va/content/francesco/en/messages/pont -messages/2017/documents/papa-francesco_20170210 _movimenti-popolari-modesto.html*. Copyright © LEV.

The excerpt and quotation on page 327 are from *Conjectures of a Guilty Bystander*, by Thomas Merton (New York: Crown Publishing Group, a division of Random House, 1966), pages 156, 158, and 157, respectively. Copyright © The Abbey of Gethesemani.

The excerpt on page 333 is from Pope Francis's "General Audience," Saint Peter's Square, November 6, 2013, at *http://w2.vatican.va/content/francesco/en /audiences/2013/documents/papa-francesco_20131106 _udienza-generale.html*. Copyright © LEV.

The quotation on page 341 is from *Mother Teresa: A Simple Path*, compiled by LaVonne Neff (New World Library, 2001), page 7. Copyright © 2001 by New World Library.

The excerpt on page 348 is from Pope Francis's *Angelus*, July 21, 2013, at *http://w2.vatican.va/content /francesco/en/angelus/2013/documents/papa-francesco _angelus_20130721*. Copyright © LEV.

Endnotes Cited in Quotations from the Catechism of the Catholic Church, Second Edition

Chapter 1
1. Cf. Mt. 18:10; Lk 16:22; Ps 34:7; 91:10–13; Job 33:23–24; Zech 1:12; Tob 12:12.
2. Gen 2:17.

3. Cf. *Gaudium et spes* 13 § 1.
4. Cf. Council of Trent Denzinger-Schönmetzer, *Enchiridion Symbolorum, defintionum et declarationum de rebus fidei et morum* (1965) 1512.
5. *Roman Missal*, Easter Vigil 42: Blessing of Water.
6. Cf. Wis 10:5; Gen 11:4–6.

Chapter 2
1. Cf. *Dei Verbum* 14.
2. Cf. Saint Augustine, *Quaest. in Hept.* 2, 73: J. P. Migne, ed., Patroligia Latina (Paris 1841–1855) 34, 623; cf. *Dei Verbum* 16.
3. Cf. *Dei Verbum* 3.

Chapter 3
1. Mt. 26:28; cf. Ex 24:8; Lev 16:15–16; 1 Jn 4:10.
2. Cf. Heb 10:10.
3. Cf. *Gaudium et spes* 29 § 3.

Chapter 4
1. *Gaudium et spes* 22 § 2.
2. St. Gregory of Nyssa, *Orat. catech.* 15: J. P. Migne, ed., Patrologia Graeca (Paris, 1857–1866) 45, 48B.
3. St. Athanasius, *De inc.*, 54, 3; J. P. Migne, ed., Patrologia Graeca (Paris, 1857–1866) 25, 192B.
4. St. Thomas Aquinas, Opusc. 57: 1–4.

Chapter 5
1. *Nostra aetate* 4.

Chapter 6
1. Cf. Jn 19:42.
2. Cf. 1 Pet 3:18–19.
3. Cf. Council of Rome (745); Denziger-Schönmetzer, *Enchiridion Symbolorum, definitionum et declarationum de rebus fidei et morum* (1965) 587; Benedict XII, *Cum dudum* (1341): Denziger-Schönmetzer, *Enchiridion Symbolorum, definitionum et declarationum de rebus fidei et morum* (1965).
4. Cf. Mt 28:9, 16–17; Lk 24:15, 36; Jn 20:14, 17, 19, 26; 21:4.

Chapter 7
1. Phil 1:27.
2. Cf. Mat 28:6; Mk 16:7; Lk 24:6–7, 26–27, 44–48.
3. Congregation for the Doctrine of the Faith, instruction, *Libertatis conscientia*, 68.

Chapter 8
1. *Gaudium et spes* 22 § 5; cf. *Lumen gentium* 16; *Ad gentes* 7.

Chapter 9
1. 1 Cor 13:12.
2. Cf. Gen 2:2.
3. *Gaudium et spes* 22 § 5, cf. § 2.

Chapter 10
1. Cf. John Paul II, *Reconciliato et paenitentia* 16.

Chapter 11
1. Cf. Jn 13:15; Lk 11:1; Mt 5:11–12.

Chapter 12
1. Tertullian, *De orat.* 1: J. P. Migne, ed., Patrologia Latina (Paris 1841–1855) 1, 1155.